The Curatorial in Parallax

The Curatorial in Parallax

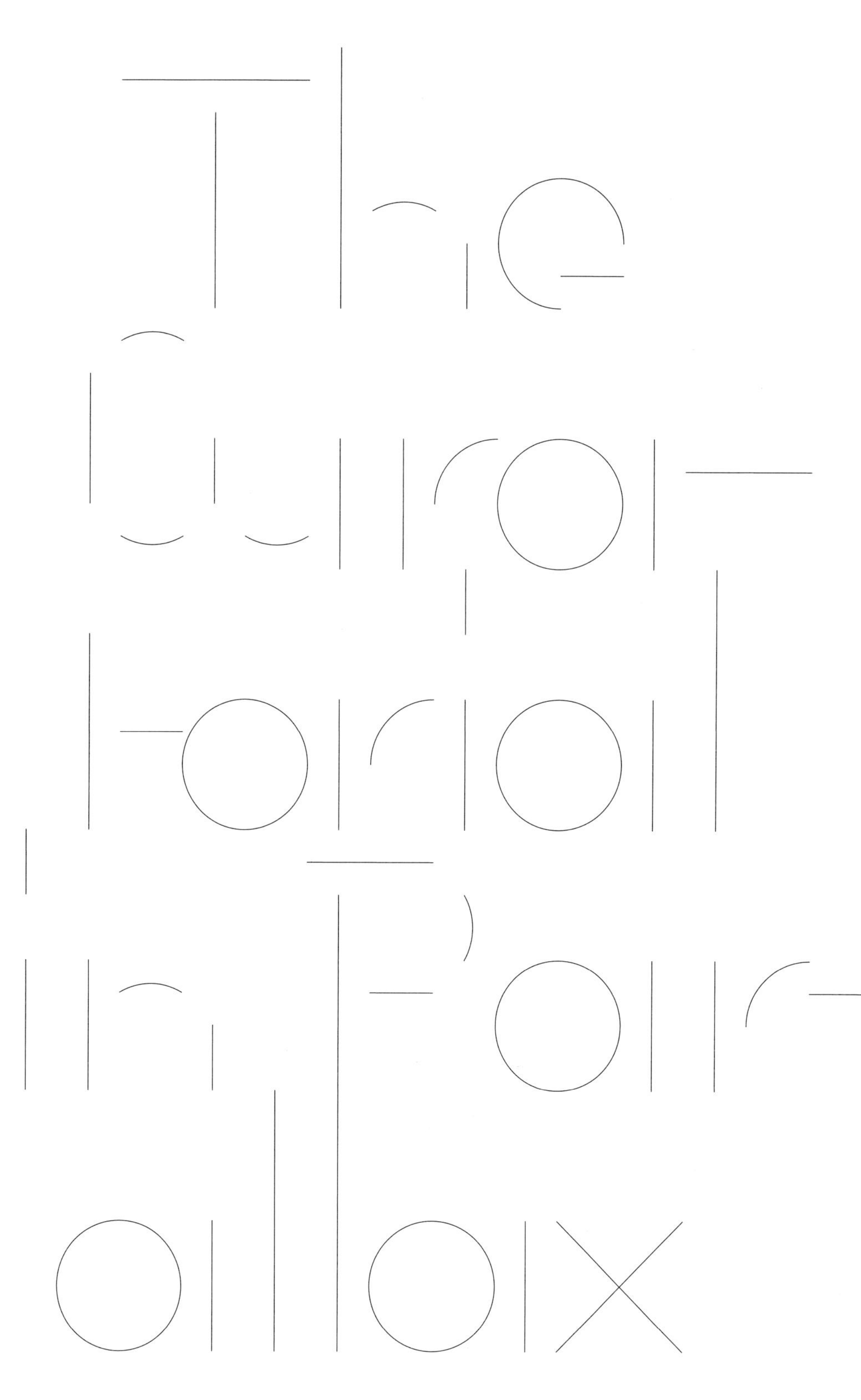

Contents

Research Practice Revisited

Museum Research—Program, Project, Platform

The Curatorial and Knowledge Production

The Imaginary of Institutions

Why Do Museums Research?

The publication that you have in your hands answers a very simple yet, for some, not so evident question: Why do museums engage in research activities? Why do they expend part of their budget on intangible, immaterial, and apparently useless actions in which curators and researchers, members of the staff, and freelancers spend time and resources? Why do museums need to hire specialists in fields that seem to be remote from the concerns of a large number of citizens? In actuality, the role of museums as institutions dedicated to public culture and enhancing knowledge mandates us to strive beyond the mere tasks of conserving and exhibiting artifacts that represent the material culture of a particular society. Whether through explicit transmission of knowledge or providing an intense experience of and with artworks, museums should never abandon their priority mission of making societies advance and improve. For this reason, the National Museum of Modern and Contemporary Art, Korea, and all museums must continuously research and innovate in our practices and the discourses about our objectives, as well as the implications and meanings of the messages we elaborate and transmit.

Globalization produced the conviction that we are all citizens of the same world (or the same planet). This presented an incredible opportunity for the MMCA to define the institution's identity with the creation of an original, precise, hopefully elegant discourse about art that could be perceived and enjoyed globally, especially after being perceived and enjoyed locally. And that discourse could not only be about Korean art: It would have to be centered around the contribution Korean artists have made, since the late nineteenth century, to the global narrative of modernity, a nonlinear narrative that does not comply with Western canons. In museums, the intellectual capacity to generate poetry, revelation, and beauty is the expression of the potential of research.

While the Korean public museum landscape is strong in terms of "hardware" (number of institutions, square meters of exhibition space, abundance of curators, etc.), it has a significant opportunity for growth in terms of "software" (intellectual production, critical debates, audience development, and so forth). In order to play a role in the global cultural conversation, we have as great a need for software as hardware. Singularity is possible when the subjects who speak and produce are well aware of their surroundings, of what other colleagues are thinking and doing. Networks and collaborative ties are essential. To this end, we decided to make the museum think, express, argue, discuss, explain, narrate, talk (and listen), act, interact, exchange, and trade—from us, with others. We call all of this "research."

What Museums Do 1: *The Curatorial in Parallax* is the first chapter in our conviction that thinking is a collective activity, that existence is relation, and that identity is permanent exchange and evolution. I would like to express our sincere gratitude to all the participants who have made this start to our initiative a true success. All of our audiences—analog and digital, viewers of live and broadcasted events, and now readers—have been and will be indispensable partners with the MMCA in this exciting endeavor. My congratulations also to the MMCA's Research and Publication Team for successfully launching this project and giving it solid continuity.

Bartomeu Marí

Director of National Museum of Modern and Contemporary Art, Korea

Song Sujong
Head of Research & Publication, MMCA

Kim Seong Eun
Guest Editor

Having secured its self-perpetuating power by lending impetus to the circumstances of history, art seems to focus more on observation than proclamation, on the lure of narratives rather than ostensible "truth," especially upon entering our contemporary times marked by pluralities and complexities. The world exists in a state of contradiction as it enters a new age of scientific revolution, with virtual reality and artificial intelligence, while also experiencing persistent economic crises and terrorism. Questions raised by these turbulent times also include concerns over the social role of museums. As institutions of art recognize that their own identity cannot be explained in terms of fixed ideas, their collections also cease to be relics locked up in art history and are instead reinterpreted in present contexts. Curatorial acts as praxis that focus on participation and process are now preferred over well-polished exhibitions in which works of art seem more like stuffed specimens.

Today, the museum is no longer a place where a select subject with a clear role completes an event; the institution of art now exists in a state of diffuseness, where all components and concepts intermingle and drift. Nonmaterial performances and data become works of art, and the act of curating itself becomes part of the exhibition. The audience, in its interaction with the work, now occupies the museum as artist or curator—or both. For this reason, it has become more usual to opt for the curatorial, rather than curators as producers of exhibitions, which encompasses all levels of idea and process, in recognition of the museum as the commons where knowledge and praxis are shared, rather than a gallery for passive viewing.

This tectonic shift has brought changes to the nature of museum publishing as well. Beyond merely presenting exhibition works, catalogues feature bibliographic notes and commentaries, now functioning as a mobile archive that transports information post-exhibition to places far from the exhibition space. As a result, the workmanship of a catalogue, not to mention its content, is regarded as part and parcel of an exhibition's degree of completeness. Expectations for museum publishing have moved a step further. Catalogues and other publications now reach beyond individual exhibitions, diagnosing the ecosystem of art as a condition that produces the exhibitions of our times. In effect, museum publishing brings together a wide variety of issues not addressed within the exhibition itself, operating as an organic platform that makes way for another kind of curatorial practice.

Echoing this shift of value within the contemporary museum, the MMCA has shored up its research and publishing functions. Here, we consider what it means to set forth the necessity of research in museums, where collecting and displaying artworks as end results has long been what the museum symbolized. We have pondered on how the museum will visualize research—a concept so broad and universal as to accompany every creative activity. How is museum research to be differentiated from research in art history and art theory departments at educational institutions?

The practice-based approach to research—unlike its traditional form of gathering provenance information or archival materials—is commonly known as "public programming." In the early 2000s, when the museum landscape underwent drastic changes, museums introduced many socially participatory programs. The museum became at once a school where theory and practice are combined by scholar or curators sharing their research projects; a place of discussion where experts from a broad spectrum of fields hold conversation marathons; and a temporary space which citizen normally situated outside the boundaries of the museum, occupy to speak out. Regardless of types and subjects, all public programs are designed to take part in the tenor of their times and pursue public values by forging relations with society through openness and cooperation.

As a starting point for this book, "What Museums Do" is a research-focused public program that the MMCA will continue to advance over time. The series is grounded in symposia, and branches out to a variety of discursive activities including pre- and post-seminars and publications for the sake of depth and sustainability. Though the subject is the museum, its approach is not limited to museology and curatorial studies. It is an attempt to profoundly explore the issues of contemporary art and thereby forecast the future and find proper coordinates for the museum. It is also a search for alternative models in an age when the race to keep up with rapid changes in visual culture can often overlook the necessary processes of investigation through reading, discussion, and criticism.

The first objective of "What Museums Do" is to focus on "research" that stems from the need for a diagnosis of reality, one that would help revise and reinforce the intertwined roles of research and publishing at the MMCA. After a preparatory work involving case studies in Korea as well as those of foreign institutions, an international symposium entitled *What Do Museums Research?* took place in April 2018, where six prominent figures in the field presented papers under the session themes of "From Attitude to Practice" and "Curating, Today and Tomorrow." The authors further developed their manuscripts, which have become the seed of this publication. As this is the first volume in the "What Museums Do" series—and, more significantly, since research is the fundamental basis for all that museums do—the editorial team invited additional authors to engage with even wider and more diverse perspectives. The space of this anthology aims to make visible the interconnectedness of viewpoints of those in the vanguard of theoretical discussions and curatorial practices.

Composed of four sections, *The Curatorial in Parallax* maps out the multiplicity of endeavors to reform and transform research vis-à-vis the museum. In the first part of this volume, "Research Practice Revisited," James Elkins and Irit Rogoff attempt a wholly new formulation of *research.* To make curatorial and museological uses of the contentious term, Elkins first delves into literature in the fields of art education and practice-led, or studio art, degrees for the principal definitions and theories of "art research." He then moves on to some significant differences between art-historical research done in universities and that performed in museums. Lastly, he raises an unusual sort of research, that is, the role played by museum visitors who wish to do their own research. For Rogoff, research is not something academic to be conducted only by the qualified; to the contrary, anyone under today's political and social conditions can, and should, be in the position of being a researcher. She claims a shifting notion of research and its growing centrality to many artistic, institutional, pedagogical, and civic practices. According to Rogoff, we all inhabit our numerous worlds differently as we inform ourselves and test out different ways to think a particular reality, which is the activity of research.

The second part, "Museum Research—Program, Project, Platform," examines public programming as a new model of research not separate from but inextricably linked to exhibitions. Beck Jee-sook's fascinating survey of what she led in different institutions and biennials in Korea in the early 2000s up to the present revolves around three axes: X for archives, Y for nonperiodical publications, and Z for programs, projects, and platforms, from which this section title is borrowed. Taking the artist collective Part-time Suite's *One Opening* as a cue for institutional critique, Beck maintains that, more than experimentality, we must now take seriously the continuity of institutional research. Paola Antonelli looks at MoMA's *R&D* initiative intended to foster productive discussion that informs the museum's programming as well as addresses wider societal discourses. Such examples as an online debate format titled *Design and Violence* suggest the potentiality and responsibility of museums to act in the public interest. She emphasizes, self-reflexively, that New York's MoMA—and, in fact, all art museums—should not shy away from promoting the curatorial path to good citizenry. Margriet Schavemaker argues for the move from a discursive to an inclusive turn. She discusses facets of the Stedelijk Museum Amsterdam, in particular, its academi infrastructure of a peer-reviewed journal and recent pubic programs devoted to issues of migration. These are a needed effort to self-critically open up the museum to other voices in order to transform it from a hegemonic space into an inclusive one in the politically polarized world From her experience of working and researching in and across both the academy and the museum over two decades, Victoria Walsh explores ho to connect theory and practice acros the two institutions. Her collaborati research projects with Tate and MeLa ("European Museums in an Age of Migrations") productively recognize the interrelations between artist, curator, and audience, and the impact of digital technology and the internet on the curatorial and cultural authority of the museum.

The third part, "The Curatorial and Knowledge Production," focuses on the theoretical notion of the curatorial posited as a mode of practice-based research and knowledge production. Beatrice von Bismarck and Paul O'Neill bring up rather philosophical notions to elaborate on the curatorial. Von Bismarck defines the curatorial as the context of meaning and action centering on "becoming-public," comprising of both human and nonhuman actors, whose sense can be well conveyed by the concept of "constellation." The characteristic structure of the curatorial constellation is transpositional, taking those involved out of their previous contexts, i.e., de- and re-contextualization; and its two procedures of "translating" and "placing outside" are especially important as politically relevant forms of critical reflexivity. In O'Neill's essay, the terms "the curatorial" and "research" are placed alongside "escape," which defines itself as an act of release accompanied by the wish to be transformed. O'Neill's escapology sees the concept of escape best embodied in the readymade. With an understanding of the "exhibition" as a form of becoming, of togetherness, the exhibition itself is thereby opened up as readymade and becomes a form of escape for the artwork as much as for the viewer to "that which is not here," in which a certain form of research is activated.

In their essays, Simon Sheikh, Kim Seong Eun, and James Voorhies combine theoretical explorations with specific curatorial forms designed for the gathering of people. Sheikh departs from Fredric Jameson's idea of theory as conceptual installation, and draws an analogy between curating and theorizing in terms of their mode of assemblage. He exemplifies this with *Former West*, a multifaceted curatorial project advanced through exhibitions, conferences, and publications as places for research. And with *Bergen Assembly*, he asserts the necessity to implement new curatorial research methods from assemblages to assemblies into instituting and institution-making. A cultural anthropologist exploring multiple possibilities to theorize the curatorial in the art museum, Kim deals with a spatiotemporal disposition for exercises of critical discussion in and with exhibitions, highlighting the role of the museum to cultivate a willingness in the public to think together. She also articulates the idea of the choreographic on par with the curatorial and formulates performances as research on permanent collections as well as the learning and unlearning of exhibitions. Voorhies proposes a new setup of research-based curatorial practices: Bureau for Open Culture and Curatorial Research Bureau. In writing flavored with personal, journal-like entries, Voorhies demonstrates the many strands of his activities, namely, artistic, administrative, educational, and editorial. All these coming into play for orchestrated connections and coordinated mediations are his means for thinking curatorially and for curatorial performance in the public realm.

The book's last part, "The Imaginary of Institutions," expands the discussion of research into the potential for museums to be changed from vertical to horizontal institutions by the very dynamics of research. Annette Jael Lehmann gives insight into collaborative research between universities and museums. In the same vein as *Black Mountain Research*, a joint endeavor of Hamburger Bahnhof—Museum für Gegenwart and Freie Universität Berlin, her current project for performance art and media is based on dialogic and interdisciplinary modeling of new knowledge experiences, with a thematic focus on new forms of narration, scenography, audience involvement, education, and digital knowledge design. Out of the urgency to make available a public critical discussion of curatorial practice and theory, Dorothee Richter has developed *OnCurating*—an initiative comprised of an online journal, printed publication, and projects with museums and institutions, all closely related to postgraduate courses. She emphasizes the unavoidable educational element of curating, addressing people through curating, as exemplified in her project *Speculative Curating* to engage museum collections together with students and museum visitors. Drawing on institutional critique practiced by artists and curators, and critical pedagogy suggested by educator and philosopher Paulo Freire and social critic Henry Giroux, Lim Shan investigates how community pedagogy can be constructed to intervene in social transformation. Marked by its performativity and social participation, community pedagogy may come in contact with participants in a way where all understand a set of shared values that allows for critical assessments of social inequality. Pascal Gielen makes an analytical differentiation between public, civil, civic, and common spaces. He delves into the gaping gulf between legality and illegality, the gray area between what is allowed and not (or not yet) allowed. These considerations reveal the specific roles that art and artistic interventions play in the political realm to create civil actions and common spaces. They mostly concern the unknown, nonregulated domains outside the white walls of the museum, if only to safeguard their own space of imagination in the museum.

The editorial premise of this book is that the curatorial—as both theory and praxis—is at the core of research, when contextualized by the art museum and distinguished from other fields. It is neither confined to exhibition-making nor too comprehensive to become an all-encompassing category of museum activities. Rather, it is a moving object of research, whose apparent position can be viewed differently; and actually, it is closer to a trajectory enabled by its constantly changing position. The ways in which the contributors to this volume respond to the curatorial manifest the differences and displacements of what the curatorial is, who engages with it and how. The commonality in their approaches, however, consists in a recognition that the curatorial can take on a specific and substantial dimension whenever a certain labor of research is set in motion. The research into the curatorial in parallax, and in transition, will thus be able to bring an alternative reality to life in the museum.

Research Practice Revisited

James Elkins teaches in the Department of Art History, Theory, and Criticism at the School of the Art Institute of Chicago. His writing focuses on the history and theory of images in art, science, and nature. Some of his books are exclusively on fine art (*What Painting Is*, *Why Are Our Pictures Puzzles?*). Others include scientific and non-art images, writing systems, and archaeology (*The Domain of Images*, *On Pictures and the Words that Fail Them*), and some are about natural history (*How to Use Your Eyes*). Recent books include *What Photography Is*, written against Roland Barthes's *Camera Lucida*; *Artists with PhDs*, second edition; and *Art Critiques: A Guide*, third edition.

James Elkins

What is Research in a Museum?

I would like to divide the question into three parts.

First, it is necessary to ask what "research" means when the word is applied to art. If we do not pause to investigate the meaning of "art research," our questions will be too general and imprecise. Luckily, there is a large literature on research in art, mostly in the fields of art education and the so-called practice-led or studio-art PhD degree. In the first part of the essay I will review, in condensed form, the principal definitions and theories of "art research," because they provide a resource for curatorial and museological uses of "research."

Second, it is helpful to ask whether there is a special kind of art-historical research that takes place in museums, as opposed to archives and universities. A Google search for the string "art research" reveals there is a great deal of interest in research for curation and exhibition, and almost no interest in research that takes place in museums. I suspect the subject of this book actually addresses research in curation and exhibition, rather than in museums. However, there are some significant differences between art-historical research conducted in universities and art-historical research done in museums. In the shorter, second part of this essay, I will make some remarks on the difference between art-historical research done in universities and art-historical research done by curators in museums.

Third, I will ask how research is conducted by visitors in museums. This subject is not as well explored, because it is usually assumed that the art historian or curator proposes the research questions and agendas. Yet visitors also do their own research, and it can be at odds with the curators' intentions.

My three-part structure is lopsided, because the first part is the longest and most philosophic; the second part is brief, and the third is anecdotal. I invite readers to consider part one as a reference guide, which can be consulted for problems that arise from the use of "research" in many art contexts. The third part, by contrast, is meant to be an informal sample of an unusual sort of research—the kind done by museum visitors, without the guidance of curators.

What is "Research" in Art?

From the enormous literature on this subject, here are six points that are especially pertinent to understanding research in museums, or research in curation.

[A] *Research is universally taken as a central method in MA, MFA, and PhD programs.*

Every PhD program for artists, and many MA and MFA programs, require students to do "art research." The literature produced for those degrees often adjusts the meaning of "art research" to fit their institution, but they rarely question what "art research" means, or ask whether the expression should be used at all. That is because departments in all subjects, in universities in most countries, require students to undertake "research" in order to discover "new knowledge." As studio-art PhD programs spread around the world, and as more universities adopt the North American tradition of including art departments, it has been both convenient and expeditious to adopt the same terminology that defines disciplines in all fields, from physics to sociology.

The literature specifically on the studio-art PhD began around 2000. One of the first books on the subject, *Thinking Through Art*, edited by Katy Macleod and Lin Holdridge, was marketed using a prospectus that notes, "it continues to prove difficult for artists both to produce art which can be identified as research, and research which can be identified as art."[1] This is an indication of how deeply ingrained the assumption was even twenty years ago: Art is assumed to be a form of research, and there is a kind of research that can be considered as art.

The largest anthology of writing on art research is *The Routledge Companion to Research in the Arts* (2010). In the book's foreword, Hans-Peter Schwarz discusses competing senses of research, but he takes research itself for granted. "It does seem to be high time," he writes, "to stop doubting whether art-based research exists at all and accept that it has long ago become an everyday occurrence in most art universities."[2] I give these examples to indicate how widespread the idea is that art, at least in the context of MA, MFA, and PhD programs, is best understood as research.[3]

[B] *The most interesting theorizing about research can be found in discussions in the UK, beginning in the 1970s.* Sir Christopher Frayling is the author of the most influential formulation of "art research" in studio-art PhD programs.[4] He distinguished "research through art" from "research into art" and "research for art":

[i] "Research through art," he said, is research in the field of art and design, for example, MPhils and PhDs that investigate technologies. Frayling calls this uppercase "Research": It is systematic, disciplinary inquiry. This first category has to do with technique, medium, and technology.

[ii] "Research into art," Frayling writes, includes art

1 Unpublished prospectus, 2003. See also my "Afterword: On Beyond Research and New Knowledge," in *Thinking Through Art: Reflections on Art as Research*, eds. Katy Macleod and Lin Holdridge (London and New York: Routledge, 2005), 241–7.

2 Michael Biggs and Henrik Karlsson, eds., *The Routledge Companion to Research in the Arts* (London and New York: Routledge, 2010), xxvii.

3 This is true internationally; see my essay "Six Cultures of the PhD," in *SHARE: Handbook for Artistic Research Education*, eds. Mick Wilson and Schelte van Ruiten (Amsterdam: ELIA, 2013).

4 For more on these categories, see the discussion in *What Do Artists Know?*, co-edited with Frances Whitehead, vol. 3 in the Stone Art Theory Institutes series (University Park, PA: Penn State Univ. Press, 2012).

history and possibly aesthetics: This is work that inquires into art; the research leads to a better understanding of historical and contemporary styles. Frayling himself was interested in Hollywood movies, and wrote several books he would have counted as "research into art."

[iii] "Research for art," according to Frayling, is work that leads to the production of art, so that the art embodies the thinking. This is lowercase "research," nonprofessional "searching."

The third of these has been the subject of continuous interest over several generations of educators. Part of the reason "research for art" has proven so fruitful is that it contains contradictory thoughts:

[iii a] It can be understood as research that leads to the production of art. This is unproblematic, but it makes "research for art" the same as "research through art"—that is, "uppercase Research," Frayling's category [i].

[iii b] Frayling also says "research for art" leads to art that "embodies" the research. This is the central problematic possibility: I will expand on this below, under headings [D], [E], and [F].

[iii c] Frayling also calls this "lowercase research" or "searching." This implies that "research for art" is free of strict research methodology but leaves it open as to how such lowercase "research" might be characterized.

[C] *There are alternative terms to "research," which could be used in curation.*

Given the ubiquity of "research" across the university and, in particular, in light of Frayling's contentious category [iii b], it is interesting that there are a number of alternatives to "research": The term wasn't used to speak about art before the 1960s, and it is hardly appropriate for most of the world's art. (Is a bas-relief from Assyria the result of "research"?

Is Jacques-Louis David's *Oath of the Horatii* the product of a research agenda?)

Here are some alternative terms, which might be useful in contexts where "research" is not necessary. Each of these could be applied to research in curation and museums:

[i] "Inquiry" or "investigation": This has the advantage of affinity with terms like "criticality," German *Kritik*, the art-world "crit," and the general term "criticism." In English-language scholarship, the journal *Critical Inquiry* has long done the things associated with "art research."

[ii] "Project": This has the advantage of corresponding with many artists' self-definition of what they do. "Projects" are short- or medium-term experiments, which artists undertake under a set of self-imposed constraints; "projects" are therefore roughly analogous to "research," but without the burden of the conceptual confusions surrounding "research."

[iii] "Practice": Of the alternative terms, this is perhaps the most common. Artists almost always have "practices" they can name and describe. The word is relatively recent and was not used much before the 1960s; it also carries the implication of theory and professionalism—but not of research.

[iv] "Work": This is a common abbreviation for "practice," and it has echoes of Marxism, of professionalization, and artists' careers.

Any of these terms could be used in place of "research." Even though the studio-art PhD and research-based MFA programs are dependent on "research," the wider fields of curatorial and museum work could possibly benefit by avoiding "research" and opting for one of these more general concepts.

[D] *Because "research" is a word borrowed from the sciences, there is widespread discussion of how close to scientific research art research should be.*

This conversation is also pertinent for the topic of this book, because there is no consensus definition of "research" outside of science. The literature has settled on three positions:

[i] Artistic research can utilize scientific research protocols, methodologies, and forms (such as the conventional division of scientific papers into "Methods," "Materials," "Results") even though it is fundamentally distinct from scientific research.

[ii] Artistic research needs to rethink scientific research protocols, methodologies, and forms, because it is fundamentally distinct from scientific research.

[iii] Artistic research cannot use scientific research protocols, methodologies, and forms, because it is fundamentally distinct from scientific research.

Each of these positions has advocates. An example of [iii] is Søren Kjørup, who has argued, "There is no scientific research to which artistic research might have to comply … artistic research should be left alone to develop its own methods."[5]

5 Søren Kjørup, "Pleading Plurality: Artistic and C Kinds of Research," in *Companion*, 24, 29; thar Erna Fiorentini for poi this out.

It would probably be a good idea for any curatorial or museum initiative that uses the term "research" to consider the relation between "art research" and scientific research, and decide how close to science, or how distant from it, the "art research" will be.

[E] *There is disagreement over whether "art research" should be defined at all.*

Here, the principal claims can be captured by these two positions:

[i] Yes, it is important to define "art research," because only in that way can conversations across the university be fruitful. In order for scientists at a university to find common ground with artists, it is necessary to agree on certain essential elements of "research." It is also important to define "art research," because otherwise it will be assimilated to scientific research, since that is the only kind of research that has been extensively studied.

[ii] No, it is not important to define "art research," because it has an intrinsic openness, which is either the result of its visual nature or of its institutional position.

This second position is the most common in the literature on the studio-art PhD. The consensus position is a mixture of this second position with the third position regarding scientific research:

> Artistic research cannot use scientific research protocols, methodologies, and forms, because it is fundamentally distinct from scientific research
>
> *is combined with:*
>
> Artistic research cannot be defined, because it has an intrinsic openness, which is either the result of its visual nature or of its institutional position.

This leads to some very complex and ambiguous claims. One of the most thoroughly pondered accounts is the Dutch scholar Henk Slager. In the book *The Pleasure of Research*, Slager writes that doctoral research can be understood as "Temporary Autonomous Research," which has "no need to be led by the formatted models of the established scientific order."[6] Slager positions artistic research outside university protocols:

> [Many] artistic research projects seem to thwart the well-defined disciplines. They know the hermeneutic questions of the humanities (the alpha-sciences); they are engaged in empirically scientific methods (the beta-sciences); and they are aware of commitment (the gamma-sciences).

They point, he writes, to a "delta-science," characterized by a "capacity … to continuously engage in novel, unexpected epistemological relations in a methodological process of interconnectivity." Artistic research is, therefore, "an undefined discipline," a "'nameless science,' directed toward generating flexible constructions, multiplicities, and new reflexive zones."[7]

I think it is clear in writing like this that what matters is the autonomy of "art research": It is not an activity that can be

6 Henk Slager, *The Pleasure of Research* (Amsterdam: Hatje Cantz, 2015).

7 Ibid., 68–69. Slager cites Agamben for "alpha-sciences."

defined, because any definition would circumscribe its political and institutional autonomy.

[F] *There is also disagreement in the relationship between the knowledge produced by art research, on the one hand, and the visual objects themselves, on the other.*

Research always leads to the production of knowledge; this is another universal component of the literature on PhDs in any subject. In terms of "art research," this leads to two principal options:

[i] Either knowledge *inheres* in the visual, so that the artist's exhibition itself is a form of knowledge, or

[ii] Knowledge is *interpreted* to exist in the visual, so that discourse reveals the objects' or exhibition's contribution to knowledge.

These two options are unresolved in the literature. In the first, the artwork itself *is* knowledge. This creates a logical difficulty for the PhD dissertation that students are asked to produce in PhD programs, because if the artwork *is* the knowledge, then there is no need for the dissertation.

In the second option, the work of the PhD program is to elucidate the knowledge that is somehow embedded, embodied, or otherwise contained in the artwork. The student learns to articulate her artwork, to reveal what in it can be understood as knowledge, what has rational content. The logical difficulty here is that if the purpose of the PhD is to reveal and articulate knowledge in an artwork, it remains unclear what is left: What is a piece of visual art when the knowledge it embodies has been put into words?

The literature on these six points is extensive, and I have only indicated it very briefly.[8] Writing on this subject has reached a point where its purpose is mainly to assert political and institutional freedom. Its self-contradictions and elisions are tactical—that is, not analytic or logical, but rhetorical. This political and rhetorical function of "research" has been inherited by curatorial and museum research. But that should not deter curators from considering different possibilities.

8
There is more materia[illegible] through [F] in *Artists PhDs: On the New Do[illegible] Degree in Studio Art* ([illegible] edition: Washington, Academia Publishing[illegible] second, definitive edi[illegible] Portions of this book[illegible] the material covered [illegible] also online at http://[illegible] jameselkins.com/yy/.

An example of the pertinence of this literature for curatorial studies is Moon Kyungwon and Jeon Joonho's *Learning Modern*, an exhibition at the School of the Art Institute of Chicago, where I work. The exhibition was conceived by the curator Mary Jane Jacob as "a form of research into the very meaning of modernism, using the exhibition as a form of research." The object of Jacob's essay is the material and spatial confluence that produces new knowledge. The knowledge itself is not described in her catalogue, because it is embodied in the "spatial and material confluence" of the exhibition. She is interested in the conditions under which "new knowledge" might appear. And yet the lack of discussion of the results of *Learning Modern*—of how, exactly, it alters the "very meaning of modernism"—implies that knowledge remains lodged in the visual. This is the same paradox that animates studio-art PhD programs: The hope is that "art research" can be described in terms analogous to those used to describe science, and that it will yield unanticipated new knowledge—but because the work is visual art, there is a reticence to say what knowledge, exactly, is produced.

What is Art-Historical Research in Museums?

I turn now to a possibly simpler subject. It has been observed that art-historical research performed in museums differs from art-historical research done in universities, research centers, and archives. A principal difference is that when research is done in museums, it is oriented toward specific objects.[9] "Object-oriented" research is not the norm in academic art history, where thematic, conceptual, social, and political themes tend to orient scholars' interests.

9
See, for example, Robert Anderson, "Truth and Meaning: Are Museums Doing Their Job?," *RSA Journal* 149, no. 5503 (2002): 58–61.

There are also social and intellectual gaps between art-historical research performed in museums and in universities. An indication of this is the fact that when museums mount large-scale exhibitions intended to rethink art-historical narratives, they seldom affect university-based art history.

Art historians in universities tend not to think of exhibition catalogues as serious contributions to the art-historical literature: Catalogues are read, but they are not always considered to be essential contributions that would warrant changes in textbooks or classroom materials.

Jacob's exhibition in Chicago is an example. Another is Okwui Enwezor's research, which he has said provides the opportunity to think about how to complicate the narrative of societies with colonial affiliations. But aside from specialists in African art, I do not think Enwezor's exhibitions at Haus der Kunst in Munich have influenced the ways modernism is taught. Postcolonial and decolonial theory are taught in art history departments in universities, and exhibitions like Enwezor's are noted, but they are not treated as viable alternative narratives. Another example is the series *The Making of Modern Art* at the Van Abbemuseum in Eindhoven, Netherlands, an ongoing project curated by Christiane Berndes, Charles Esche, and Steven ten Thije. In an online video, Quinsy Gario asks ten Thije, "Can you re-present the notion of modern art, the modern art museum, as something that is healing or reparative, rather than using it for the abject project of national socialism?" This kind of question is pertinent for contemporary discussions of modernisms, but so far the series has not provoked art-historical responses.

The exceptions to this disconnect between university and museum research are academically sited galleries and curators who speak directly to academic art history, for example, the work of Molly Nesbit at Vassar or Ellen Tang at Bowdoin, both in the United States.

An example of an initiative that blends academic and nonacademic research is the artist Joseph Grigely, who has the long-term project of managing the Hans Ulrich Obrist Archive at the School of the Art Institute of Chicago (fig. 1).[10] Obrist and Grigely have been friends since the early 1990s, and Obrist has been sending Grigely everything he has been producing. The result is a growing archive of materials, which Grigely uses to teach classes on curating the curator.

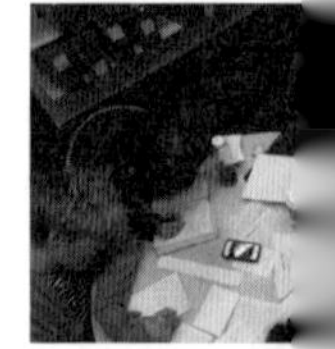

Fig. 1. Joseph Grig
a seminar in the H
Obrist Archive, Sc
Art Institute of Ch
Courtesy of Joseph

10
See http://www.hu

Grigely says that his initial interest was the difference between an exhibition and a publication, which became the difference between an archive, an exhibition, and a publication. "The biggest part of the project," he told me, "is taxonomic: creating a bibliographical model for the archive that involves mapping and visualizing data. So this is a very specific kind of research related to models of filiation developed by textual critics and bibliographers."[11] For Grigely, the project evolved into a way of showing "how the documents reflect upon Obrist's curatorial practice of creating links between people, disciplines, venues, and continents—essentially, a practice of hyphenation." The Obrist Archive is a hybrid entity, poised between art history, curation, and several other disciplines. More commonly, "research" differs in curation and in academic art history. The two tend to share general concerns—the nature of modernism, inclusivity, multiple modernities, and so forth—but art-historical research in museums remains distinct and is not consistently influential outside of museums and galleries.

11 Interview with Joseph Grigely, spring 2018.

What is Research for a Visitor?

My third topic is the least studied. Here, research means something like "inquiry," in the sense of informal or unsystematic investigation. The question is what an interested viewer might conclude from an exhibition, if she is not following the brochures or other narrative prompts.

My example is the Louvre Abu Dhabi, which I visited just before its public opening in autumn 2017. It is a very unusual museum: the first new universal museum, perhaps, in a generation, and a sort of incarnation of André Malraux's imaginary museum.

On the surface, it proposes to tell the history of the art of all cultures, but it has a strong Francophone bias, and its categories and many of its curatorial choices reflect specifically French ways of understanding art history. A visitor might not be aware of the French inclination of the museum, except in the trilingual labels (Arabic, French, English); but few engaged visitors could be unaware of the museum's universalizing intention.

The opening gallery, called the Grand Vestibule, has a series of small, freestanding vitrines, each of which is dedicated to a specific theme: Prayer, Motherhood, Writing, Horses, and so forth. A typical vitrine has three objects in it: one Islamic, a second Christian, and a third European antique or tribal. I do not imagine it would occur to many visitors that this triad, which is putatively universal, is Eurocentric and Islamocentric. But viewers who read the labels in the first room, and note that the floor decoration is a scrambled map of the world, with city names in the original scripts (Tokyo in Japanese, Delhi in Hindi, and so forth), will realize they are being asked to contemplate the essential unity of all the world's art. The vitrine "Motherhood," for example, includes a fourteenth-century French Virgin and Child statuette, an Egyptian figurine of Isis nursing Horus, and a small statue described only as "Phemba, maternity figure" (fig. 2). The text asks, "What is the secret of the universal gesture of love from a mother to her child?" Given this degree of historical unspecificity, a visitor might well conclude that the museum is a place to learn about universal, transhistorical values and ideas.

Fig. 2. "Motherhood" vitrine in the Grand Louvre Abu Dhabi. Photo: James Elkins.

The museum proposes a single linear narrative for all of art history, because its twelve rooms are to be visited in order. There are six rooms, then an "Intersection," and then six more rooms, culminating in contemporary art. Given this structure, what might a visitor research? I will limit myself here to some examples. (A full analysis of the Louvre Abu Dhabi needs to be published, but this is not the place.)

Room 4, "Universal Religions," generally keeps to the same groups of three artifacts. In this case, one gravestone is from Mecca, 700–900 ACE; a second is from Tunisia, twelfth century; and a third, placed in the middle, is from Paris, thirteenth century. The remarkable thing here is that the Parisian one is in Hebrew. The label identifies it as a "funerary stele of Dame Florie, daughter of Rabbi Benjamin." The isitors shown in figure 3 were discussing the strangeness of ıe Hebrew inscription together with the Arabic. They were, ı effect, assessing the possibility that cultures considered as ivergent might belong together. A visitor who read all the .bels in Room 4 might conclude that all religions are equal in nportance, and that they are comparable in form and perhaps .so in content.

Fig. 3. Women looking at grave stelae in Room 4, Louvre Abu Dhabi. Photo: James Elkins.

After the first six rooms comes the "Intersection," called Cosmography." It is intended to show how Islamic and uropean explorers used instruments to navigate the world. A eflective visitor would be able to determine that Islamic and uropean navigation were not entirely equivalent, and that oint would be made even more strongly by the next room, umber 7, "The World in Perspective." Together with the ntersection," these are the two most important rooms in the ıuseum, because they propose the partnership and parallelism etween medieval Islam and early Renaissance art and science. .oom 7 makes this explicit by pairing a medieval Islamic text n optics with an Italian Renaissance text that exhibits linear erspective. Above each is a picture: a northern European deal city" with careful perspective, and an Ottoman ceramic f a mosque (fig. 4).

Fig. 4. Two books and two images paired in Room 7, Louvre Abu Dhabi. Photo: James Elkins.

A visitor intent on comparing Islamic and European ılture would notice that linear perspective, which is linked ere to exploration, science, and the Enlightenment, is not uite present in the Ottoman image. While I was in the oom, one seemed to draw that conclusion, mainly because ıe hang in the "Intersection" and in Room 7 clearly proposes partnership or convergence. (Room 7 is also the location of ıe museum's most important and politically significant object, eonardo da Vinci's *La belle ferronnière*—as of spring 2018, was scheduled to be joined by the newly acquired *Salvator undi*.)

I will close with one more example: At the end of .oom 9, "A New Art of Living," two paintings usher visitors ıto Room 10, "A Modern World?" (fig. 5). On the right Gilbert Stuart's portrait of the first American president,

Fig. 5. The end of Room 9 and the passage to Room 10, Louvre Abu Dhabi. Photo: James Elkins.

George Washington (actually, it is one among twenty-four surviving such portraits Stuart did of Washington). Farther down the passage is Jacques-Louis David's equestrian portrait of Napoleon (actually, one of five such paintings). The Stuart painting is smaller and hangs on a side wall. The implication is that the modern world was introduced mainly by France, and secondarily by the United States.

Again, unreflective visitors would conclude that the "modern world" began after the American and French revolutions; but a visitor "researching" the museum's layout and choices could easily conclude that France is the patron of modernity, and America is its less important predecessor.

These sorts of conclusions may be reached dozens of times in the course of a tour of the museum's twelve rooms. In each case, there is a difference between the narrative that the curators apparently intended—universal, with minimal interruptions for politics, cultural contexts, regionalisms, or parochialisms—and the narrative that can be read by "researching" the placements, texts, and choices of objects. Conclusions like the ones I have mentioned lead to a sense of the museum that is very different from the official, public one: a good reason, I think, to consider visitors' research alongside that of curators.

Concluding Thoughts

I hope these three perspectives contribute to this book's purpose, and to the wider subject of curatorial theory and practice. It matters, I think, that "research" itself is so contentious and so poorly understood, and perhaps the literature on "art research" can help there. My second and third topics also have to do with subjects that are often marginal in conversations about radical and innovative curation: the alienation of curation and university-based research, and the part played by visitors who wish to do their own research.

Irit Rogoff is a writer, educator, curator, and organizer. She is Professor of Visual Cultures at Goldsmiths, University of London, a department she founded in 2002. Rogoff works at the meeting ground between contemporary practices, politics, and philosophy. Her current work is on new practices of knowledge production and their impact on modes of research, under the title of *Becoming Research* (forthcoming). As part of the collective freethought, Rogoff was one of the artistic directors of the Norwegian Triennial *Bergen Assembly* (September 2016) and editor of *The Infrastructural Condition* published in its wake. Rogoff also cofounded the European Forum for Advanced Practices in 2017.

Irit Rogoff

Becoming Research*

Singularizing Knowledge[1]

In the past, we assumed we knew what "education" was about: an encounter with the world at another level through a set of personal transformations. We also assumed we knew what "research" was about: an investigation into the world around us in order to ground bodies of knowledge.

Research used to be thought of as an academic practice, one that took place in advance of an event or manifestation in order to ground it in knowledge. Research also used to be thought to be a highly academic activity: consulting great tomes of knowledge, burrowing in dusty archives, interviewing certified actors in certain scenarios, conceptualizing experiments in a laboratory, or relying on expertise from elsewhere to give credibility to a claim.

But research has changed all around us—both in cultural and intellectual practices as well as in the protocols of daily existence, among so many. One of the reasons I have been trying to conceptualize new models of research in our

1 Irit Rogoff, "Practicing Research: Singularising Knowledge," *MaHKUzine*, no. 9 (Summer 2010): 37–42.

* [Th]is is a short version of the opening [ch]apter of *Becoming Research* (Cambridge, [M]A: MIT Press, forthcoming 2019).

lives is my sense that to think of ourselves as researchers allows us a small amount of agency within a world whose rampant neoliberal drives have taken away both agency and the ability to actually argue points in terms of content and substance. The shift from someone who expresses themselves individually to the position of being a researcher is a shift in which one doesn't simply acquiesce or protest against but allows oneself to get involved with the workings of institutions, of protocols, of memory, and of community—not in compliance or in defiance but in efforts to rewrite these through their very workings. This encapsulates the performativity of the various research projects I will briefly refer to here and of the many I have worked with over the years.

When we claim research for ourselves as an activity, we actually inhabit our numerous worlds differently as we inform ourselves and test out different ways to think a particular reality, which is the activity of research. With the advent of ever more virulent neoliberal managerialism and rampant cognitive capitalism, we have had to constantly revise our understanding of both, so as not to lose their capacity for critical and resistant invention. If we pursue a model of knowledge as singularity, never universal and constantly reinventing its alliances with far-flung insights, practices, and protocols, we might have a form of learning that is not so easily captive by dominant cultures of evaluation and prediction.

The climate and values of neoliberal managerialism make their presence felt within education in numerous ways. These include the culture of constant evaluation through mechanisms of student satisfaction, research outputs, careers developed directly out of courses of study, and funding brought into institutions. All of these entail a huge inflation of management structures and a steady demise in the position and significance of academic and intellectual input. Wendy Brown has called this permeating intensity of neoliberalism's holistic capture "a stealth revolution"—"it is governing conduct as if it were granting liberty."[2]

The claims made for this "stealth revolution" are that

2
Wendy Brown, *Und[...]* *Demos: Neoliberalism[...]* *Revolution* (Brookly[...] Books, 2015), 48–4[...]

we have, it would seem, more space in which to succeed, to expand, to be entrepreneurial, to act on our ambitions, to financialize everything, which in turn grants us more revenue, which in turn feeds the management by algorithms with data that serves as indicators for targets or for achievements. The opposite realm is that of subjectivity, the tension between multi-positioned knowledges and subjects, and the undefined realms that takes place at the interstices of named positions, identities, and knowledges. As André Lepecki has argued in his timely and captivating study *Singularities*, "In permeating our actions, neoliberal conditioning shows how it has captured subjectivity."[3] If subjectivity had previously delineated the arena of stakes and relations, of affinities and solidarities, of shared imaginations and shared criticalities (the multiple and often dissonant positions of the subject), in its hijacked form it is geared to achievement, success, forging new markets and new desires for more than commodities: for affects, for energies, for spectacles, for expansion, growth, reach, brand recognition, and credit. Above all, for credit.

Education, then, could potentially offer the possibility of deconditioning from neoliberalism's permanent logistical conditioning. It is initially a form of gathering, a transgenerational set of exchanges, of what Stiegler calls "transindividuation."

For Stiegler, the concept of transindividuation is one that does not rest with the individuated "I" or with the interindividuated "We" but, rather, is the process of co-individuation within a preindividuated milieu in which both the "I" and the "We" are transformed through one another. Transindividuation, then, is the basis for all social transformation and is therefore a way of addressing what happens within education.[4] As Stiegler views it, education is a set of transgenerational exchanges that provoke and question rather than pass on the baton. Therefore, it is not the knowledges but the embodied relations between them, their ability to group and regroup (thus avoiding the demographic aspect of grouping), that enables transindividuation. And it

3 André Lepecki, *Singularities: Dance in the Age of Performance* (London and New York: Routledge, 2016).

4 Bernard Stiegler in conversation with Irit Rogoff, "Transindividuation," *e-flux journal*, no. 14 (March 2010): 9.

is in these transgenerational encounters that subjectivity can find a place from which to shape and influence rather than be captured and instrumentalized.

On that account, let us be less occupied with who is coming together for what reason—some want to be transformed, some want to obtain very specific knowledge, some want to be professionalized, some want a pathway to employment through obtaining degrees, some want the credibility, status, and confidence they associate with having a degree—and recognize that regardless of why we have come, we are together: sharing space, sharing online teaching platforms, sharing libraries, sharing pints in the pub, sharing complaints about the overload of assessed work, sharing an understanding of the woes of the world. At moments of crisis, there have been so many of these recently: Syria's civil war, Brexit, Trump, North Korea, political crises around migration the world over, collapsing healthcare systems, the depression and anxiety suffered by students facing huge education fees, a shrinking job market, a chronic inability to get into adequate housing, the death of our colleague Mark Fisher.[5] In these crises we find ourselves together, able to turn the spaces of teaching into spaces of questioning, analyzing, raging, and mourning. We enact Stefano Harney and Fred Moten's "fugitive study" using the urge to learn, to turn away from disciplinary curricula, outcomes and exams, and towards an engagement with the conditions we are living out.[6] We learn the conditions and we learn from them, and we allow them to dictate other rhythms, ways of listening that aren't about gathering information but of a sharing of concerns we didn't quite know how to articulate.

Education, then, as a form of deconditioning, becomes not "knowledge transfer" but the possibility of fully living the conditions in which we are immersed. In this process, we (students, teachers, support staff, artists, and practitioners) are all *becoming researchers*. It is important to me to refrain from trying to salvage from past eras what was some form of nostalgic and idealized "freedom," which was never that free to

5
Mark Fisher, writer and our colleague in the dep of Visual Cultures at Goldsmiths, committed in January 2017. He wa a figure through whom political burdens and a cultural excitements of moment flowed and m He was a critical intell our students and for us colleagues, and his loss links with the political in Britain are acutely f

6
Stefano Harney and F Moten, *The Undercomm Fugitive Planning & E* (New York: Minor Compositions, 2013), www.minorcompositi wp-content/uploads/2 undercommons-web.

egin with. And not because it is defunct but because it might ot be up to the specific conditions we have to contend with ow, largely to do with financialization and marketization of tudy and research, of display and exhibition. These changes ffect the move away from the notion of "public" and towards rivatized revenue, whether it be fees, external research unding linked to predictable outcomes, business partnerships, isitor numbers, or media chatter and digital clicks.

For me, *deconditioning* (borrowed from Lepecki) omes in the form of *becoming research*. It also comes with an nderstanding that research is not the purview of the privileged ı institutions of research but a matter of necessity: for example, necessity for migrants to survive; for those transitioning ender to understand what they are facing biologically, legally, nd civically; for those who fight for justice or those who imply want to do no harm; and for those who develop an nderstanding that knowledge as spectacle, as revenue, as randing, even when it is about harm, actually does harm.

The thoughts I would like to share with you in this essay ircle around a shifting notion of research and its growing entrality to many artistic, institutional, pedagogical, and ivic practices. There are so many forms of such research, rom fictions that intervene in historical moments to rotate hem away from their normative understandings towards nother form of possible insight.[7] Or through the invention f institutions, and forums and protocols, that challenge the uthority of existing institutions in whom we trust. Or in he sweep of "relational geographies" that we see between nconnected moments of radical thought and action, which an provide inspiration or comfort for those who are not sure hat they have a place to start from. Or the moments in which races of erased memories materialize and begin linking with ontemporary manifestation. Everywhere, at every time, we ee that the victims, the pariahs, the erased, the forgotten, he subsumed, and the speechless need to find a place to start om, since their place within a normativized narrative has een lost or evacuated.

7
There is an immensity of writing on fictioning, parafictions, and the work of fictionally subverting historical narratives within the arts. For a few sources, see the following: Carrie Lambert-Beatty, "Make-Believe: Parafiction and Plausibility," *October*, no. 129 (Summer 2009): 51–84; Henriette Gunkel, Ayesha Hameed, and Simon O'Sullivan, eds., *Futures and Fictions* (London: Repeater, 2017); and Jon Shaw and Theo Reeves-Evison, eds., *Fiction as Method* (Berlin: Sternberg Press, 2017).

History, to paraphrase Walter Benjamin, is the chattels and spoils of war that are dragged behind the chariots of the winners of that war. Research within the realm of the arts, then, is the mode by which one defies the predominance of the winners, inserts oneself and one's insights into an arena in which you do not have a designated space. There are so many spaces and situations in which the binary opposites of winners and losers, victims and perpetrators, in their simple divisions between total opposites, simply have no purchase. Instead, there is the complex archaeology of who was there and is barely present now, who has been erased and silenced and driven from view, denied a history, who is perceived as permanently *emerging* in the present, whose presence never accrues in the long term. Through the many different projects that artist Theater Gates has generated, one continuous thread is his understanding that while African Americans have had much of their history erased—from slavery to Civil Rights to ongoing racial genocide and murderous violence in North American cities—there are nevertheless moments plucked from the atmosphere that can provide starting points for a project to make these manifest in the present.

This is not recuperative work, or restorative work, but work that is called forth by the present. "Even erased memories," says Gates, "leave behind a rhythm," and that rhythm becomes a place from which to start pulling together the traces and the odd ephemeral, barely recognizable moments that have been free-floating in the absence of a framing narrative. Gates performs the work of reconcretizing these ephemeral rhythmic traces in a dizzying array of modes of research: archival, performative, sculptural, social organizing, and urban regeneration that is not for profit or for the rewards of cultural diplomacy. There are musical histories and urban histories and archives rescued from within the bowels of odd institutions that have no visible connection to these archives; there are art institutional platforms and university platforms and municipal platforms and moments of gathering that belong to no platform. So much labor goes into the locating

Theater Gates in his C
Studio, 2013. Photo: S
Wilkes.

Black Monks of Mis
St. Laurence Church
Performance, Chicag
2014.

of site and the conceptualizing and planning and bringing together—and it is that work that constitutes research, not simply the materials that are unearthed.[8] The effort materializes before our eyes. It draws us in, it makes manifest, it is nothing less than "world-making," in Jean-Luc Nancy's parlance.

What might on occasion have been seen as "community work" or "social and political practice" is here posited as research because of the centrality of investigation and knowledge production and the new ways of performing knowledge that are at its center. It is research because it is an insistence on changing a perspective, a point of entry, a mode of engagement that is the production of knowledge rather than the accumulation of additional information.

People gather around the desire to investigate and to know; they use their wide-ranging knowledge not necessarily to climb up the ladder of a discipline or institution but with the recognition that numerous forces make up the world they live in and we need to have relationships with these forces. Some twenty years ago, philosopher Gilles Deleuze said, "Participation is the process of laying the grounds for a claim"[9]—and, to me, this is what research in the arts is doing in increasingly imaginative and inventive ways. It is not making claims but laying the ground for speaking them otherwise.

The art world I inhabit now straddles great institutions and reading groups, think tanks and community gardens, supranational forums and weekly salon-like meetings in pubs. The students in our curating programs think the model of nongovernmental organizations (NGOs) suits their aspirations more than exhibiting institutions do. Collective reading, writing, investigation, sharing information, blogging, learning skills like woodwork, metalwork, and horticulture, going on urban study walks of gentrified parts of the city, etc., are the stuff of daily life for many of my students—not set up in antagonism to either the art world or the university and art academy but in recognition that we are surrounded by failing systems and failing ecologies. Rather than protest

8 See Michael Darling, Matthew Day Jackson, and Carolyn Christov-Bakargiev, *Theaster Gates: 12 Ballads for Huguenot House* [a project for dOCUMENTA (13)] (Cologne: Buchhandlung Walther König, 2012); Theaster Gates, *Theaster Gates: Black Archive* (Cologne: Walther König and Kunsthaus Bregenz, 2017); and Theaster Gates, "How to revive a neighborhood: with imagination, beauty and art," TED 2015, http://www.ted.com/talks/theaster_gates_how_to_revive_a_neighborhood_with_imagination_beauty_and_art?language=en/.

9 Gilles Deleuze, *The Logic of Sense*, trans. Mark Lester (New York: Columbia Univ. Press, 1990).

them, we need to learn about them, understand their workings and intervene in them. So, it is *research* and not activism, communitarianism, or protest—a need to know, differently and from another perspective, and to communicate that knowledge and share it in imaginative, enticing, sociable, and compelling ways that draw one in rather than keeping people at a distance, lecturing facts at one another.

One of the things that compels me about the different forms of activity I see around me and take part in is how many varied knowledges—high theoretical ones, philosophical, economical, logistical and organizational ones, technical ones, scientific ones, pedagogical and communal ones, sensory and immersive ones—come together in such activities. Knowledges that are not hierarchized but find ways to dance with each other, at each turn finding different arrangements to the movement.

This is part of an ever-growing proliferation of practices whose aim is not the production of objects, or images that take their place alongside other objects, but whose focus is to make manifest in the world, by all means, what is urgent and important to our lives. Artistic practices have become modes of drawing attention to altered conditions and of making sites perform differently than they are designated to. For example, the New Cross Commoners, a loose collective of people who have had relationships with or through Goldsmiths, University of London, attend sites of former civic culture like public libraries and schools that have been turned into businesses and residences as part of local regeneration schemes, job centers that have closed, and reservoirs that have been privatized, and they read or study in them for long hours. They force the sites to perform their previously intended civic lives rather than their current financialized ones. They generate collective "schools" that point to other sources of knowing and other, circular modalities of pedagogy, such as the *School of Healing*.

The art students involved at our university garden plot grow things and produce long lines of connection to colonial routes, genetic modification, taxation, and trade agreements

New Cross Common[...] *for Healing*, 2018. Cou[...] Paolo Plotegher.

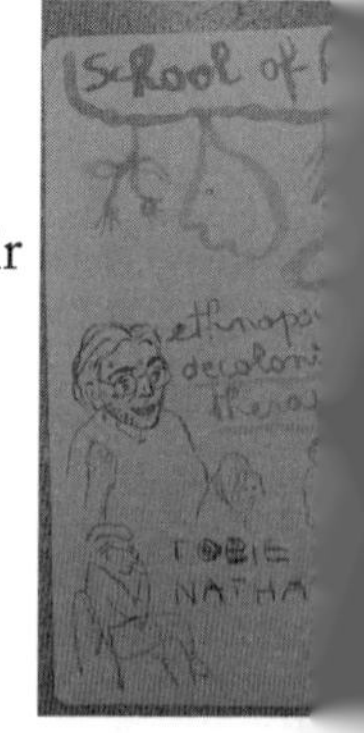

New Cross Commo[...] *of Healing*, "Decolon[...] Therapy." Courtesy [...] Plotegher.

as defining factors in food production. They see dominant supermarket policies as shaping the landscape of how we eat and how we disconnect from the environment. There are artists working in advocacy of fair-trade farming, producing new modes of representation, and other artists working with groups of political activists that have been designated as terrorists by their own governments, lawyers who espouse the cause of human rights for national liberation, by creating what Jonas Staal has called the *New World Academy*, a backdoor perspective on the legal map of human rights around the globe.[10]

Jonas Staal, *New World Summit*, Berlin Biennial, 2012–ongoing.

Jonas Staal, *New World Academy*, 2012–ongoing.

10
Jonas Staal, *New World Academy* (2013–17), http://www.newworldsummit.org/.

For Staal, existing structures such as the International Court of Human Rights, or other international forums that have the status of arbitrating crimes and misdeeds within international law, repeat the hegemony of national state legislature. Instead, he sets up summits and academies that operate differently, using the official forums as a photographic negative for the ghostly, less-than-acknowledged presences that actually can do the work of representing outlawed interests. In the *New World Summit*, the ghostly presences were those who are forbidden to travel due to accusations of terrorist activity, in most cases emanating from the political demands they represent for sovereignty and rights. It is the work of extracting the figures and their struggles out of one logic and producing an alternative structural logic in which they can be represented. The constitution of such alternative forums requires a vast amount of research: about global politics and legal systems and the bureaucracies that can outlaw and decree political actors to be "terrorists," about structures of representation and pedagogies that can reverse-engineer assumed compliance with security-driven fears about who can and who cannot circulate freely.[11] What is of great interest about this mode of research is that it reinvents the very structures it is researching, and it posits a modus operandi that is based on the assumption of "as if"—as if we were different and these were actually the institutions through which we had the capacity to operate.

11
BAK (Basis voor Actuele Kunst) in Utrecht has worked closely with Staal on all of his projects and has published many volumes of the results of this research, all available as PDFs on http://www.jonasstaal.nl/. Among these are *Stateless Democracy* (2015), *The Art of Creating a State* (2014), *Leaderless Politics* (2013), *New World Summit* (2012), and *Towards a People's Culture* (2013).

My friends teach classes in parking lots and seminars in pubs, and set up schools whose curriculum is a curated, thematic program of free public events taking place in London every day as part of rethinking what are the actual public spaces of study and research. A Curating PhD project by Leire Vegara (head curator of Bulegoa z/b in Bilbao), researching Spain's sovereign islands off the coast of Morocco, unearthed maps, walked the terrain, and ran reading groups on the coastal rocks while looking on at the military-occupied islands from the closest permitted distance.[12] The knowledges that she and her collaborators produced were cartographic, photographic, historical, land-related, and included literary and philosophical readings and storytelling. When the project concluded, these "Sovereign Plazas," shrouded in mystery for having been unreachable and unviewable, became legible and otherwise knowable.

Leire Vergara, Reading
Morocco, 2016.

12
Leire Vergara, *Dispositi*
Touching: Curatorial Im
in the Time of Expanded
(curatorial research pro
conducted at Trankat i
Tétouan, Morocco, 201

A hallmark of all this activity is its collaborative nature, of the fact that it operates more like a seminar and a form of exchange than of isolated work by someone in a studio. "Collaboration, or more specifically, collectivity—a scene of some kind—is also crucial for this operation," says Simon O'Sullivan. "How else can one make something that is of one but not of one at the same time? That is intended but produces the unintended?"[13] Like all knowledge production, it takes place in the relational interaction *between*—between perspectives, familiarities, estrangements, hopes, and the many legacies that intermingle to make up what it is to *know*. Knowing is performing the event of knowledge, expositing its efforts and not just its results.

13
Simon O'Sullivan, "M
Science and the Fictio
Reality," *Paragrana* 2
(2016): 80–93.

We stage summits that emulate the protocols of nonaligned nations who had reached out to one another to carve out a space that was otherwise entirely designated by superpower divisions, and when asked what we are doing, we say we are *practicing*. Architects, geologists, maritime law experts, climatologists, filmmakers, and marine biologists come together to produce another layer of complex understanding of what are "oceans," as in TBA21's establishment of the

"Current Institute," named for the invisible forces that propel waters and aimed at understanding how oceans are places from which to read everything.[14] Other artists try to visualize the Anthropocene, or the satellite communication of surveillance systems, or to spatialize moments of great violence, or they try and turn the spaces of venerable museums into laboratories for communal research, as in *Cosmopolis #1: Collective Intelligence* at Centre Pompidou in Paris.[15] Inspired curators, such as Maria Hlavajova, turn their spaces into pursuits of large-scale remappings of inherited global relations as in *Former West*.[16] Everywhere I look, I see practitioners turn to ways of working, involving collective research and collective study and their performance—performances that are not framed by one kind of discipline, or one kind of institution, or one kind of market. So, when I come to speak of what I perceive has become of "research," I speak of concrete shifts in which study and research and creation have together become agents of changing environments and changing perceptions, and perhaps, most importantly, of a sense of permission to speak in many languages and many forms of where we perceive of urgencies. Some of the practices that have caught my attention are exposed in large-scale international museums, and others are elsewhere, in basements and parking lots and classrooms. What they have in common is not their standing in the art world but their commitment to research as a mode of engaging with their contemporary realities. Research, it would seem, does not require so much tenacity as we were taught as students but, rather, it requires audacity—the ability to envisage and to know from elsewhere and otherwise.

14
TBA21–Academy, *The Current II: Spheric Ocean* (a three-year expedition cycle through New Zealand's North Islands, led by curator/art historian Chus Martínez), Thyssen-Bornemisza Art Contemporary, Vienna, http://www.tba21.org/.

15
Centre Georges Pompidou, *Cosmopolis #1: Collective Intelligence* (Paris, 2017).

16
Maria Hlavajova and Simon Sheikh, eds., *Former West: Art and the Contemporary after 1989* (Cambridge, MA: MIT Press, with BAK, Utrecht, 2017), http://www.formerwest.org/.

Research as New Realities

So far, this argument has been expository, briefly touching on some of the ideas and practices that together sketch out a new notion of complex and multifaceted research within the expanded field of art. Now, I would like to bring together its strands in a slightly more prophetic voice. The prophetic (the predictive) isn't held so much to its truth claims as to its urging for change, and might enable us to make the leap that posits that research rather than that which takes place in advance of the main event—whatever that main event might be—is actually the constitution of New Realities.[17]

Research, as we experience it now in both institutional and culturally active contexts, has moved away from stable bodies of knowledge to be excavated as well as away from recognized subjects whose validity is universally recognized.

Research is now the arena in which we negotiate knowledge we have inherited with the conditions of our lives. Those conditions, whether economic, geographical, or propelled by subjectivity, have become the drive (not the subject matter) of the work. And it is here, in the immersion in conditions, that research transforms from an investigative impulse to the constitution of new realities. It is thus that we recognize that research is not some elevated activity requiring a great deal of prior knowledge, nor is it simply the urge to "find things out." It is, in many ways, the stuff of daily life. Every form of hardship encountered—whether one is an immigrant or living out catastrophic conditions, affected by emotional sea changes or crises of identity or of security—generates *research*, and everyone *researches*. And the forms of current research have equally shifted as contemporary, multivalent research moves between archival, documentary, conceptual, and performative modes and utilizes everything from fictioning, docudramatizing, to mimicry, the queer animation of archives, and to structural self-instituting to produce new realities of knowledge. Moving farther and farther from the assembling of information, research has undergone a process of singularization, becoming relational in form, shifting as it changes locations and experiences unexpected encounters, no longer framed by how it originally came into the world, the discipline or professional practice that once named it. It is, in the words of Giorgio Agamben, "whatever" knowledge. In Agamben's terms, "whatever" is

17
The first iteration of thes thoughts of "research as realities" appeared in *To Seminar*, ed. Henk Slage (Utrecht: Metropolis M MaHKU, and BAK, 201

"being such as it always matters"—"Singularity is thus freed from the false dilemma that obliges knowledge to choose between the ineffability of the individual and the intelligibility of the universal."[18] So, contemporary research practices occupy neither exclusively; neither the realm of universally acknowledged formal learning nor the realm of pure self-expression. They are, instead, a harnessing of both in a new relation to one another, a relation that cannot be contained by scholarship or by individual experience but plots out the ground for shared, social communication of conditions, drives, and lines of flight. New research, then, is the inhabitation of conditions in another modality, one that responds to formal knowledge but does not adhere to it, as well as one that invokes the subjectivity of those conditions but does not narrate it as such.

18
Giorgio Agamben, *The Coming Community*, trans. Michael Hardt (Minneapolis: Univ. of Minnesota Press, 1993), 1.1.

It is crucial to insist on this fundamental change in both the impulse that propels research and the new forms it takes, because institutions of higher education and museums have instrumentalized advanced research practices for a host of pragmatic ends: in order to have reasons for expansion and variety, in order to satisfy public sector demands that knowledge be produced and be shown to circulate, and in order to garner whatever resources might be available and to claim greater numbers for their programs. Using the creative industries terminology of "innovative" and "imaginative" and "cutting edge," emergent research practices, as they are presently framed within institutions, are losing their critical potential as they become the latest cog in the wheel of cognitive capitalism. They are increasingly public-relations sound bites in the endless pursuit of "the new" for higher education and cultural institutional market ends.

Instead, we can keep in mind the many potential contributions that new forms of research in the art world have been able to introduce:

– The possibility of making the art world more than it is, of being less captive by the market, of being about more than tangible art, but instead having concrete forms of indicating immersive processes rather than celebrating products.

— The recognition that these new forms of hybrid and imaginative research activity require an entire new vocabulary in which we begin to understand how we have gained permissions for exiting the older formations of knowledge and re-forming the world around us through urgent concerns.
— The understanding that we now need to articulate new models of research as well as those for performing, delivering, displaying, and viewing of new practices. How can displays be constantly productive rather than passively informative? What does it mean to be the viewer of research, and can it provide us with an alternative form of participation?—one that is less institutionally located and more interior, seeing ourselves as fields of amalgamated knowledges.

It is as such that *research*, in the contemporary sense, is both a set of new relations as well as a set of critical insights. It is as such that research links hands with the ongoing desire for criticality in a world in which one cannot step outside of the problematics, cannot ever exit and have an external viewing position. Research, in the final analysis, is the potential for immersion and engagement without drawing conclusions and making predictions, the potential for making the world our own.

Museum Research—Program, Project, Platform

Beck Jee-sook is a critic and curator based in Seoul and Charleston, South Carolina, US. She was Artistic Director of SeMA Biennale Mediacity Seoul 2016 *Neriri Kiruru Harara* a the 4th Anyang Public Art Project (APAP) *Public Story*, held from 2013 to 2014. Previously, she was Artistic Director of Atelier Hermès (2011–14), Director of the Arts Council Kore (ARKO) Art Center and Project Director of Insa Art Space (2005–8). She served as Curator of Insa Art Space and Chief Curator of the Marronnier Art Center from 2000 to 2004. She co-curated *Activating Korea: Tides of Collective Action* (Govett-Brewster Art Gallery, New Plymouth, 2007), *The Last Chapter-Trace Route: Remapping Global Cities* (6th Gwangju Biennale, 2006), and *The Battle of Visions* (Kunsthalle Darmstadt, 2005). 2002, she organized the international symposium on alternativ spaces titled *Memory of Cities, History of Spaces*. A collection of her critical and curatorial essays is forthcoming from Mediabu in 2018.

Beck Jee-sook

What Museums Don't Research: A Survey Through *One Opening*

This essay is a meaningful opportunity for me—as someone who (perhaps in a very Korean manner) generally only looks forward instead of backward—to reflect on my activities over the last ten years. Of course, I am well aware of the hazards of gazing backward. In cases where everything can easily become historicized, it is difficult to avoid the double-edged sword of either empowerment or exhaustion. In that sense, seeing that the word "survey" is being used more often than the word "retrospective" in exhibitions these days, I would like to treat this opportunity not as a retrospective but, rather, as a field to survey.

Part-time Suite, still image from *One Opening*, 2015 (HD video, sound, 30 min 2 sec), 01:23.

For me, the text that evokes this survey is not a specific book or document but, instead, a work by the artist collective Part-time Suite titled *One Opening* (2015). The video, which comes from the archive of Insa Art Space (IAS) and which I encountered in 2015 while conducting research for SeMA Biennale Mediacity Seoul 2016, appears to take its title from a document that mistranslated the term "exhibition opening" to a (physical) "opening." It was produced about seven years after IAS Archive went dormant and the artists explain:

> … the video follows a series of performances that form loose patterns out of the preparation process for an exhibition in parallel with scattered montages of images and words from catalogues, documentations, and managerial papers dating from 2000 to 2008 that were extracted from IAS Archive. At the same time, it transforms the remnants of attempts to adapt to globalization among the intense legacy of art practices from the past, together with vestiges of guidelines for artists to grow as artists, into an inquiry regarding the present status of art.

This work reflects the ideal relationship between an archive and an artist's commissioned works that IAS Archive aspired to embody in its most active period, which followed a bit later. At the same time, it brings in "double bind" language, in other words, schizophrenic language, as if the artists believe the words at face value. It may be that these circumstances are a result of the temporal difference between IAS's past and present. I hope that this thick yet flat space, which has been created by layering different time periods, can be utilized as yet another opening through this essay. I would like to gradually walk through the turning points of my survey by tracing the axes X, Y, and Z, which comprise the majority of the artwork.

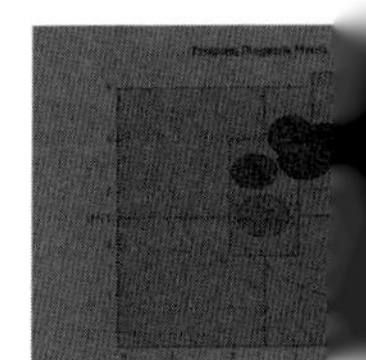

Part-time Suite, still i[…] from *One Opening*, 20[…] (HD video, sound, 30[…] 2 sec), 02:36.

This survey aims to reorganize or re-form, in hindsight, the three-dimensional relationship between the work of archives and nonperiodical publications and art institutions or biennials through the lenses of several projects that I led within the Korean "contemporary" art scene, taking a long view from 2000 up to the present, or a short view of about ten years from 2005 to 2016. Long or short, both periods reflect the contemporaneity that Korean art has sustained since the 1990s; in other words, it is a period characterized by expanding art institutions, the expansion of the art market, and flourishing international biennials, as well as a time when alternative spaces, public art, emerging spaces, and self-organizing activities performed their individual roles as negotiators and outliers with institutions in their respective positions.[1]

In my view, a political and economic variable arose after the democratization of Korean society—a fierce impetus toward global competition, or a variable of neoliberalism and unequal standard of living—that has made a significant impact on various trajectories of art. Meanwhile, based on my experience, it is hard to deny that the power of realpolitik represented by elections has affected the contemporary Korean art scene to a far greater extent than the market economy. Above all, the public sphere in institutional contexts—e.g., government-run museums, government funding, and local government-run contemporary art events—takes the lead with regard to the contemporary art landscape in Korea. Realpolitik has had a thorough and persistent effect not only on the art system's policy-framing and practice but also on institutions' exhibitions, collections, and programs, as we can observe from the blacklist incident under the last administration.[2] If we presume that museums in Asia (under the aegis of corporations) lead with large collections, publicly funded institutions appear to be latecomers, and art centers without collections are relatively common, then I would argue that Korea is an exception to the norm.[3]

In this context, I would like to clarify that the archive and publication projects I have led and will discuss here—at IAS under Arts Council Korea, Anyang Public Art Project (APAP), and Mediacity Seoul hosted by Seoul Museum of Art—have had their staff and budgets fully funded by the City of Anyang and the City of Seoul. In fact, the funding of the organizations that run these events—Arts Council Korea and local museums—is situated within a cultural arena where right-wing populists, government officials who are indifferent to art, and progressives with impetuous dispositions all insist on receiving their own share of benefits. Nevertheless, because

1
Moon Young Min, "Situating Contemporary Art from South Korea 1980–2015," in *A Companion to Korean Art*, eds. Park J.P. and Rhi Juhyung (Malden, MA: Wiley-Blackwell, forthcoming). I would like to thank Moon for letting me read the manuscript.

2
See the former Korean president Park Geun-hye's blacklist of artists.

3
Claire Bishop, *Radical Museology: or, What's 'Contemporary' in Museums of Contemporary Art?* (London: Koenig Books, 2013), 11.

these organizations are positioned relatively on the periphery,[4] they have been able to secure a certain degree of flexibility.

Furthermore, from the start, this flexibility has not been willingly given in recognition of the autonomy of art or the autonomy of the curator or art director. Instead, it involves a peculiar institutional situation where these projects operate with public funding and, as such, they must consistently demonstrate the differences and distinctions between themselves and already established institutions and biennials, resulting in their flexibility. Skipping ahead to my survey's conclusion, the projects that I will introduce took this precariousness and risk as a starting point or opportunity, and constructed their archives in the process of rethinking their institutional identity in parallel with critical publication projects. In addition, by overlapping these platforms and projects to activate a sort of "constructive citizenship of artistic thinking," I have sought to engage in institutional projects as a critical practice for contemporary art, regardless of their success and sustainability.

4
Strictly speaking, IAS was neither a government-run museum nor an alternative space, and APAP and Me[illegible] Seoul are still unstable as latecomers to the biennial format. This is reflected in APAP changing its hostin[illegible] from two- to three-year intervals, and in Mediaci[illegible] Seoul constantly changin[illegible] name.

X—Archive

Part-time Suite, still i[illegible] from *One Opening*, 201[illegible] (HD video, sound, 30 [illegible] 2 sec), 04:26.

IAS Archive, which operated pilot programs starting in 2005, built its framework and interior facilities in collaboration with the artist Lee Meekyoung and developed its direction and basic inventory in collaboration with the Pidgin Collective, which was organized by artists Lim Minouk and Frederic Michon. Artistic perspectives and interpretations were deeply rooted not only in the archive's structure but also in its foundational principles and programming; thus, from its beginning, IAS Archive did not aim to become a traditional storage archive that manages, preserves, and maintains documents and physical materials in a rigid and hierarchical manner.

At the time, the Pidgin Collective presented a manifesto for an active and dynamic archive: one that would facilitate the realization of radical projects, enable provocative collaborations between artists and researchers, and aspire to a fluid and intermittent network. Following this framework, all of IAS's exhibitions, talks, workshops, screenings, and performances were initiated on the archive concept and, then, also integrated into the archive.

In 2015, the critic Yoon Wonhwa interpreted IAS Archive's activities as follows: "At first, IAS Archive was more a sort of portal traversing spatial intervals, borrowing the form of documents and generating new points of access, than a breakwater against the flow of time. It … was always collected as a database, and then it dreamed of a multidimensional network twinkling with the sparks of unexpected encounters."[5]

In fact, IAS arose from a predictable and sustainable network. Created from a special fund of the Ministry of Culture to support young artists suffering economic difficulties following the IMF crisis, IAS emerged alongside the activities of alternative spaces that spontaneously came into being around the same time, weaving new patterns into the fabric of Korean contemporary art in the 2000s. IAS served as a hub for

5
Yoon Wonhwa, *1002th Night: Arts of Seoul in the 2010s* (Seoul: workroom press, 2015), 104.

alternative spaces, from curating the international symposium on alternative spaces titled *Memory of Cities, History of Spaces in* 2002 which featured exhibitions and workshops, to organizing the Non-profit Art Space Association in 2005. Throughout this period, IAS took the initiative to complement and challenge the limitations of other alternative spaces that were unable to engage in activities outside of holding exhibitions; in doing so, IAS attempted to build and program an archive with institutional resources and manpower in a way that alternative spaces were unable to do alone.

As such, IAS represented a changeover in the artist support structure that focused on "the exterior of the exhibition." However, this method was more than just circuitously supporting artists by utilizing an archive; in fact, it understood the archive as not only an exhibition that artists participate in and contribute to but also a "curatorial" practice in itself. In 2007, the IAS Annual Report stated that the archive's documents, which are constantly being organized, are waiting for users' hands and memories so that they may be written and transformed.[6] However, once Lee Myung-bak was inaugurated as the new president of Korea, IAS Archive abruptly ceased all activity.

Again, Yoon noted that even though IAS was helpless to prevent the closure of the archive, there was nevertheless a triumphant sense of victory, of defenseless euphoria without regard for what the future might hold.[7] If there was, in fact, euphoria, it would be for the archive; more accurately, this captivation really started with the name "archive." As you may know, an art archive is related to forms of knowledge, such as books, documents, and information, and thus directly intervenes to a significant extent in the process of knowledge production in contemporary art. Furthermore, because of the originality and physicality of an archive, it can have an existential and indexical relationship with incidents, objects, and figures that comprise history and society beyond the mediative characteristics of art, such as icons, representations, and symbols.

6
Cho Jiyoung, *IAS Arch*
(Seoul: Insa Art Space,
Council Korea, 2008),

7
Yoon, *1002th Night*, 1

In a situation where postcolonial history constantly adheres to our bodies like phlegm or moisture, the archive that young artists could imagine laid claim to a will to penetrate a huge absence or void—or a certain opening—rather than to defy the passage of time and bestow immortality. IAS Archive was a kind of fake genealogy that was necessary for "an orphan child with no family history."[8] Yet, if there was a triumphant sense of victory, it might have been nothing more than the promise of the future before an orphan who glimpses the momentary shimmering of this fake genealogy. Rather than emphasizing the hierarchies of knowledge, the value of documents, and the weight of preservation, this "archival impulse"—which seeks to create a new archive by interconnecting fragmented information where a certain relatedness is difficult to establish—logically heads toward the future.

8 Lee Kyung-sung, "What Crops could be Harvested in a Weedy Field," *Pyonghwa shinmun* (December 26, 1956), quoted in Shin Chunghoon, "Art of the 1990s and 'Historical Necessity,'" in *X: Korean Art in the Nineties*, ed. Yeo Kyunghwan (Seoul: Seoul Museum of Art/Hyunsil Publishing, 2016), 45.

X-2—4th Anyang Public Art Project Archive, Anyang Foundation for Culture & Arts, 2013–14

If IAS Archive was heading toward an unknown future, then APAP's archive made a turn to the ambiguous past as a tool to save common memories and edit the present. However, when I took the position of art director of the fourth APAP in 2012, constructing an archive was not included in the plan. Over the course of three APAP events since 2005, feelings of fatigue and disconnection from the APAP artworks had multiplied within civil-society organizations, as well as public pessimism among the Anyang City Council and local community after the local government elections. Thus, APAP was almost driven out of existence by a reduction in its total budget and the uncertainty of its maintenance. In this situation, the burden to prove the reason for its existence and identity became my responsibility as art director. I would say that APAP, which was initiated amid the ebullient mood of other international biennials in Korea, suffered a predictable crack from its very establishment.

As it was unable to solve the complex relationship between public art's aesthetic and activism, and, moreover, as its goal of branding for the purposes of regional redevelopment and tourism lost direction, Anyang citizens effectively became indifferent to APAP, and ultimately the artworks became neglected where they were sited in public space.

Eventually, the fourth APAP gave up on adding new outdoor works or organizing public art projects in collaboration with the community. Instead, we started to collect, sort, and review the preserved documents, photographs, and videos related to the past three APAP events. While conducting this "study," we were able to arrive at a plan for organizing APAP's archive, proposing it as a platform for public approval—not an agreement that reaches the same opinion but, rather, the potential for a minimum degree of public consensus that would allow for discordance and different views—and we finally proposed this plan as a common ground from which to research and practice the connection between the public and art. While the users of IAS Archive would be mainly young artists, prospective artists, and students, APAP's archive had to build up its interface not only with people from the art world but also with regular Anyang citizens in mind. Accordingly, we created *Park Library* and *Making Lab* in the Anyang Pavilion. Also, APAP's archive reflected the lessons learned from IAS Archive—namely, the necessity of a backup plan for continuity. Now, after several missteps, there is presently an attempt to establish a new structure and move forward as a public art archive.

In the meantime, there has been a major shift in the understanding of and environment around archives within the Korean art scene. The trend and overuse of archives has been a topic of frequent criticism, but diverse kinds of archives are now accepted as fundamental elements not only in art museums and biennials but also in large and small events and exhibitions. Taking place within only a few years, this change reflects an exceptional confidence in art history and the contemporary art system in Korea to the point where the dispute over genealogy has fallen by the wayside. I think that this is a result of Korean contemporary art embodying contemporary methodology in real time; this arises as the sense of the 1990s period of postmodernism and post-Minjung Art has ripened to maturity,[9] and the interchange and prevalence of international biennials reveals this sense in a global manner.

9 Shin, "Art of the 1990s," 49.

Y—Nonperiodical Publications

Along with *One Opening*, we chose nonperiodical publications as the Y-axis. If archive work, as the X-axis, rethinks and mediates institutional identity according to its context and condition, then publications, in response to this, suggest a coordinate that more directly externalizes the critical views and statements about contemporaneity that Korean art generates. Instead of choosing the form of academic publications based on long-term research and regularly published journals, we followed the form of nonperiodical publications, which are able to respond in an instantaneous and timely manner with a focus on an extended network and circulation method. Also, the factor of the allocation and management of participating manpower and of the institution's capacity had a significant impact on this nonperiodicity. As the two archives discussed above had left us with a lingering affection and concern about their sustainability and continued existence, we set up two kinds of nonperiodical publications with their lifecycles structured so that they could continue as independent texts after completing their publication cycles.

Part-time Suite, still image from *One Opening*, 2015 (HD video, sound, 30 min 2 sec), 11:30.

Y-1—IAS, *Journal BOL*

From 2005 to 2008, IAS published *Journal BOL*, totaling ten volumes in Korean and English (or mixing in a third language, depending on the circumstances), in the format of a nonperiodical publication of around 300 pages including essays, cartoons, photographs, poems, novels, and artist pages from domestic and overseas writers.

Journal BOL emerged out of strong criticism of and discontent about Korean art journalism. The editorial board viewed typical art journalism as the listing of events, and individual events only exist as fragments, with no vision of the connections between the events or the currents they create as a whole. We believed that art must serve as a channel for the fierce competition of values in society, and determined that *Journal BOL* would focus on defining the intellectual currents of contemporary art.[10]

Incorporating the critical mindset of an editorial board, the *Journal BOL* team chose its topics by researching and developing new agendas, such as "Panic," "The Call of History," "Justice," "Resonance," and "Ghost," and by relating to exhibitions curated by IAS and other area art institutions, such as *The Middle East and "Us"* and *Vietnam and "Us."* In the latter case, catalogues and other exhibition materials were published separately, and *Journal BOL* independently created a plan for the publication project with writers and page allocations based on the editorial direction. Instead of considering publications to be the byproducts of and supplements to exhibitions, *Journal BOL* published elements where knowledge and layers of sense, previously embedded in the form of exhibitions, collide with the editorial axis and are thus revealed. We expected a level of criticism and acceptance where, presupposing the exhibition-as-artist, texts stemming from this perspective are read without the artist's intention and at times deconstruct exhibition auteurism.

In research dissertations by Korean art historians who study the recent past, *Journal BOL*—together with *Forum A*, published by Alternative Space Pool (a Korean alternative space, now known as Art Space Pool)—is evaluated as an attempt to produce autonomous discourses reflecting on Korean cultural and social situations.[11] It is true that *Journal*

10
Editorial Board, *Journ*
no. 1 (Winter 2005): 6

11
Park Eunyoung, "K
Globalism," in *Kor*
Contemporary Art
(Seoul: Sapyoung
House, 2017), 46.

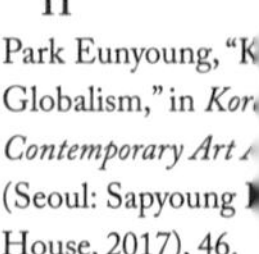

BOL was founded at the time when *Forum A* ceased its publication, and a considerable portion of *Journal BOL*'s editorial team overlapped with *Forum A*'s. However, there is a difference between the two. *Forum A* paid attention to critical theory focusing on the artist and reality, emphasizing criticism of reality in contemporary art through intense criticism of artworks and exhibitions, whereas *Journal BOL* did not deal with specific genres, essays on artworks, or reviews of exhibitions. Instead, *Journal BOL* took interest in the direct region-to-region networking without going through the global art world, and attempted to deconstruct homogenized globalism. Furthermore, by calling forth a historical perspective—one that is gradually fading—it tried to tease out the complex relationship between art activity and common memory. Meanwhile, *Journal BOL* generally maintained its view embracing both art and visual culture, but it emphasized that art is nevertheless important because it has a certain ambitious attitude and a historical intention to possess the peak of culture in its concepts and sensory world, as the self-consciousness of visual culture.[12]

Although we did not declare it when we started *Journal BOL*, we knew that its life would end after the tenth edition was published. We expected that there would be a limit to the available domestic writers due to the selectivity of our topics, as well as a limit to the energy and motivation of the editorial team, which operated with a collective-minded attitude. However, in contrast with our expectations, or perhaps aligned with our predictions, the direct trigger for disbanding *Journal BOL* was the inauguration of Korea's new president, just as with the discontinuation of IAS. As I was preparing this essay, I browsed through the journal and found that the last issue, no. 10, introduced the upcoming topic for issue no. 11 as "The Female's Space." Seen from the fervor of feminism in Korea, which is now making cracks in Korean civil society, the uncompleted issue no. 11 seems especially prescient.

12 Editorial Board, *Journal BOL*, no. 1: 7.

COULD BE, which originated from the *Open Editorial Meeting* during Mediacity Seoul's pre-biennale in 2015, was published in four issues. Whereas the ten editions of *Journal BOL* were distributed by Korean bookstores in a thick-bound series, *COULD BE* was published in the format of a fifty-page free pamphlet/newspaper that could essentially travel anytime, anywhere. *Journal BOL*'s emphasis on horizontal networks transformed into *COULD BE*'s editions where guest editors from Korea, Thailand, Myanmar, South Africa, Costa Rica, and Peru each took on the responsibility of editing their respective issues according to their selected themes: new art spaces and art writing, high-school students and participatory textbooks, science-fiction graphic novels, and the language of gender and queer politics.

COULD BE NO. 1: Trios of Guides emerged from the response to new art spaces that blossomed before and after 2015. Unlike the alternative spaces that emerged at the end of the 1990s, these new art spaces demonstrated a major difference in terms of their reactive methods even though they shared the same experiences of political and economic crises. The 1990s alternative spaces, each with its own distinct direction, organized an official network in order to proactively change the topography of the Korean art scene, whereas the new art spaces, interconnected through social media, reject identity politics and have no specific associations. However, sharing the recognition that "it is possible for artists to create paths to show their own works themselves," they tend to directly connect artists' livelihoods and their artworks' distribution systems through events like *GOODS* (a 2015 art fair) instead of holding symposia and exhibitions.[13]

Symbolically drawing the site characteristics of Seoul as a media city into this discussion, if the alternative spaces from the 1990s targeted remnant domains such as rooftops and vacant lots for public ownership, then the new art spaces from the 2010s could be attempting to occupy invisible and

13
Song Yoonji, "Conte[illegible] Art and Mass Cultu[illegible] *Korean Contemporar[illegible] the 1990s* (Seoul: S[illegible] Publishing, 2017), [illegible]

latent spaces such as *banjiha* (semi-basements) and cyber "dungeons" as forms of collective time. *COULD BE NO. 1: Trios of Guides* was initiated when Hyun Seewon, cofounder of Audio Visual Pavilion (one of the new art spaces), invited fourteen writers to cowrite texts as a temporary writing-production gathering called *Trios of Guides*. This group work was initiated by walking around the sites of Mediacity Seoul and, according to Hyun, attempting to embody fragments that cannot be placed into a single vessel: women, SF (science or speculative fiction), Seoul, new art spaces, changes in society and the art world, and the history of Seoul.[14] Among the publication's issues, *Trios of Guides* is the only one composed of texts without images; thus, it is more like a "zine" that utilizes various forms of writing and expresses practical knowledge in written form.

14
Kil Yekyung, "Editorial," *COULD BE NO. 1: Trios of Guides* (Seoul: Seoul Museum of Art, 2016), 7.

Z—Program, Project, and Platform

The X-axis archives and Y-axis nonperiodical publication projects individually organized exhibitions, talks, and workshop programs, and they intersected with individual projects over the long term. Moreover, they hovered over other platforms, such as libraries, laboratories, villages, schools, and so forth, and thus tested the feasibility of a form of cultural production where the characteristic of commons is revealed. Through the three-dimensionality of this Z-axis, the possibility of a functional transformation emerges where the art institution's identity does not stop at the repetition of fixed self-affirmation but, instead, moves animatedly so as to exchange influences with the changing environment.

Part-time Suite, still image from *One Opening*, 2015 (HD video, sound, 30 min 2 sec), 26:43.

The Artist Portfolio (within IAS Archive) diversified artist support channels by combining with annual projects such as *TOOL BOX for emerging artists* (2005–8) and *IAS media* (2006–8).[15] *Journal BOL* focused its critical view of the institution through another editorial criterion not yet mentioned, a holistic exploration of topics while organizing

15
TOOL BOX for emerging artists, curated by Kang Sung-eun, and *IAS media* by curator Kim Hyunjin, followed by Kang Yumi.

a series of programs with international biennials and overseas art institutions. First, issue no. 5, "Bare Life," was a special issue in which *Journal BOL* participated in documenta 12 magazine project before undergoing publication. Issue no. 9, "Dongducheon," which ISA researched for two years at the invitation of *Museum as Hub* (an inter-institutional network and partnership initiative conceived by the New Museum in New York) introduced the Korean city of Dongducheon—the site of acute conflicts while the US Army was stationed there after liberation and up to the time of its departure—to the other participating overseas institutions as their "neighbor."[16] The last issue, "8008," was published via a series of Guerrilla Salons and Plenary Sessions organized by *Journal BOL* as the Gwangju Biennale's academic events in 2008. While questioning what "languages" we're using at the present time when speaking about Korean contemporary art, tracing this inquiry, and endeavoring to "repeat" the Minjung Art of the 1980s, editor Park Sohyun wrote that, in the manner of Slavoj Žižek, to repeat the 1980s is to accept the failure of particular solutions in the 1980s, and to distinguish what had actually been done from the field of opportunities opened up by that era.[17]

Although APAP's archive operated various programs interpreting and reorganizing the archive (as demonstrated in its byname, Project Archive), its physical location was crucial in terms of establishing the archive. The fourth APAP restored Anyang Pavilion, the work from the first APAP, to its original name—it had previously been called Alvaro Siza Hall—in the process of archiving previous APAP events and creating a public art center that would secure a foothold to enable the continuity of a civil festival. Installing the function of a platform in *Park Library* and in *Making Lab* (both 2013–14), APAP's archive was created along with "Books on Contemporary Public Art" in *Park Library*. *Park Library* utilized books and boxes as its tools and organized a package program made up of publications and art materials for APAP Friends volunteers and APAP Tours docents. In this process, APAP's archive was able to provide its users with a unique and memorable experience.

16 Kim Heejin (guest edit… *Journal BOL*, no. 09, "Dongducheon" (2008).

17 Park Sohyun (guest ec… *Journal BOL*, no. 10, "… (2008): 9–10.

Mediacity Seoul 2016's nonperiodical publication *COULD BE* circuitously intersected with the platforms of *Uncertainty School* (2015–16) and *The Village* (2015–16). Taking its starting point as pre-biennale, Nam-Seoul Museum of Art's *The Village*, organized by artist Ham Yang Ah, consisted of elements and phases that included creative learning, circulation of learning, museums and *The Village*, everyone's dining table, Saturday open class, interview, and archive exhibition, and culminated in the printed curriculum *School for Everyone: The Village Project*, a book that included the project's elements and entire process. The main participants in *The Village*—art teachers from middle and high schools, educators from national and private museums and art institutions, artists organizing education programs, and so on—promoted the circulation of learning. *Uncertainty School*, organized by artist Choi Taeyoon, gathered individuals who have different, special ways of communication, movement, and thinking. *Uncertainty School* brought together participating artists, social workers, activists, and disabled and able-bodied people for a summer camp premised on unlearning processes regarding established knowledge, recognition methods, and emotional exchange methods at the Buk-Seoul Museum of Art. In this manner, *Uncertainty School* explored the concept of a school utilizing the biennial as a resource.

The stages I've discussed—organizing, operating, and evaluating archive formations, publications and their related programs, projects, and platforms—were, of course, realized through teamwork and collaboration, but each project involved different working methods and standards. Most prominent s the interdependence of artist-ness and the curatorial n a collaborative process involving people from diverse lisciplines. Kim Jinju, who not only organized the program ut was also project director for APAP's archive, Ham Yang h of Mediacity Seoul's *The Village*, and Choi Taeyoon of PAP's *Making Lab* and Mediacity Seoul's *Uncertainty School* re all artists. They maintained a distance from their individual ractices when they led these projects, and they fully performed their respective roles as archivists, educators, and organizers. However, regardless of whether or not they were engaged in making artworks, their auteurism/spirit/attitude/outlook led these cultural productions in new directions that were different from established practices or concepts. These new and different directions were evidenced in a variety of ways: the conflicts and oppositions arising between professionals during concentrated and intensive collaboration; the differing views and conflicts regarding the exclusiveness of the artist-author; and the differences over evaluation standards traversing ethics, aesthetics, and politics, to name a few. Moreover, when these artists rearrange languages, thoughts, objects, and experiences within the contexts of history, life, sensitivity, and the unconscious, it is difficult to separate their works from curatorial performativity in that they reconstruct transitional experiences, thus allowing for the interpretation of individual places and for temporal encounters regardless of their platforms, e.g., a library, a laboratory, a village, and a school.

I have not counted the number of the affiliated programs and projects, but they are numerous, with participants in each program numbering around thirty people at most. In evaluating these institutional efforts, there was some dissatisfaction expressed over the efficiency of the programs' operations and pessimism about their overall impact. Although separate discussions are required to conceptually define and address issues related to the public and people, citizens and audiences, the most urgent matter at present when institutions operated by public funding lead the flow of Korean contemporary art is how we may comprehend differences in the public and map them.

In this context, there is the peculiar Korean condition embracing art and realpolitik on opposite sides. While changes in national and local government leaders greatly affect art, Korea's cultural bureaucrats, who have stable positions regardless of the administration in power, are largely indifferent to art. To speak rather cynically, most bureaucrats are more interested in protocols than exhibitions, and more interested in awards than artworks. Under these circumstances, in order to make art oscillate between autonomy and heteronomy—and be accepted as a unique language and way of practice that constructs civil society—citizens should take action, even though there is still a long way to go. Ideally, citizens would become more discerning toward art, and cultivation and knowledge about art would interpenetrate other parts of life without boundaries, thus becoming a site for public discourse. In this view, borrowing the pragmatic vocabulary of the archive that Kil Yekyung, chief librarian of *Park Library*, an editorial member of *Journal BOL* and a guest editor of *COULD BE NO. 1*, drew on in the preface, the principle of public mapping we employed was to scatter myriad access points to the already changed artistic culture in Korea over its citizens.[18]

18
Kil, *COULD BE NO. 1*, 4.

If we assume that *One Opening* is an institutional critique that Part-time Suite performed as an artist-agent, then it is essential to have a view that critically approaches the institution itself in order for the practical knowledge of this kind of work to properly take root. It means that each institution should have a political, aesthetic, and critical view about their activities as a cumulative process, including the production of artworks, research and publication, education, archive, and so on, beyond criticism about artists, artworks, exhibitions, collections, and macroscopic views of institutional critiques. Given the circumstances in Korea, where public museums and biennials are becoming more and more bloated, it is impossible for institutions to have their own directions and to change themselves; indeed, it is far easier to get lost in the process. Yet because of this fact, paradoxically, Korea may indeed be a place to actively diagnose the critique of neoinstitutionalism.

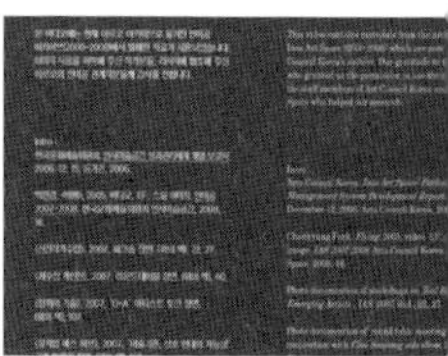
Part-time Suite, still image from *One Opening*, 2015 (HD video, sound, 30 min 2 sec), 28:47.

In considering *One Opening*, the thing I took most seriously from this survey was the issue of the continuity of institutional works and the "continuity and commonness of culture." In lieu of a conclusion, I will refer to my fragmented thinking in connection with this. First of all, I discovered that the archives I examined have relocated to other platforms where they remain active: IAS Archive moved to Arko Archive; APAP's archive moved to the APAP Welcome Center; *The Village* moved to Donuimun Museum Village in Seoul and DEPO Istanbul. Also, there are several spaces leading programs in the manner previously used by *TOOL BOX for emerging artists*.

Next, in an online chat, a curator who had experienced IAS as a student intern and who now works in the field told me that, through her experience at IAS, she came to realize how it was possible for something—a project, an initiative, an institution—to become better than it was initially. The common memories and shared experiences (having gone through this, we came to know the dialectics of friendship and loneliness) have changed our methods of working together, the language that we use, our tastes, and even a little bit of our future. Experience, in a way, is more solid and lasts longer than any institution.

However, I was shocked while chatting with an artist who is actively engaged with new art spaces in Korea and who traveled to the United States to participate in a residency program. As the artist was relating sour memories of the experience of selling artworks and complaining about always having the sense of starting from scratch, I was suddenly struck by a sense of déjà vu when I recognized the very same words that my colleagues always used as they were initiating art activities at the beginning of the 1990s.

According to *Journal BOL*, the word "bol" is not intended to be a contraction of "something to see" (*bol goet* in Korean) but, rather, a contraction of "to want to see" or "must see." In fact, if the word reminds one of the future that we "must see" from the here and now rather than an artwork or exhibition that one wants to see, that would be even better.

Translated from Korean by Lee Sunghee.

Paola Antonelli joined the Museum of Modern Art, New York, in 1994 and is a Senior Curator in the Department of Architecture & Design, as well as MoMA's founding Director of Research & Development. With a Master's degree in Architecture from the Polytechnic of Milan, Antonelli has also earned Honorary Doctorate degrees from the Royal College of Art and Kingston University, London, the Art Center College of Design, Pasadena, and Pratt Institute in New York. She has curated numerous shows, lectured worldwide, and has served on several international architecture and design juries. Her most recent exhibition, *Items: Is Fashion Modern?*, devoted to 111 items of clothing that have had a strong impact on the world in the past 100 years, opened at MoMA in October 2017. She is currently working on the next Triennale di Milano, entitled *Broken Nature* (March 2019); on the book *States of Design;* and on a new Theory of Everything for design.

'aola Antonelli

Museums (and Design) as the R&D of Society

1 2012, MoMA's *R&D* initiative was launched—with a self-eflexive emphasis—to explore the potential and responsibility f museums, and of the Museum of Modern Art in particular,) act in the public interest. We have a vision of establishing ur institutions as the "Research and Development" epartments of society, R&D signifying investment in long-erm harmony and prosperity for all citizens. While R&D is 'aditionally found in the realms of business, technology, and ie sciences, we are convinced that museums are equipped to onfront the crucial conflicts of our time and prepare society or the future.

This idea began in 2008 during the US financial crisis, in art as a reaction to the deprioritization of the cultural sector 1 a time of upheaval and uncertainty. MoMA recognized 1 opportunity to demonstrate how cultural institutions can rovide the kind of slow, dependable, sustainable progress iat can truly benefit society. Ten years after, the recession is ld news for the lucky few yet still fresh for the multitudes iat have lost a lot, besides their innocence. Socioeconomic, political, and humanitarian crises still proliferate. Their continued presence should undermine the public's confidence in other sectors (government, finance, etc.) to resolve these issues on their own. As museums can be safe havens for all those who have a stake in the future, regardless of race, gender, religious, or class boundaries, our voice in this conversation becomes that much more vital.

Cultural institutions have played pivotal roles in civic life by cultivating dialogue around critical issues, even going so far as building diplomatic bridges for international relations where politicians alone could not succeed. At the height of Cold War tensions, the Centre Georges Pompidou organized the exhibition *Paris-Moscou, 1900–1930* (1979), highlighting the commonalities and cross-pollination between the French and the Russian avant-garde at the beginning of the twentieth century. The Pushkin Museum, a state museum in the USSR, chose to display this exhibition in full, despite its controversial subject matter. The Moscow iteration transpired despite the rampant censorship and political surveillance of the early 1980s; this is demonstrative of how an exhibition can bridge divergent ideological systems and create space for cultural exchange that might otherwise not occur.

Similarly, MoMA's own R&D department acts as a launching point, fostering productive discussion that will inform the museum's programming as well as wider societal discourse. Part of the R&D initiative at MoMA involves organizing a series of salons that tackle themes pertinent both within the museum walls and beyond. The audiences for these salons are not invited to be passive listeners but, instead, are asked to read and research in advance, and to join their peers ready to participate in and contribute to the discussion. We are now at Salon 26: "Friction." Previous salons have examined, amongst other topics, the role of curators; hybridity; the effectiveness of protest in communicating civil discontent; death; truth; and, most recently, why words matter in negotiating and inhabiting our role in the world today.

Outside of specific public programs, the Museum of

Modern Art, historically and still today, has not shied away from promoting the arts' ability to address social issues. Design, in particular, has been deployed by MoMA curators as a bridge between art and everyday life. Several iterations of the exhibition series *Useful Objects of American Design under $10* (1940) suggested the best-designed and most functional, affordable household objects, along with directions on where to purchase them. During World War II, the series adapted to wartime rationing to suggest goods that were not made of metal or leather, and renamed the exhibition *Useful Objects in Wartime under $10* (1942). After the war, the museum launched the "International Competition for Low-cost Furniture Design" of 1948 to accommodate a booming middle class benefiting from the GI Bill, an educational and financial benefit reserved for veterans returning from war. Between 1950 and 1955, as part of the so-called Good Design program, MoMA curators in collaboration with buyers from the Merchandise Mart in Chicago awarded a "Good Design" designation and label to those they deemed to be the best objects in current production. Throughout the twentieth century, the American public was consistently confronted with and engulfed by new models for living, spurred by world-changing events, and with these competitions and exhibitions, MoMA asserted its role as an ambassador committed to educating and to developing these new models for the benefit of the public. At the center of everything, design remained constant in its ability to impact real change in society at large.

When people think about architecture and design at MoMA, there are a few iconic pieces that always come to mind. Often, the images conjured are foregrounded by traditional and historical examples of furniture, which prioritize the beauty of the object over the beauty of the object's function. While there is value in beauty, what we appreciate so deeply about design is its function—the reality rooted at its core. This "reality check" is what allows design to so directly address society and engage citizens, and perhaps why MoMA curators have consistently shown an interest in discussing design's potential to support social and technological growth.

MoMA's founding director, Alfred H. Barr Jr., advocated that having design in a museum was of paramount importance because design presented the opportunity for everybody, regardless of economic status, to have art in their lives. In design exhibitions at MoMA in the 1930s and 1940s, almost every object on display could be encountered in real life. Often, design is characterized by detractors as "commercial," as if being obtainable for a price were a lowly, contemptible trait. In fact, availability is the very essence of design, the quality that makes it so poignant. One of the earliest design exhibitions at MoMA, organized by architect Philip Johnson, was a show that presented machinery such as propeller blades, springs, ball bearings, and a variety of hidden components that run and create our built environment. The show, *Machine Art* (1934), presented to the public a kind of design that had never before been highlighted in a museum setting. The pieces were displayed as if they were sculptures, shown on white pedestals, against white walls. The display created a "shock of the familiar," where everyday objects were decontextualized from their use, allowing the public to appreciate them like they would works of art. The public was invited to reflect on the beauty of the tools, mechanisms, and parts that facilitated functions across all spheres of life, from the private to the commercial, from the industrial to the scientific, and therefore their own relationship to the machine.

The objects displayed in *Machine Art* were some of the first objects in the collection, and many of the pieces exhibited in subsequent exhibitions have found a permanent place in the museum's holdings. I've come to understand that the collection of the Museum of Modern Art, especially when it comes to design, is not simply a collection of objects or designers. Rather, MoMA's is a collection of ideas that are supported by objects. The museum's defining, albeit ineffable, attribute—"modern"—allows us to be selective in what we preserve and what we promote; MoMA's collection has woven one particular narrative of twentieth-century modernism through these objects.

My own working definition of modern comes from Kirk Varnedoe, an exceptional scholar and Chief Curator of Painting and Sculpture when I started at MoMA, who was quoting someone else. Though I do not know whose words they were originally (and they will remain unattributed because Varnedoe regrettably passed away in 2003), he would say, "Modern is everything that does not hide the process of its making." For a design curator, that's a marvelous definition; it means that for an object to be called modern, regardless of its function, for the betterment of society or its detriment, it has to demonstrate why it was made in a particular way. In examining each object, you are able to read the mind of the designer, and viewers are left with a new understanding of one's own (and the object's own) position in the world.

When I started at MoMA in 1994, there was a prevailing attitude in New York City that design's primary purpose was for decoration and embellishment; furthermore, design was considered a luxury reserved only for the social elite. Coming from Italy, where the so-called secret of design is no secret at all—it is fully embraced and integrated into everyone's daily life—I wanted to convey that sense of normalcy to the audience of the museum. I also wanted to reengage with the legacy of curators who had come before me, and those early MoMA exhibitions, to show that good design was for everyone and could be a real force in manifesting action towards the betterment of society.

Exhibitions must be an opportunity to learn through objects and the ideas they represent. While the objects themselves can be innovative, museums too can be innovative in the ways information is disseminated to the public. Whether its purpose is to elicit an emotion, or cut a potato, good design must fulfill its function; so too must museum exhibitions clearly communicate their subject matter, lest they fail to disseminate the information at hand. My first exhibition at MoMA, *Mutant Materials in Contemporary*

Design (1995), brought together objects either made with innovative materials, or made using traditional materials in an innovative way, and more importantly, took on a new approach to exhibition display that allowed visitors to touch samples of these materials and learn through interaction. The exhibition was a centralized archive of new material manufacturing processes and techniques, but it also demonstrated how these new materials empowered designers to take control of the entire process of making objects.

The monographic show on the prodigious designer Achille Castiglioni followed in 1997. It presented an interesting opportunity to tell the history and creation story of the objects in a way that was understandable to an audience primarily versed in art. Mindful of Varnedoe's quote, in order to engage audiences in the objects' design process, we hired illustrator Steven Guarnaccia to depict the story of each object's making. Every object in the exhibition had a label with an illustration to depict why, for example, the Arco Lamp is an ingenious solution for lighting a dining room table in a rental apartment where you can't drill any holes.

In the legacy of *The Taxi Project: Realistic Solutions for Today* (1976), an exhibition for which curator Emilio Ambasz commissioned designers to rethink New York taxicabs, the exhibition *Workspheres* (2001) took up the mantle of advancing the societal discourse by looking at the office of the new millennium and proposing solutions to more effectively balance work and life away from one's desk. This was at the nascency of mobile technology, and as with any new technology, it offered so much promise and simultaneously so much frustration. Formulated with the help of a distinguished advisory committee, six questions about the way we work were posed to the contemporary designers best equipped to answer the tensions of technology and the workplace with a new design. The impact of technology on our lives remains profound; in tasking designers to examine this relationship, *Workspheres* became an opportunity for designers to demonstrate that technology is a tool, not a goal.

The designs that most impact our lives and propel society forward are not always the flashy and new; they are sometimes things, like the objects in *Machine Art*, that are both ubiquitous and unnoticed. *Humble Masterpieces* (2004) gathered objects that so perfectly fulfill their function that they are almost ignored as triumphs of design—things like the Bic pen, Band-Aids, the zipper, and Q-tips. The idea behind the exhibition was to show people that if we pay attention we might realize just how much our lives are consistently impacted by the collection of design objects that, at any given time, fill our homes or our bags.

During the exhibition, we set up a few books where visitors could nominate the humble masterpieces that were indispensable in their own lives, inviting participation in the discussion started (but not set in stone) by the exhibition. The catalogue for *Humble Masterpieces* continues to spark engagement and the dissemination of these ideas long after the exhibition closed. I believe that as curators of contemporary design and architecture, our job is not necessarily to tell people what's good or bad but, rather, to help people develop their own critical tools for examining their own existence.

A few years ago, we took this desire for direct communication and discussion online with the launch of a curatorial experiment called *Design and Violence* (2014–15). *Design and Violence* was an exploration into the manifestations of violence in contemporary society, challenging the idea that design is always a force for good while also shedding some much-needed light on current events. Like anything else, design can be turned into a weapon, a force for evil, or something in between. People are the moral compass of design, not the objects themselves. Together with my co-curator Jamer Hunt, we looked for design objects that have an ambiguous relationship with violence. They ranged from architecture to industrial design, from a prison to the Toyota 4×4 that has become the car of guerillas and narcotraffickers worldwide, and from plastic handcuffs to a map of refugee camps all over the world.

Perhaps the most successful part of the project was the format, which facilitated discussion in a way that is almost never possible in a traditional museum exhibition. Each week, a design object was published online alongside a text authored by someone authoritative on the topic. At the end of every post, we asked a question as an invitation to readers to respond and discuss in the comments section. We asked questions that were deliberately provocative—Is execution always ugly? Can we design a violent act to be more humane?—giving space for audiences to engage in a charged but meaningful debate.

As MoMA approaches its ninetieth anniversary, it continues to confront and challenge accepted norms by expanding the scope of arts discussed within its walls and by its audiences. Curators must operate on the collection like surgeons, inserting objects that represent new methodologies and new fields that perhaps had been discounted in the past. The exhibition *Design and the Elastic Mind* (2008) inaugurated several new strains of design in the collection by highlighting work one may not expect to find within a modern art museum—for example, design dealing with biological entities, objects constructed with additive manufacturing processes like 3D printing, and contemporary models of speculative design. *Design and the Elastic Mind* was an experimental exhibition postulating that something surprising could happen by bringing designers and scientists together without the interface of engineers or technologists. Technology is frequently the bridge or membrane found in the space between design and science, and just as often, something is lost in translation as a result.

One particularly alluring work acquired from *Design and the Elastic Mind* was Oron Catts, Ionat Zurr, and Guy Ben-Ary's *Pig Wings Project*. Inspired by the English idiom "when pigs fly," the designers developed a small set of wings grown from porcine stem cells. Though we couldn't acquire the biological entity directly, we instead acquired a print of the work as a surrogate. As is already common practice in architecture, we've adapted by acquiring proximities for design that, for philosophical reasons or very practical reasons, cannot be acquired in a traditional manner.

When I first started at MoMA, some of the most interesting materials being employed by designers were still rooted in the physical realms. Now, very often, the materials and building blocks of design are digital, biological, or intangible. Each new acquisition presents a unique set of challenges to collect and preserve. But as the art of our time, these acquisitions are not only about innovation but represent a whole universe of possibilities for education, knowledge sharing, and reflection. Furthermore, each acquisition is an attempt to ensure that MoMA's collection mirrors the full spectrum of the design field.

To this end, we've begun collecting interfaces and examples of visualization design—fields that are becoming increasingly important with the proliferation of data sets that need interpreting and analyzing. We've started collecting video games—beautiful examples of interaction design that, in and of themselves, are tied to space, time, and behavior, and therefore morals and ethics. In 2010, MoMA acquired its first digital typefaces, all designed to respond to the technological advancements of the digital revolution both in functionality and in social significance. *Items: Is Fashion Modern?* (2017) was the first exhibition at MoMA to tackle fashion in more than seventy years, and subsequent acquisitions ensure that future museum audiences may discover fashion's ability to address such topics as cultural biases, politics, labor, and identity.

Possibly one of the most controversial acquisitions, and also one of the acquisitions I'm proudest of, is that "at" sign—@—though, really, we shouldn't call it an acquisition at all. In reality, "collecting" the at sign is an anointment, because it is a symbol that belongs to everyone and remains part of the collective sphere. In anointing works to MoMA's collection, we must reexamine our role as curators. Curators need not be hoarders scouring the globe for precious objects to hide away from the world but, rather, as the wonderful curator Ambasz likes to say, hunter-gatherers foraging for things to share with the world. I like to think of curators as guides, gently but intelligently pointing people in a new direction, and providing the tools necessary to help each individual figure out the world on their own terms. In order to remain a relevant and beneficial public actor for society, cultural institutions must continue to cultivate opportunities for meaningful exchanges. As the arts have followed the development of society throughout the centuries, so too must our institutions reflect upon social developments and progress.

MoMA is an institution—established by three progressive women in 1929—that sees the arts as a path to progress, freedom, and equality. The first director Barr believed in the Bauhaus ideal that the unity of the arts could help build a better world; indeed, we believe that museums and cultural institutions must use the power of their platform to do good. We believe that arts and cultural institutions have a commitment to act as centers for research and development, advocating for meaningful developments across disciplines. It is a privilege to serve such a large and diverse audience as MoMA does, and we must proceed responsibly knowing the scope of our influence.

Margriet Schavemaker has been working at the Stedelijk Museum Amsterdam in various roles (a.o., Head of Collections) since 2009. As Manager of Education, Interpretation and Publications, she is currently responsible for all forms of education and knowledge production in the museum. Her curatorial projects comprise exhibitions and collection presentations such as *The Stedelijk & the Second World War* (2015), *ZERO: Together Let Us Explore the Stars* (2015), *Jean Tinguely: Machine Spectacle* (2016–17), *Nalini Malani: Transgressions* (2017) and *STEDELIJK BASE* (in collaboration with Beatrix Ruf and Rem Koolhaas) (2017–22). She was the co-initiator of the acclaimed lecture series entitled *Right about Now: Art and Theory since the 1990s* (2006–7), *Now is the Time: Art and Theory in the 21st Century* (2008–9) and *Facing Forward: Art and Theory from a Future Perspective* (2011–12), which all three resulted in publications. To further the interaction between academia and museum practice, she in 2014 launched the online peer-reviewed magazine *Stedelijk Studies* of which she functions as the editor in chief.

Margriet Schavemaker

Changing the Game: Museum Research and the Politics of Inclusivity

Over the past two decades, the notion of a "discursive turn" has been shaping museum research all over the world. Instead of focusing on exhibitions as key "output," museums now seem bent upon transforming themselves into networked organizations, which entails (co-)conducting research of all possible shapes and forms. In the theoretical discourse surrounding the aforementioned discursive turn, one finds a strong focus on institutional critique and antagonism, bringing counter-voices inside the museum. The museum criticizing itself from within has been a familiar description of the changes that were taking place. However, one might also argue that despite their potential for criticality and depth, these practices ultimately remained somewhat unchallenging and homogenous when it comes to both audience and outreach.

Currently, a more radical turn towards diversity and inclusivity seems to be shaping our field. Not only in museums but across all of our institutions and social interactions, new and suppressed voices are demanding access, fundamental research, a rewriting of conventional narratives, and the deconstruction of the hegemonic powers that be. Is now the time when museums will actually begin to open up and museum research will finally liberate itself from the constraints of "preaching to the choir"?

In this essay, I will discuss some core programs and programmatic trajectories that have been developed by the Stedelijk Museum Amsterdam, firstly in order to bridge the gap between the museum and the academic world (including peers and professionals), and secondly to implement a more radical and self-critical opening up of the museum in order to counter social inequity and broaden accessibility. It will become clear that fundamental changes on many levels in the organization are still necessary, and we must prepare ourselves for some fundamental shifts as well. Or, to put it more strongly, the move from a discursive to an inclusive turn may appear to be a foundational game changer.

The Stedelijk Museum Amsterdam was founded in 1895. It is the largest modern and contemporary art and design museum in the Netherlands, and is located in the cultural heart of Amsterdam, adjacent to the Van Gogh Museum and the Rijksmuseum. *Stedelijk* means "municipal," but, like many public institutions in the Netherlands, the museum has been privatized in order to foster a more entrepreneurial attitude. This occurred in 2008, but the collection and the building are still owned by the City of Amsterdam. Moreover, the City remains the museum's greatest benefactor.[1] Aside from this public funding, the museum generates revenue via ticketing, the bookshop and restaurant, and additional fundraising. The governance of these public/private hybrids is a challenge for similar institutions globally. It became a major issue at the Stedelijk in the second half of 2017, when director Beatrix Ruf stepped down. She was hired by the supervisory board in 2014 because of her remarkable international network and track record in bringing in private funding. However, it came to light that she had been gaining income from private collectors during the two years preceding 2017, while also directing the

Stedelijk Museum Am
Photo: John L. Marsha

1
Around 50 percent of budget is granted to th museum. The funding structured in four-yea proposals. The current runs from 2016 to 20 the next from 2021 to

Stedelijk Museum. Ruf was accused of not being sufficiently transparent about this fact.[2]

When I joined the Stedelijk in 2009, the museum had already been closed for over five years due to an extensive renovation and the construction of an additional wing. There was frustration in the community about this prolonged closure, and when it was decided that the museum would temporarily open the now renovated original part of the building, preceding its grand reopening in 2012, research and the implementation of the discursive turn was a key component. A small organization was set up to program lectures, book presentations, screenings, symposia, conferences, and performances on Thursday evenings and weekends. This so-called public program collaborated with various partners in the city, such as festivals, academics, artists, and art schools, and aimed to offer a platform for the more performative and ephemeral forms of art and design, as well as enhance critical thinking and research in the field.

In order to make the research outcomes of this public program (and the many other forms of research conducted by the museum) more sustainable and build upon the new connectivity with academic partners in the Netherlands, the idea arose to launch a peer-reviewed magazine. Yet this idea needed more time; it was not until 2014 that the first issue of *Stedelijk Studies* (https://stedelijkstudies.com) appeared. The online journal offers high-quality, peer-reviewed academic research related to the Stedelijk Museum's collection, its institutional history (such as education and conservation practices), and topical themes such as globalization and the borders of Europe. It is open access and presented in a comprehensible and attractive format geared towards international audiences of (up-and-coming) art professionals and those with an interest in art theory and history. The journal aims to publish two thematic issues a year, and an international call for papers is issued for each edition. Between six and twelve papers are then selected and reviewed by two academics in a double-blind process.

2
Independent research into the matter has since been conducted, which led to the conclusion that Ruf had been mostly transparent about everything and that it was the supervisory board that was to blame for lack of clarity and inadequate governance. See J. A. J. Peeters and S. E. Eisma, "Governance en de WNT bij het Stedelijk Museum Amsterdam," City of Amsterdam, June 4, 2018, and https://www.stedelijk.nl/nl/nieuws/bericht-van-de-raad-van-toezicht-2/.

As mentioned in the editorial of the first issue of *Stedelijk Studies*, the journal also signaled that the role of research in museums was changing. Such research currently occupies a greater and more autonomous role than it once did, and is no longer restricted to supporting exhibitions and the collection.[3] It has become an independent, often interdisciplinary program with its own curators and budget. The trend is, among many things, part of the so-called New Institutionalism in which museums adopt a self-reflective approach to their strategies as institutions and incorporate research into their everyday practices. Although this often involves a form of critical self-reflection, we see that the academic world is frequently a partner in such programs.

A collaboration with the art history departments—together with the critical theory departments, whose orientation is more interdisciplinary—of six Dutch universities has enhanced the academic programs in the museum (resulting in more collaborations on the level of exhibitions, conferences, lectures, etc.), while international attention for the online journal is growing. The last three issues were visited by over 12,000 readers, and a recent improvement allowing individual essays to be downloaded as PDFs has increased this usage tremendously.

Although I am very proud of these research-driven programs at the Stedelijk Museum, I have also become progressively self-critical of their impact. The prevailing feeling is that we have foremost managed to create an infrastructure that allows the museum to collaborate with its academic partners and reconnect to its audiences comprising peers and professionals. However, should the goal not also be geared towards a more radical opening up to a broader public? To engage with voices that are not normally heard in the museum, and thereby cocreate new knowledge?

When the discursive turn was theorized in the beginning of the new millennium, the British philosopher Chantal Mouffe was often quoted. She spoke about the museum as a space for "agonistic pluralism," arguing that

3
For a more in-depth explanation of the missic vision of the journal, see Margriet Schavemaker, "Editorial: Topical, Urge High-Quality," *Stedelijk* no. 1 (Fall 2014), https:/ stedelijkstudies.com/jou stedelijk-studies-editori

Screenshot of the onlir platform *Stedelijk Stud* https://stedelijkstudies

society has reached a state in which people will always disagree and that sharing differences is the most constructive way forward. The museum is the ultimate place in which to do this: Both public and private, within and outside society, various voices can be uttered in a safe space.[4] A "safe place for unsafe discussions," as director of the Jewish Historical Museum in Amsterdam, Emile Schrijver, calls it.[5]

But do we really have unsafe discussions? Are we not in agreement and talking with our peers, most of the time?

In my essay "Curating Interactivity: Models, Motivations, and New Institutionalism" (2014), I set out to address this issue.[6] I brought critic Jan Verwoert to the table, who argues that the art world is lying about many things, but most of all about its impact. In this harsh and polarized world, in which too many people doubt the merit and relevance of art and want to cut its funding, we, the art professionals, feel inclined to mislead others: We say that art is good for people (actually, an unproven claim). Currently, my feeling is that we are lying about the fact that we are open to all possible audiences.

How can we stop this? First off, we should stop lying about the fact that we are lying. Honesty about dishonesty seems an indispensable step in this process. However, we cannot leave it at that. It would be cynical to cling to this fake "publicness" and truthfulness; further steps must be taken. We should instead begin to acknowledge the fact that museums are in crisis due to a lack of relevance and impact. Moreover, efforts must be made in terms of the repressed "ghosts of the past" in their collections, funding structures, buildings, etc.

Yet, at the same time, these are opportunities as well. In this day and age of polarization, the museum could be the ultimate place dedicated to helping these ghosts from the past to speak. Moreover, the museum can begin dedicating itself to social and sexual equity, and be open and accessible for all. Or, for example, as Tate director Maria Balshaw formulates it, a place where art and visual culture at large can help people to live their lives in a better way and society can renew or rejuvenate itself.[7]

4
Chantal Mouffe, *Deliberative Democracy or Agonistic Pluralism*, Political Science Series, vol. 72 (Vienna: Institute for Advanced Studies, 2000).

5
Emile Schrijver, in debate with this author at the Stedelijk Museum Amsterdam, February 11, 2008, https://www.stedelijk.nl/en/events/sunday/.

6
Margriet Schavemaker, "Curating Interactivity: Models, Motivations, and New Institutionalism," in *Interactive Contemporary Art: Participation in Practice*, ed. Kathryn Brown (London and New York: I.B. Taurus, 2014), 239–55.

7
Maria Balshaw, "Museums of the Future," in MMCA Research Project 1, Symposium, *What Do Museums Research?*, April 8, 2018.

In other words, more radical steps need to be taken in order to make the public turn a success and help museums to become relevant.

In *The Art of Relevance*, American thought leader and Santa Cruz Museum of Art & History director Nina Simon sees cultural institutions as rooms with doors that can be opened by various publics with a key.[8] Every visitor needs a key in the right shape and size, which can be handed to them proactively by the institution. Of course new doors can be produced as well, in order to create new pathways to existing programs (e.g., innovative tours, apps, public programs), and in many cases entirely new rooms need to be shaped in order to bring in new groups (e.g., radically different exhibitions and collection presentations).

A radical opening up of the museum can take many different shapes and requires a large amount of research. Put differently, this opening up takes the shape of research projects, which are often conducted with many different partners in any given city. Consider, for example, *Tate Exchange* by Tate Modern. Since the opening of the new wing in 2016, this large-scale program has offered an entire floor to over fifty cultural and educational partners in London, each permitted to meet and actively program in the museum for a period of one week. Another good example is the "Special Guests" project at the Van Abbemuseum in Eindhoven, a frontrunner in the field of accessibility, social equity, and inclusion. Years of intensive research with partners in the field resulted in radical new approaches regarding how to welcome people with hearing and visual disabilities.[9]

In 2017, the Stedelijk Museum and the Van Abbemuseum joined forces in *Studio i: Platform for Inclusive Culture*.[10] The initiative sets out to investigate best practices in the field of inclusivity and accessibility on a global level, supported by doctoral research devoted to an international comparative study on the impact of such projects. Moreover, the Stedelijk and the Van Abbemuseum use the platform to

8 Nina Simon, *The Art of Relevance* (Santa Cruz, C Museum 2.0, 2016).

9 See https://www. vanabbemuseum.nl/e mediation/inclusion/

10 More information is https://www.studio-

offer their successful inclusive programs as easy-to-implement "modules" (e.g., the *Unforgettable* project in which people with Alzheimer's and their caretakers can visit the museum and experience a tailor-made interactive tour and workshop).[11]

To diversify audiences also means diversifying content, adding new readings and layers of information. Regarding the collection, this shift in the Stedelijk Museum has taken shape in presenting the collection in two distinctive ways. Since December 2017, the museum has staged *STEDELIJK BASE* in the new wing, a large-scale exhibition that will remain for five years and presents highlights from the museum's 125-year-old collection. This presentation of the canon (displayed in an experimental exhibition design by AMO/ Rem Koolhaas and Federico Martelli) is complemented with small-scale, research-driven collection presentations under the heading *STEDELIJK TURNS*, through which the museum sheds light on hidden or suppressed stories and unseen or rarely exhibited artworks. The two models are in dialogue with one another; fueled by the new research, the alternative perspectives offered in *STEDELIJK TURNS* will inspire changes in *STEDELIJK BASE*. Consequently, *STEDELIJK BASE* will be in flux over the next five years, inviting visitors to experience the transformation of the canon.

In 2017 and 2018, *STEDELIJK TURNS* consisted, among other things, of a series of exhibitions devoted to the theme of migration. Departing from the topicality of this theme in terms of international political agendas, it aimed at bringing out multiple perspectives from the collection, reexamining and restaging works that had, in many cases, not been on show for a long time. For the first exhibition, Nalini Malani contextualized her video/shadow play *Transgressions* (2001; acquired by the museum in 2002 but never displayed) in which she departs from the forced migration of her family caused by the partition of India and Pakistan in 1947.[12] *Solution or Utopia? Design for Refugees* presented a generation of designers who strive to offer solutions for the continuing stream of refugees attempting to make their way to Europe,

The workshop *Unforgettable Stedelijk* makes art accessible to people with dementia. Photo: Tomek Dersu Aaron.

11
For more information, see the online publication and academic research on this project: https://www.stedelijk.nl/en/museum/inclusive-programming/unforgettable-stedelijk/.

12
This show led to the first infusion from a *TURNS* to the *BASE* collection presentation via the work *Utopia* (1969/1976) by Nalini Malani, which had been donated to the museum in honor of the *TURNS* exhibition *Nalini Malani: Transgressions* (March 17–June 18, 2017), https://www.stedelijk.nl/en/exhibitions/nalini-malan/.

fleeing violence and poverty in the Middle East and Africa.[13] The series concluded with a large-scale collection presentation titled *I am a Native Foreigner*, in which the effects of migration on artists both past and present were considered, revealing how they dealt with and depict the impact of displacement.[14]

In this series of exhibitions, migration was brought into play in various ways, offering a range of different visualizations and investigations by many different artists. Showing there is not one way to define or frame migration, by revealing the many questions raised by artworks from the collection, the museum aimed to provide a more nuanced consideration of the often harsh opposition between those in support of and those resistant to welcoming refugees.

Since 2016–17, the public program also opened up more radically for a multitude of voices from outside of the museum. In the series *Stage It!*, the key of the museum is offered to local cultural and educational institutions like the Gerrit Rietveld Academie, the National Opera, Mama Cash, and Sonic Acts for the presentation of new productions. Additionally, the *Stedelijk Statements* series offers the museum's key to a mix of artists, designers, writers, and academics who present (artistic) research in any possible admixture of performances, discussions, and Friday-evening events. It explicitly offers space to alternative readings of the collection, as was provided, for instance, by artist Joseph Semah. Semah has dedicated over thirty years of his research to the excavation of the Jewish context in works by modernist artists like Kazimir Malevich, Mark Rothko, and Barnett Newman. Various debates and performances, curated and performed by the artist and his network, adhered to these alternative readings and also critiqued the museum for neglecting these perspectives.[15]

The opening up of the museum to Semah stems from a longer relationship between this particular artist and the museum. The Stedelijk, which owns several of his sculptures, functions as an important site and text. Semah positions himself in relation to the museum via what he

13
Solution or Utopia? Desig Refugees, May 20–Augus 2017, https://www.stede en/exhibitions/solution-utopia-design-for-refug

14
See https://www.stedeli news/i-am-a-native-for aspects-of-migration-in collection-of-the-stedel

15
See https://www.ste events/stedelijk-stat joseph-semah-2/.

calls "footnotes." In recent years, these critical commentaries have transformed into sometimes rather aggressive appeals. Semah demands that the museum change its core narratives, going as far as hiring a lawyer and making appeals to the media to move the dialogue forward.[16] Giving Semah the key of the museum for a *Stedelijk Statement* can be seen as an acknowledgment of the fact that the world has changed. These conversations are not always safe, equal, or pleasant. As I wrote in Semah's publication on the relationship between the artist and the museum, "The new encounters can distort and become uneasy, often questioning, attacking and reformulating the conventional relationships between all players."[17] However, in this day and age, this is exactly what the museum needs: By radically opening up to these critical and "other" voices, the museum can shake off its identity as a neutral white cube speaking with a single, authoritative voice. Instead, the museum becomes a production house in which a myriad of voices can interact.

This goal became even clearer in another *Stedelijk Statement* that was developed with writer Arnon Grunberg and seventeen newcomer artists and designers who recently moved to the Netherlands (the majority from Syria). Under the moniker *Give us the Museum*, they extended the *Stedelijk Statement* through the entire month of May 2018, during which they worked in the museum, culminating in a final statement on the evening of Friday, June 1st. In the mornings, the participants acted in several capacities, ranging from security guards to art restorers, and covering anything from the marketing department to the current directorship. In the afternoons, they worked on their own projects at the museum. In addition, debates, performances, and other interventions took place while they worked in the galleries. Visitors had the opportunity to engage in conversation with the artists, and vice versa.

The inspiration for the project came from the fact that Europe has been entangled in a migration crisis since 2015, meaning refugees have become a central subject in European debate. Yet these people are mostly talked about in

Peter Baren participating in the work of Joseph Sassoon Semah, during *Stedelijk Statement*, October 20, 2017. Photo: Ernst van Deursen.

MaKOM, The Doubling of the House performed by Joseph Sassoon Semah, Jom Semah, and Peter Baren, October 21, 2017. Photo: Ilya Rabinovich.

16
For an analysis of the relationship between Semah and the Stedelijk Museum, see Margriet Schavemaker, "Dwingende voetnoten: Joseph Semah en het Stedelijk Museum," in *On Friendship/ Collatoral Damage II* (in Dutch), ed. Linda Bouws (Amsterdam: Metropool, 2017), 141–53.

17
Ibid., 141.

terms of numbers, figures, quotas, and costs. In the rare cases when refugees are permitted to take part in the discussion, rather than be discussed, they are primarily viewed as "token refugees." What if this could be radically reversed? What can we learn from newcomers in Europe—and not just about them but also about ourselves, our identities, and our cultures? The title of the project arose from several conversations between Grunberg and the newcomer artists. When asked about the meaning of the Stedelijk to the artists who had recently arrived in Amsterdam, the answer was clear: "Give us the museum and we will show you."

Grunberg asserted that *Give us the Museum* was "a research project, improvisation, performance and dialogue."[18] With his daily column about the project in the Dutch national newspaper *NRC*, Grunberg shared his encounters with the Dutch elite (*NRC* is the most highbrow newspaper in the Netherlands). In many of his writings, he reflects upon the rules that govern a museum institution like the Stedelijk, depicting a sanitized place where people are scared of dirt, trying to create some sort of hospital or mausoleum for precious art from the past. Yet, at the same time, the entire project was about people. We met frequently with all the people involved (artists, Grunberg, the Stedelijk team, assistants, representatives from various organizations, etc.), and the morning "shadowing program" was also about connecting museum staff to the participating artists. This focus on the human aspects also took shape in the daily reports penned by Grunberg, which included many personal stories about museum colleagues and the artists. The art objects in the museum were humanized as well, described as "sick patients."[19] In other words, not only did *Give us the Museum* reflect upon the museum as a sanitized institution but also transformed it into a lively and warm home. The latter aspect became increasingly visible in the course of the month as well, as the gallery space where the artists and Grunberg were working was domesticated by bringing in curtains, carpets, plants (normally not allowed in the museum), games, and so forth.

18 See https://www.stede events/stedelijk-x-mak unite-x-forum-europe culture/.

19 Arnon Grunberg, " is a terminally ill pa *NRC*, May 8, 2018, www.nrc.nl/nieuws/ 08/het-kunstwerk-i doodzieke-patient-

The aspect of the personal and the human also became the nucleus of frustrations: Within the group, some artists began to feel annoyed by the fact that not all of the artists were spending enough time in the museum, whereas for others the feeling arose that the museum expressed too little individual appreciation for their work. As artist Mazen Al Ashkar formulated it during the final debate, on the night of June 1st, "I refuse to be a token despite all good efforts and willingness to change by the museum."[20]

Writer Arnon Grunberg introduces the participating artists of the project *Give us the Museum*, May 1, 2018. Photo: Maarten Nauw.

20
Because the museum questioned its usual hegemonic criteria, the artists were not selected by the museum on the basis of their individual work but, rather, as a group by the MakersUnite organization (https://www.makersunite.eu/).

Besides this self-criticism, the museum had anticipated criticism about the *Give us the Museum* project from the right side of the political spectrum. Surprisingly, this was not the case. However, right-wing responses had been triggered one year prior by the inauguration of the first exhibition in the aforementioned series on migration. The museum issued a press release in March 2017, wherein the series was framed and explained as critical nuancing of the unified populist perspective on migration, quoting director Ruf:

> It is important to always tell new stories, both with our collection and with separate exhibitions. Especially now, as populism is taking hold in Europe. I believe it's important that, at the Stedelijk Museum, you can see how art addresses this issue, and how art can confront us with how we think and allow us to reframe our thinking.[21]

21
See https://www.stedelijk.nl/en/news/press-release-in-2017-the-stedelijk-museum-amsterdam-dedicates-five-exhibitions-to-the-theme-of-migration/.

It evoked strong responses from populist right-wing politicians via Twitter (i.e., Theo Hiddema), arguing that the museum was siding with left-wing politicians and was therefore too exclusive (despite its public funding). To contextualize these issues, a radio news program invited the museum for a discussion with Thierry Baudet, leader of the new populist party Forum voor Democratie (Forum for Democracy).[22] In the discussion, Baudet, like Hiddema, strongly objected to the fact that the museum, in his

22
"Dit is de Dag," radio 1, April 8, 2017, https://www.nporadio1.nl/dit-is-de-dag/onderwerpen/402735-ophef-over-politieke-exposities-stedelijk-museum.

perception, was taking sides with left-wing voters, offering no room for more conservative and populist perspectives. I represented the museum in the debate and did my best to convince Baudet that we tried to counteract a one-dimensional and unified voice with offering multiple perspectives, forms of art, and questions to enhance critical thinking. Baudet, however, was not convinced, making the assertion that the museum was "only showing left-wing abstract art" and offered no opportunities to more conservative, realist art, which he personally appreciated.

The issue of being overly left-wing oriented and exclusive also popped up in another critical response by Kate Sinha that same year. In an op-ed for the right-wing opinion website TPO.nl about who should be the new director of the Stedelijk Museum after Ruf stepped down, Sinha made an argument that it was not Ruf who was the problem but the corrupt left-wing ideology building upon a genuine disinterest in art. As an example, she critically refers to the exhibitions Ruf organized with artists from her circle, such as Seth Price, Jana Euler, Jon Rafman, Jordan Wolfson, Ed Atkins, and Avery Singer, who, in her eyes, share "left-engaged indifference." The epitome of this trend was embodied by the museum's exhibition of work by Zanele Muholi,[23] which demanded that visitors be interested in the "lazy figments of a spoiled brat, only because she is from South Africa, lesbian, and black."[24]

Although published in October 2017, the essay became world news in February 2018 when Amsterdam's Gerrit Rietveld Academie decided that Sinha and her partner, Stefan Ruitenbeek, with whom she forms the duo Kirac (Keeping it Real Art Critics), were disinvited to present their latest video blog on art collector Bert Kreuk. The reason for the cancellation was that students at the art school believed that Sinha was a racist, based on her remarks about Muholi. Ultimately, the school held a debate with Sinha and her partner about the whole affair, which in turn became fuel for a new video blog by Kirac.[25] Moreover, Sinha wrote an additional op-ed for the left-wing national newspaper

23
Zanele Muholi, Stedel Museum Amsterdam October 22, 2017, htt stedelijk.nl/en/exhibi zanele-muholi-2/.

24
"De toekomstige dire het Stedelijk Museu *Post Online*, October https://cult.tpo.nl/2(toekomstige-directe museum/.

25
Kirac 13, "Stigma," https://www.youtul watch?time_contin QS5Ws5ShnNw/.

de Volkskrant in which she explains that she believes that artists with talent, who also fall under the categories black, woman, or LGBTQ, have a high risk of falling prey to being presented as "tokens" in the art world. In other words, they will be selected for what they represent without respect for their talent, and Sinha calls on these artists to use their talents to take responsibility for this.[26]

Although I do not agree with the right-wing typecasting of the art world as exclusively left-wing, such as formulated by Baudet and Sinha, I feel uncomfortable with the silencing of such voices. I grew up in a predominantly white suburb of The Hague (Zoetermeer), raised by white, intellectual parents—left-wing voters who strongly believed in the freedom of speech—but at the same time did not feel kinship or alignment with the middle- to lower-class environment in which they were living. These circumstances inspired me to bridge this gap by searching for common ground, including talking to those that did not like me, or even pestered me. I try to mediate, again and again.

26
Kate Sinha, "Token én talent," *de Volkskrant*, February 13, 2018, https://www.volkskrant.nl/columns-opinie/opinie-kate-sinha-token-en-talent~b0d3416b/.

This is also the reason why I think the Stedelijk Museum should engage in discussions with both Sinha and Baudet about their ideas. In the case of Baudet, I invited him to the museum at the end of the radio interview. I must admit I felt discomfort the day after, when I saw the headline on the website of the populist newspaper *De Telegraaf*: "Baudet makes mincemeat of museum babe." What followed was an edited version of the radio discussion from the previous day, in which only Baudet was speaking and my comments were largely deleted.[27] This sexist typecasting and willful silencing—on top of the unfounded accusations used by Baudet in the interview—are as unpleasant as they are common in these current times of "fake news." Should one therefore stop engaging?

27
De Telegraaf online, April 9, 2017.

Grunberg wondered about this as well, when he worked with the Stedelijk advisory board for inclusivity and accessibility in the context of the *Give us the Museum* project. This advisory board consists of a group of fifteen museum

Arnon Grunberg in conversation with visual artist Noor Issa (Syria) during *Give us the Museum*, May 9, 2018. Photo: Maarten Nauw.

employees, a cross section of people taken from every possible team at the Stedelijk. Since the beginning of 2018, they have advised the Stedelijk director and management team on how to become more diverse and inclusive at the levels of programming, partners, staff, and audience.[28] In his column about the meeting, Grunberg raises the issue of how the museum should also become a relevant place for angry right-wing white men.[29] In order to kick-start the museum in this quest, he set out to organize two therapy sessions for these EU-, immigrant-, and art-hating populist voters for the final event of the *Give us the Museum* project.

In his humorous open application to become the new director of the Stedelijk Museum, artist Jan Hoek expresses a similar idea. His focus will be on making the museum relevant again, via engaging young artists, inspiring sexual exchanges in a "sex/art cave," and an extensive program of African art (as the latter is absolutely amazing in his eyes, and should be on show in order to counter its invisibility in the West). However, he will also offer programming for populist voters:

> I don't want to get the complaint that I only program politically correct leftish art (what I most certainly will be doing), and I therefore want to consciously engage with getting art-hating Geert Wilders voters [the most prominent populist in the Netherlands, M.S.] to the museum. In order to do so, I will open a special gallery in which, every three months, a Dutch artist will be commissioned to make a work that is both layered and high level, but also pleases Geert Wilders voters. The artists are forced to talk to a special comity of angry white voters on a regular basis, who, in the end, will judge the work.[30]

Not everybody agrees with this kind of engagement with the right-wing spectrum. In earlier presentations on this topic for, among others, students of the Sandberg Institute and in meetings with the Stedelijk editorial board for public-

28
The board was installed i
to implement the Dutch
for cultural diversity in t
museum. See https://ww
codeculturelediversiteit.
the-code-english-versio

29
Arnon Grunberg, "Ah, d
witte mannen," *NRC*, M
2018, https://www.nrc.
nieuws/2018/05/26/ah-
boze-witte-mannen-a1

30
See https://www.vic
article/pa3q3m/mijn
sollicitatie-voor-dire
het-stedelijk-museu

program events, I was confronted with the fact that my plea for an open attitude towards those criticizing the left-wing *Gutmensch* and its dedication to incomprehensible art and minorities (e.g., the aforementioned Baudet and Sinha) led to heated discussions. For some, the idea prevailed that when a fundamental line is crossed regarding mutual respect, this functions as a disqualification and excommunication from the public forum that the museum offers. One should not open the door for those who do not respect the ground rules was the core message. Especially not in this day and age, when museums are finally challenging their own hegemonic positions.

For others, my tolerance was framed as a hidden intolerance, something so omnipresent in Dutch society. This perspective is probably best described by Gloria Wekker in her book *White Innocence* (2016), in which she explains how the Dutch have long cultivated an image of themselves as an exemplary model of tolerance, despite evidence to the contrary:

> I am intrigued by the way that race pops up in unexpected places and moments, literally as the return of the repressed, while a dominant discourse stubbornly maintains that the Netherlands is and has always been colorblind and antiracist, a place of extraordinary hospitality and tolerance toward the racialized/ethicized other, whether this quintessential other is perceived as black in some eras or Muslim in others. One of the key sites where this paradox is operative, I submit, is the white Dutch sense of self … [31]

In other words, the dominant groups see themselves as tolerant and will not consider themselves or their freedoms under threat from intolerance, because they are not. Although I do consider myself an avid (self-)critic of this Dutch mentality, the discussions with my peers did open my eyes to the fact that my desire for a radical freedom of speech is, in

31
Gloria Wekker, *White Innocence: Paradoxes of Colonialism and Race* (Durham, NC: Duke Univ. Press, 2016), 1.

fact, grounded in a hegemonic position that I did not perceive as hegemonic.

However, I strongly believe that radically stepping aside and opening up to other voices, as described above, is a solution. If the museum and its staff is willing to relinquish (some of) its ownership/power, this shows it to be an institution that can be transformed, that can be and become an inclusive platform, an agent of change, and thus prove itself not to be an immutable tool simply working to maintain and reproduce hegemony. However, one of the most probing challenges that remains unsolved for these (semi-)public institutions is how to radically open up for all and yet also be a safe space where the repressed and counter-voices can speak up, challenge, and change the institutions from within.

Perhaps it is an impossible combination. Can these two fundamentally different paradigms be united?

Issue 8 (Spring 2019) of *Stedelijk Studies* will deal with these topics. The call for papers is titled *Towards a Museum of Mutuality* and begins with the assertion that "engendering integration while acknowledging differences is one of the biggest challenges facing museums globally today."[32] We ask researchers and practitioners to reflect upon a reconceptualization of museums' relationships between their collections and the engagement with (new) audiences at all levels, thereby aiming to shed light on shifts in the museum model, both theoretically and on the level of institutional arrangements, from the museum as a site of authority to the post-museum as a site of mutuality.

It is wonderful to deploy the academic infrastructure of the peer-reviewed journal to critically discuss fundamental issues as described in this essay and assess both best practices and those in need of improvement. However, I hope it is clear that a different kind of research is necessary, as well, in order to open up our museums more radically and move forward. Finding new narratives in the collection and staging new public-program events like *Give us the Museum* are just the beginning. In this polarized world, practice-based research

32 See https://www.stede studies.com/beheer/w content/uploads/2018 CFP-Stedelijk-Studi pdf/.

projects provide us the mirrors and the game changers needed to transform our cultural institutions from hegemonic spaces into inclusive spaces.

Victoria Walsh is Professor of Art History and Curating and Head of the Curating Contemporary Art program at the Royal College of Art, London. She previously worked at Tate where she played a key role in creating Tate's Research Department, subsequently leading Tate's first major national research-funded project *Tate Encounters* (2007–10). This led to the publication *Post-Critical Museology: Theory and Practice in the Art Museum* (Routledge, 2013). Focused on questions of how digital and networked culture is impacting on the art museum and curating more generally and, building on a second Tate research project *Cultural Value and the Digital*, she is currently co-developing a research project with the Centre for the Study of the Networked Image (at LSBU) and The Photographer's Gallery in London, and Rhizome in New York.

Victoria Walsh

Situated Research: Curating, Technology, and the Future

Why Do Museums Research?

The UK Context

In response to the original conference question—"What do museums research?"—I'd like to begin by considering *why* museums research, specifically in the UK context. My own position in answering this is based on my experience of working and researching in and across both the academy (the Royal College of Art) and the museum (Tate) over two decades. This research has been consistently defined by my long-term interest in how to usefully connect theory and practice across the two institutions to create new models of curating and curatorial knowledge that productively recognize the interrelation between the artist, curator, and audience.

There always has been, and I am sure always will be, an established and dominant culture of research by individual museum curators—what is often called the "lone scholar" mode. This research was, and continues to be, rooted in the work of a museum's collection or exhibition program through the practices of cataloguing, archiving, interpreting, and mediating a collection or work's provenance, specificity, and significance. Over the last two decades, however, new forms of corporate research, usually commissioned from specialist consultants and problem-solving or speculative in nature, has been focused on business planning, public-space development, partnership building, marketing, income generation, and, most recently, digital interaction.

Towards the end of the twentieth century, the UK government began to publicly recognize that the work of the museum was extending well beyond museological concerns of collection care and display, and the government began to demonstrate its understanding that the role, function, and place of the museum was rapidly accumulating both a national and international profile. The imperative for museums to change was invariably defined by their own changing relation to government funding and new demands placed upon them to create sustainable financial models comprised of one-third government funding, one-third sponsorship, and one-third income generation. By the end of the twentieth century, the government regarded museums, particularly national museums, as valuable assets and reassessed their importance and contribution in terms of their cultural, educational, social, and economic value.

Following the immensely successful opening of key, high-profile millennial projects supported by the government through national lottery funding, including the creation of Tate Modern and the spectacular architectural extension of the British Museum, the government began to understand that the kind of self-initiated, corporate research that museums were driving was producing much greater levels of knowledge production, innovation, and entrepreneurship than the university sector and academic research. As the government perceived, this museum-generated knowledge and innovative practice was not being sufficiently or usefully shared between or across other sectors—particularly between the museum and the university sector—and subsequently not fully exploited, either nationally or internationally. Internationally, these untapped resources needed to be fully exploited if the UK was to sustain a leading position in the increasingly competitive and new global markets of the knowledge economy. The government also recognized that academia (universities) were developing and reproducing knowledge independently of museum and cultural practice and educating students without any clear application value of what they were teaching.

The government consequently created a new national research funding agency—the Arts and Humanities Research Council (AHRC)—which advocated new models of "collaborative research" that would bring the university and museum together to share knowledge and to increase the range of fields, sectors, and audiences the research would have an impact on. This collaborative approach invited new models of "practice-based," or at least "practice-led," research (researching while doing) in order to overcome the separation of practice and theory, of academic thought from practice situated in the museum. Although initially there was some resistance, particularly in the academy, today this kind of research has become the norm.

In 2006, in recognition of the sustained quality and impact of the research carried out by certain national museums, including Tate, ten national institutions were designated as "Independent Research Organizations" (IROs)—granting them the equivalent status as universities to directly apply for research funding, run doctoral programs, and initiate major research projects. As of 2017, there were twenty national museums constituted as IROs, and as the AHRC's tenth-anniversary publication noted,

> The UK's cultural and heritage organisations, including our galleries, museums and conservation bodies, are central to our national life and are a vital part of our identity across the globe. For most of these organisations, research plays a key role in supporting their activities: without research, they would not be

able to engage audiences in the same way, or make their many other contributions to public life. Without research, our culture and heritage organisations would not have had such a positive impact on the UK—on our economy, on our quality of life and on our influence overseas. Cultural organisations and practitioners contribute £27 billion to the UK economy each year and the cultural sector employs around 624,000 people.[1]

Collaborative Doctorates

One of the major initiatives of the AHRC was the creation of the "collaborative doctoral award scheme," which provided fully funded PhD scholarships for students to study with two co-supervisors, one in the university and the other in the museum. This scheme emphasized the opportunity for students to undertake "situated research," that is, to be situated within the museum as the critical site of inquiry and to provide privileged access to the museum as a working organization. It also embraced ideas of the "embedded" researcher, that is, the student who becomes immersed in the everyday working life of the museum in order to understand how the museum operates, how decisions are made, and values created. The scholarships emphasized the value of interdisciplinary research in order to mutually expand and diversify the knowledge base of both academia and the museum—to move beyond the limits and confines of traditional disciplines such as art history, visual cultures, and literature; disciplines that no longer adequately reflected what the museum did, the interests of contemporary artists, the nature of contemporary culture, or the social and cultural life of visitors. Since 2005, the scheme has awarded over six hundred fellowships.[2]

In 2005, as Head of Public Programs at Tate Britain, I secured two of the first collaborative doctoral awards for Tate in partnership with the London School of Economics Cities program (LSE Cities). It is worth noting that before the Tate Research Department was established, externally funded research activity was located in Public Programming

1 See *A Decade of Success: Supporting Research in th Major Culture and Heri Organisations* (London: and Humanities Resear Council, 2017), 3, http: ukri.org/documents/pr reports-and-reviews/a- of-success/ (accessed A 2018).

2 See http://www.ahrc newsevents/events/c cda10thanniversarye (accessed August 30

the Tate Learning Department, where it has again recently turned. These fellowships were focused on the vision and atronage of Tate Modern—how it was conceived, built, ıd became so internationally successful.[3] The second PhD so focused on Tate Modern but, in this case, as a new ban cultural phenomenon looking at how Tate developed model of cultural regeneration with a major impact on ondon's urban planning, environmental responsibilities, ıd community development. In 2010, and building on two the research projects to be discussed below, another two ollaborative doctorates were secured at Tate in collaboration ith my research partner, Professor Andrew Dewdney at ondon South Bank University (LSBU), looking at the npact of technology and marketing on curating at Tate and ıbsequent practices of audience development in the museum.

3 See Caroline Donnellan, *Towards Tate Modern: Public Policy, Private Vision* (London and New York: Routledge, 2017).

Four Collaborative Research Projects (2007–18)

Tate Encounters—How Audiences are Created and Excluded

s Head of Public Programs at Tate, I also had the pportunity to develop with Professor Dewdney and Dr. avid Dibosa (Chelsea College of Art) the museum's first ıajor collaborative research project funded by the AHRC, *ate Encounters: Britishness and Visual Culture* (2007–10). his subsequently led to ten years further research, along with rofessor Dewdney, in designing new models of practice-led search into key questions facing the European museum of ıodern and contemporary art.

The problem at the heart of the *Tate Encounters* project as that despite considerable investment of government ınding, significantly increased levels of targeted audience rogramming, and extensive market research, Tate remained nable to diversify its audiences to meet the national emographic of Black and Minority Ethnic population, part of the government's cultural diversity policy. The interim analysis of the problem of Tate's inability to diversify its audiences identified three particular facts. Firstly, that despite high levels of discursive programming rooted in academic discourses of postcolonialism, critical museology, and institutional critique, academic debate had had little or no impact on audience engagement with the museum. Secondly, that although high levels of curatorial and education programming were designed and based on market research targeted at particular audiences, there was no long-term change in audiences. And thirdly, that although policy formation around cultural diversity and social inclusion was informed by significant academic research in the Social Sciences, the dominant framing of the individual subject based on categories of race and identity held no meaning with Black and Minority Ethnic audiences themselves. Constructed as "problem-solving research," *Tate Encounters* identified the need to develop a new model of research that was

— Situated (the full team of seven and a further twenty-five participants were all based inside Tate)
— Collaborative (the research team brought together Tate, Chelsea College of Art, and the Social Sciences and New Media Departments of LSBU)
— Practice-led (the project involved target audiences over two years awarding them the status of co-researchers rather than objects of study)
— Interdisciplinary (the project brought together art history, curating, and visual cultures with science, technology studies, and new media)

Collectively, the ambition of the project was also to enable the research process itself (practice-based research) to become a "performative tool of change"—that is, to create the conditions of change during the research process itself. We defined this approach as "post-critical museology" (and published a book with this snappy title) to distinguish it from the European interest in "institutional critique," which treated the museum as an object of study rather than as a collaborator in the research process. Five years on, and to our surprise, the project's websites, online resources, and publication *Post-Critical Museology: Theory and Practice in the Art Museum* (Routledge, 2013) continue to gain currency and readership as students studying and curators working in museums of modern and contemporary art grapple with how the museum should engage increasingly diverse audiences produced through the globalization of culture and migration to cities.[4]

One of the key findings of the project centered around the crisis of representation brought about by the distributed nature of online digital culture, along with the globalization of culture, labor, and capital. These factors have led to new conditions of subjectivity, transculturalism, and transnationalism for audiences who no longer find meaning or interest in the ahistorical logic of aesthetic modernism, which, at the time, defined Tate's curatorial practice—think white walls, single well-spaced-out works of art, and celebration of individual artists. This key finding underpinned two further collaborative research projects: MeLa/*Transfigurations* with the Museu d'Art Contemporani de Barcelona (MACBA), and "Cultural Value and the Digital" with Tate in London.

4
Andrew Dewdney, David Dibosa, and Victoria Walsh, *Post-Critical Museology: Theory and Practice in the Art Museum* (London and New York: Routledge, 2013). See also *Tate Encounters: Britishness and Visual Culture*, http://www.tate.org.uk/about-us/projects/tate-encounters/; and http://www.process.tateencounters.org/ (accessed August 30, 2018).

Curatorial and Artistic Research in an Age of Migrations—The Impact of Technology on Contemporary Art and Its Display and Collection

In 2013, a second research project, funded by the European Commission as part of the *European Museums in an Age of Migrations* (MeLa) four-year project, offered a further opportunity to expand upon the findings of the *Tate Encounters* research, particularly in relation to the crisis of representation, the shifts in artists' practices towards new technologies, and the need to identify new collaborative models of both curatorial and artistic practice in "problem-solving" research. MeLa was a multidisciplinary and collaborative research project involving nine European partners from 2011 to 2015. As its website notes, "The objectives of the MeLa project focused on the impact of the contemporary migration(s) of peoples, objects, information and cultures on museums, and on the identification of innovative policies and practices enhancing the role of these institutions towards a changing social, political and cultural context."[5]

As Head of the Curating Contemporary Art program (CCA) at the Royal College of Art at this time, the focus of my research shifted to questions about what new forms of exhibition/display practice could be modeled to overcome the representational pull of the exhibition form, a key concern in relation to how the work of migrant or diasporic artists were being presented in museum exhibitions and displays. That is to say, how could curators avoid creating displays that ghettoized or racialized artists and audiences who did not wish to either self-identify or be presented through a status of difference in a policy climate championing positive inclusion? And equally, why were artists increasingly turning to technology as a means to overcome conditions of difference and representation? To address these questions, a series of artist and curator collaborations were commissioned from across Europe, including the UK, France, the Netherlands, and Spain, which as part of the process included the exhibition *Transfigurations* and a publication.[6]

Amongst the questions this project asked were the following:

- How are globalization, digital media, and changing patterns of migration affecting our understanding and experience of the contemporary work of art?
- How are contemporary artists engaging with curators to think about the condition of the contemporary through their work, its display, and collection?
- How are curators working with new forms of artistic production, particularly "immaterial" intangible works of art that fall outside conventional forms of display, collection, and archive?

As each artist/curator collaboration highlighted, the

5
See http://www.mela-pr polimi.it/ (accessed Aug 2018).

6
See http://www.mela polimi.it, Research F the publication *Trans Curatorial and Artisti in an Age of Migratio* http://www.mela-pro polimi.it/upl/cms/ attach/20140902/16 3882.pdf/ (accessed 2018).

extent to which artists draw on and remediate an ever-expanding repository of digitally generated content—be it playlists of music compiled through iTunes (Kader Attia), museum-collection image banks (Camille Henrot), or broadcast and amateur video footage and sound recordings (Lawrence Abu Hamdan)—has made it increasingly difficult for the museum to display and collect this work, destabalizing as it did the values and idea of the modernist art object. As with *Tate Encounters*, this project was funded and designed as "problem-solving" and "challenge-led" research in order to generate findings that could inform future national and European cultural and research policy. This was, of course, pre-Brexit (the UK's vote to leave the European Union) and before the politics of representation and inclusion became reframed by discourses and the interests of nationalism and localism. At the interim stage of the project in 2014, the collaborative research "exhibition" took place, and in the accompanying publication (not a catalogue), the following observations and future needs were put forward:

- The fluid and undefined practice of the artist has assumed new value and agency in a global context to mediate (and remediate) cultural and political issues that professionalized and institutionalized positions often cannot
- The postcolonial persistence of curatorial engagement with the artist on the level of cultural identity—not subjectivity— … is implicitly determined by modernist teleological narratives
- The need for greater interdisciplinary collaboration and risk-taking between museum curators and artists
- Desire for greater collaboration by both curators and artists with other disciplines, knowledge spheres, and research alliances
- More flexible and informal spaces within museums for more provisional activity than fully formulated projects and public display

— New museological thinking in relation to the conceptualization of public forms of display and engagement (durational issues of liveness, event, hybrid forms of commission/exhibition)

And in relation to technology and the digital:

— The need for increased critical awareness by museums of value systems operating in the administrative management of collections—the opportunity of digitization to rethink collection management through reconceptualization of function and design of database systems and online networked practices
— The need for more ambitious engagement and understanding of the digital, not only as a tool but as a medium through which to reimagine cultural relations and cultural heritage in a global context (including "intangible" cultural heritage)
— The need for a reconfiguration of museums' practices in relation to collection, and exhibition management of artists' practice and collections in relation to immaterial practices, as defined by museological traditions centered on the object

Cultural Value and the Digital—The Impact of Technology on the Curator, Artist, and Museum Audience

Taking up the findings of the *Tate Encounters* and the MeLa research projects focused on the impact of digital media on the art museum and its audiences, a second, smaller research project—"Cultural Value and the Digital"—was subsequently developed in 2014 following an invitation from Tate to collaborate with the CCA program and LSBU.[7] This project was again funded by the AHRC, which issued a short-notice call for digital research proposals as part of a larger national research project into "cultural value of the arts." This national research initiative had two objectives: first, to identify the

7
See "Cultural Value Digital: Practice, P Theory," http://ww uk/about-us/projec cultural-value-and- practice-policy-anc (accessed August 3

various components that make up cultural value; and second, to consider and develop the methodologies and the evidence that might be used to evaluate these components of cultural value.[8]

In 2014, the digital was still considered a separate field of practice rather than an integral condition in which all practice and work takes place. As both previous projects had found, while the art museum's curatorial practices were (and still are) rooted in the narratives and cultural logic of aesthetic modernism based on ideas of expert knowledge grounded in Art History, such models of curatorship no longer held authority over how contemporary audiences viewed or interpreted works of art. This situation has, invariably, been produced by the impact of the digital on the visual realm through the visual saturation and circulation of imagery—via smartphone cameras, online culture, and social media platforms.

Building on the *Tate Encounters* research method of bringing artists, curators, and museum practitioners together with academics, theorists, funders, and policymakers, the project also expanded to include online curators, social media companies, digital designers, and the Google Art Project. As with the MeLa project, the participants came from European cultural and academic institutions. These thirty-seven participants were invited to contribute to panel discussions that prioritized a discursive over a presentational mode of interaction in order to examine how connected or disconnected the language of each field and sector was to the others, or how the nature of each participant's questions resonated or not with those from a different vocation or perspective.

As figure 1 outlines, our design of these sessions was led by taking the three key research policy themes set by the funding council—new media, digital access, and coproduction—and mapping these against our own analysis of the key research strands we related them to: representation, network, and archives. As figure 2 presents, these themes and

8
See "Cultural Value Project," http://www.ahrc.ukri.org/research fundedthemesand programmes/culturalvalue project/ (accessed August 30, 2018).

strands were then further analyzed and separated out into session themes that reflected the practice domains in which the research questions were primarily located or the conditions through which they were defined.

Cultural Value and Cultures of Network Participation: Research Matrix

		Strands: Dimensions of the research problematic		
Themes: Cultural value policy perspectives		**1. Representation** Crisis of analog value systems	**2. Network** Collapse of public/ private realm	**3. Archives** Challenge to cultural authority and expertise
	New Media	Remediation	Interface	Distribution
	Digital Access	Computing/Code	Circulation	Collections
	Coproduction	Subjectivities	Collectivities	Agency

Fig. 1. Mapping of the (AHRC cultural value strands (selective litera review)

Research strands and AHRC themes combined		
1. New Media Representation/Crisis of analog value systems	**2. Digital Access** Network and the collapse of public/private realm	**3. Coproduction** Convergence/Challenge to cultural authority
1. Producing Culture POLICY FRAMING	5. Online Collectivities identifying and working with new formations	9. Converging Practices virtual and real spaces, communication models
2. Digital Culture histories, medium specificity	6. Online Collections analog and digital collection, problems curation	10. Digital Economies ecologies, experience, scale, globality, finance
3. Digital Channels marketing & programming the digital	7. Coding Cultures software as culture	11. Agencies new subjectivities, definitions, practices, authorship, status
4. Digital Tools uses of medium, education, learning	8. Networks/Interfaces visualizing data, working with data interfaces, politics of data	12. Digital Politics FUTURE POLICY

Fig. 2. Synthesis of st methods used to defin programs

As the published report of this project highlighted, the museum's and cultural institution's understanding of the digital as multifarious and contradictory, ranging from the digital as "tool," as a "medium," as a "technology," and as "culture." This eneral confusion about what constitutes the digital underpins ıe confusion of how to work with the digital in relation to ıdiences and to understand how cultural value is produced . a post-digital culture. The report also noted the following ɔservations:

- A false binary opposition persists between the concept of culture and the concept of the digital, which is rooted in the historical separation of art from technology—a separation that continues to underpin the traditional distinction between high and low culture.
- Museums predominantly understand and employ the digital as a tool and continue to adopt the analog broadcast model of one-to-many transmission based on traditional models of institutional cultural authority and disciplinary expertise.
- Cultural institutions are trying to adapt to the two-way, many-to-many model of digital networked communication through which new collectives and collectivities are redefining the idea of the social and publics, but they struggle to identify and find ways to work with these new users/visitors.
- While cultural heritage is understood to hold exceptional national cultural value, there are conflicting positions about how this value can be sustained in contemporary digital culture.

As the project rapidly discovered, the museum's struggle • move beyond the historic broadcast, enlightenment model ⁻ the transmission of knowledge (of the one to many) and its efault position to think of the digital and technology as a tool ther than a culture—and, specifically, a distributed-network ılture—highlighted Tate's bigger struggle to recognize ıe legitimacy and new cultural authority of the audience, hich held little or no interest in the modernist system of museum classification and value. "Coproduction," one of the funding research criteria, also emerged as an important aspect of new modes of production, distribution, circulation, and consumption of cultural value as a result of the application of digital technologies and development of the internet. How museums relate to such practices, what forms of coproduction are taking place, and whether they reproduce or challenge existing models of cultural value were central questions. From the research point of view, coproduction was underpinned by a concern to articulate the challenge to cultural authority represented by convergent practices, new economies, ecologies, and digital politics.

Collective Findings

Collectively, these projects have led our research to conclude that there are three major challenges facing the European museum of modern and contemporary art today:

— The challenge to curatorial value and expertise
— The challenge to museum modernism and modernist time
— The challenge to established ideas of audience

The Challenge to Curatorial Value and Expertise

So, historically, museums of modern and contemporary art have claimed their authority through the status and expertise of their curatorship. Academic expertise rooted in the Humanities (more often than not, History of Art) combined with curatorial expertise gained in a national institution directly aligned the curator with the work of art as its mediator and translator. Theory and practice, combined with knowledge and experience, have historically acted as a guarantee of cultural and curatorial authority. But in the "post-digital," "post-internet" moment, however, the curator's claim to holding specialist, unique knowledge and experience is no longer fixed or valued in the same way.

As theorist and writer Jean-François Lyotard anticipated back in 1984 in his *Report on Knowledge*, legitimate and legitimized knowledge now circulates in all directions in many different forms due to the impact of technology.[9] For visitors and audiences, the digitization of collections, and thus online access to ever-changing and ever-increasing bodies of information and interpretation, means the curator (and museum) are no longer the unique site of encounter or producer of the knowledge of an artwork. How we encounter, engage, mediate—and remediate—the work of art is inextricably and inherently tied into our everyday visual culture defined by technology: by our smartphone cameras, by Instagram, and by networked culture.

9
See Jean-François Lyotard, *The Postmodern Condition: A Report on Knowledge*, trans. G. Bennington and B. Massumi, Theory and History of Literature, vol. 10 (Minneapolis: Univ. of Minnesota Press, 1984). Originally published in French, *La Condition postmoderne: rapport sur le savoir* (Paris: Les Editions de Minuit, 1979).

This poses new questions and demands for both greater transparency and greater clarity as to what constitutes the expertise of the curator. What gives the curator the authority to bestow value on one work and not another, particularly at the level of national collection or museum? This challenge is not new to curators (questions of value and canon formation dominated the 1980s and 1990s in Europe and the United States), but the conditions driving such questions today are. As knowledge—the foundation of expertise—is superseded by the proliferation of access to knowledge online, professional experience and technical knowledge become more important to distinguish the curator from other types of practitioner. This knowledge, however, is still firmly attached to the unique analog art object—with all its added ideological and museological investments and attachments to the art market and patronage.

From the research we gathered, art museums predominantly still regard the digital and the internet as "tools"—tools of organizational and operational management, public communication, content distribution, and marketing. There is little or no investment in fostering knowledge in and of the post-digital and post-internet moment, nor curatorial training. The museum curator has little knowledge of, or interest in, computational culture, which rules the network.

The Challenge to Museum Modernism and Modernist Time

One of Tate's responses to this changing culture of communication has been to accelerate its public programming, as in Tate Tanks and the Art in Action program in 2012 that promoted the opening of the Switch House, the Tate Modern museum extension. The transition and flux of spatiotemporal relations within the museum through accelerated programming and performance-based event culture is continuously taking place, and, as Boris Groys has noted, "the function of the museum becomes one of staging the flow—staging events that are synchronized with the lifetime of spectators."[10]

This was exemplified in June 2016 during the opening events and projects at the Switch House, and the launch of a new long-term project, *Tate Exchange*, to which one floor of the new building is now entirely dedicated. As our research showed, for the modern and contemporary art museum, event-based projects invariably prompt analog behaviors of materialization through the processes of documentation to ensure the production of a material asset—be it for online publication, archival collection, or collection acquisition.

But in these moves to document and rematerialize the content of programming, the art museum is struggling to recognize that the internet user/visitor has already bypassed the curatorial processes of archiving and validation through their own uploaded documentation, supplanting the historical role of the museum as the arbiter and owner of cultural value. As Groys has noted, the internet, has as in this instance, assumed the historic universalizing archival function of the museum. In short, distributed-network culture and the age of the internet have undone the control and authority of the art museum; to some extent, one could argue that the museum of both modern and contemporary art is now the new "heritage."

10 Boris Groys, "Entering the Flow: Museum between Archive and Gesamtkunstwerk," *e-fl[ux] journal*, no. 50 (Decemb[er] 2013): 11.

The Challenge to Established Ideas of Audience

In the post-digital, post-internet moment, the expertise of

the curator is further compromised and complicated by two key transformations of the analog artwork: its conversion into a "digital image" and its circulation and proliferation as a "networked image" online. A further challenge is posed by the "born-digital" artwork. In all three circumstances, traditional bodies of knowledge (art history, humanities, museum-based experience) are again challenged in the claim to curatorial expertise. In the post-digital, post-internet present, there are very few curators whose knowledge and experience is rooted in the fields directly aligned to either the computational culture of digitization or the networked cultures of art production and consumption online in which artists and audiences are now interacting directly. In this current moment, the historic claims of the curator to firsthand knowledge and situated experience now demand not only technical knowledge of the artwork but also an understanding of its digitized image and the networked ecology in which it moves.

Again, we might want to ask what is the difference between this and the emergence of photographic reproduction and mass-publishing in the 1950s and 1960s? Curators were not expected to hold a technical understanding of photography or the photographic image. But the crucial difference here is that the camera and the photographic image were not the default form of mass visual communication as it is today. Now, the image is both "poor" and inherently social, as artist and writer Hito Steyerl has alerted us:

> The poor image thus constructs anonymous global networks just as it creates a shared history. It builds alliances as it travels, provokes translation or mistranslation, and creates new publics and debates. By losing its visual substance it recovers some of its political punch and creates a new aura around it. This aura is no longer based on the permanence of the "original," but on the transience of the copy. It is no longer anchored within a classical public sphere mediated and supported by the frame of the nation state or corporation, but

floats on the surface of temporary and dubious data pools. … The poor image is no longer about the real thing—the originary original. Instead, it is about its own real conditions of existence: about swarm circulation, digital dispersion, fractured and flexible temporalities.[11]

11
Hito Steyerl, "In Defense [of the] Poor Image," *e-flux journa[l]* 10 (November 2009): 8.

As our research highlighted, in addition to the new digitized and digital "ways of seeing" that define culture today, it is the radical shift from the historic analog broadcast ways of communication (one-to-many) to the many-to-many model of communication, which Web 2.0 and the internet established, that again undermines the authority of the curator—and the museum.

Throughout our research at and with Tate, it was clear how hard the museum was trying to adapt to the two-way, many-to-many model of digital networked communication through which new collectives and collectivities are redefining the idea of the social and publics. As Tate curator Catherine Wood discussed in our project "Cultural Value and the Digital," the introduction of the BMW Live online performance commissions for Tate Online was fraught with problems as audiences "didn't turn up" at the scheduled and advertised performance time, and when they did, "they were the wrong kind." At the core of this was the misidentification of network-culture behaviors as if they are the same as those of traditional broadcast culture.

The question here is how do we move to understand the audiences of the network? And how do we understand the audiences not as members of the analog public sphere but as hypermodern individuals of the accelerated present?—that is to say, as both living and consuming the rapid production of heritage within the museum, and as part of new online collectivities and communities.

Conclusion—The Location of Cultural Value has Shifted

In reviewing the crisis in curatorial expertise as outlined, and the impact of the remediated networked image of the artwork, we begin to see the extent to which the curatorial and cultural authority of the museum has been disturbed by the digital and the internet. This cultural authority was predicated on the understanding that cultural value was located in and validated by the art museum. But in the post-digital and post-internet present, these processes and claims are significantly under threat. Understanding how cultural value is being produced within the network through computational ways of seeing, networked distribution, and curating online is now an urgent issue.

To address this, we constructed a new collaborative research proposal that brought together the CCA program at the Royal College of Art, the Centre for the Study of the Networked Image at LSBU, The Photographers' Gallery in London, Rhizome in New York, and Google. In setting up these collaborations, we recognized that as curators and academics we need to engage with both the public and commercial sector—the latter of which is driving the production of cultural value online more than ever through its constant modes of research and innovation, enhanced distribution, global reach, targeted audiences, and creative user-driven development and user-centered design. If such collaborations are not forged, the art museum can only continue to reproduce itself in the image of itself and its own histories, rendering itself the new heritage, albeit the new contemporary heritage.

To develop the audiences of today and the future, the opportunity presented to the MMCA to take on these issues and research challenges confidently and creatively is significant. Where Tate Modern set the agenda for audience development in the art museum in the UK and Europe, and further internationally through the last two decades, the potential for the MMCA to pick up the baton as a national museum in a country that has not only embraced technology and digital culture but has been a global leader in hardware design is both exciting and important.

The Curatorial and Knowledge Production

Beatrice von Bismarck is Professor of Art History and Visual Culture, and Cultures of the Curatorial at the Academy of Fine Arts in Leipzig. Main curator of twentieth-century art at the Städel Museum in Frankfurt from 1989 to 1993, she then co-founded and directed the project-space "Kunstraum der Universität Lüneburg," associated with Lüneburg University (1993–99). She is also co-founder of the project-space "/D/O/C/K-Projektbereich" (2000) and initiator of the MA program "Cultures of the Curatorial" (2009). Her current research interests are the curatorial, the modes of cultural production connecting theory and practice, the effects of neoliberalism and globalization on the cultural field, and postmodern concepts of the "artist." Recent publications include *Cultures of the Curatorial* (ed. with Jörn Schafaff and Thomas Weski, Berlin, 2012), *Timing: On the Temporal Dimension of Exhibiting* (ed. with Rike Frank, Benjamin Meyer-Krahmer, Jörn Schafaff, and Thomas Weski, Berlin, 2014), *Hospitality: Hosting Relations in Exhibitions* (ed. with Benjamin Meyer-Krahmer, Berlin, 2016), and *Now-Tomorrow-Flux: An Anthology on the Museum of Contemporary Art* (ed. with Heike Munder and Peter J. Schneemann, Zürich, 2017).

Beatrice von Bismarck

Constellations and Transpositions: On the Political Potential of Curatorial Practice

Today, neither the presentation format of the exhibition, nor the activity of curating, nor the curator's status as a subject can be assumed to have clear definitions. Since the late twentieth century, the aims and methods of discourse surrounding the exhibition's history and function, its conditions of time and space, its protagonists and the ways they are required to act, have been too diverse to allow us to speak of a clearly outlined medium. An exhibition neither merely serves the end of giving an audience access to artworks and artifacts nor can it be fully explained in terms of the claims and gestures of the artists and curators. Moreover, museums and galleries have forfeited their prerogative as exhibition venues; private views and closing events are still potential end markers of the exhibition period, but by no means the only options. Instead of fixed exhibits and displays, the exhibition situation is now increasingly structured by the duration, movement, and timing of its various elements.[1] Finally, the exhibition itself is now commonly considered a work in its own right, a view that goes hand in hand with heightened awareness and appreciation of the creative

1 On the diversification of the current debate surrounding the exhibition format, see Okwui Enwezor, *Großausstellungen und die Antinomien einer transnationalen globalen Form* (Munich: Fink, 2002); Beatrice Jaschke, Charlotte Martinz-Turek, and Nora Sternfeld, eds., *Wer spricht? Autorität und Autorschaft in Ausstellungen* (Vienna: Turia & Kant, 2005); Gwen Allen, *Artists' Magazines: An Alternative Space for Art* (Cambridge, MA: MIT Press, 2011); and Beatrice von

potential associated with exhibition-making. Such an understanding makes it necessary to distinguish between the meaning of the individual works on show and the meaning of the exhibition-as-work: the exhibition always shows something (i.e., the exhibits), but it also shows itself. In this way, it goes beyond what is presented in and through it, opening up additional contexts of its own within which it positions itself. Being not only the result and the medium of exhibition practice but also its tool, the exhibition format has an inherent potential for action, helping to shape the relations of which it consists.

This potential has implications for the definition and evaluation of subject positions in the field of the curatorial, as well as for the activities carried out there. As part of this practical and discursive development, author status was assigned to curators, sparking a controversy over this status and making the curator's profession both one of the "sexiest"[2] and most disputed. Processes of professionalization and differentiation in the art field caused "curator" to become a hierarchically structured job description. Beginning in the late 1960s, the emergence of "independent curators," who realize exhibitions without being employed by an institution, is seen as a turning point in the history of the profession, as the (sometimes almost cultish) elevation of the curator can seem to relegate artists and critics to a subordinate position in the field of art.[3] Rather than being a one-sided increase in the power of a single profession, this is the result of relational repositioning involving all of the positions adopted within the art field: While the profession of the "independent curator" was taking shape, there were also diverse crossovers between curating and various artistic and academic disciplines, as a result of which the remits, qualifications, and methods of curators have been and continue to be reviewed and redistributed. This has seen artists become curators, publishers, networkers, and theorists, and the roles of artist-curator and curator-choreographer, for example, have become familiar models.

Corresponding with this diversified role, the definition of the activity of curating also became broader, now applicable

Bismarck, Rike Frank, Benjamin Meyer-Krahm Schafaff, and Thomas W eds., *Timing: On the Tem Dimensions of Exhibiting* (Berlin: Sternberg Press

2
Suzana Milevska, "Be Curator," in *The Curat Philosophy of Curating* Jean-Paul Martinon (Bloomsbury, 2013), 6

3
On the debate surro relationship between curators, see also Da "Exhibiting Exhibiti Dan Fox, "Being Cu *frieze* 154 (April 20 www.frieze.com/issu being-curated (acce 9, 2018) (originally German as "Ausstel Ausstellung" in the for documenta 5, K Jens Hoffmann, "W Artists?," in *The Ne Should be Curated b* (Frankfurt am Mai 2004), 26–31; Beat Bismarck, "'The M Works': Daniel Bu Contribution to dc Kassel, 1972," *On* (June 2017), http: curating.org/issue- the-master-of-the- daniel-burens-con documenta-5-in-k html/ (accessed A [originally publish as "Der Meister d Daniel Burens Be

to many and varied areas of life. Thanks to this semantic elasticity, it is possible to curate not only consciousness but also urban development and church services.[4] And finally, the term's association with individual practices of self-improvement and self-presentation ("curate your résumé") or lists tailored to personal purchasing habits ("curated shopping"[5]) gives its popularity a grounding in the everyday (online) world.

This increased popularity and expanded definition of the curatorial must be understood within the context of major changes in society since the 1960s—above all, the dictate of visibility and self-promotion driven by mass-media technology, the valorization and growth of immaterial forms of labor under post-Fordist conditions, and altered requirements related to gathering and processing the wealth of data generated by globalization and digitization. The resulting social and economic living and working conditions are reflected in the curatorial. Here, too, procedures and techniques of mediation are called for within a framework of mobile, collective, and project-based structures. If curating is understood as a cultural practice with the potential for self-reflection, then it also has the ability to portray, comment on, and alter prevailing conditions, such as current forms of subjectivization, socialization, and economization. In this essay, the concepts of "constellation" and "transposition" are described as the potentially political dimensions of curatorial practice.

documenta 5 in Kassel 1972," in *Jenseits der Grenzen. Französische und deutsche Kunst vom Ancien Régime bis zur Gegenwart. Thomas W. Gaehtgens zum 60. Geburtstag*, eds. Uwe Fleckner, Martin Schieder, and Michael Zimmermann (Cologne: DuMont, 2000), 215–29]; Susan Hiller and Sarah Martin, eds., *The Producers: Contemporary Curators in Conversation* (Newcastle: Baltic, 2000); Anton Vidokle, "Art Without Artists?," *e-flux journal*, no. 16 (May 2010); and Beatrice von Bismarck, "Response," in "Letters to the Editors: Eleven Responses to Anton Vidokle's 'Art Without Artists?,'" *e-flux journal*, no. 18 (September 2010).

4
Marcia Brennan, *Curating Consciousness: Mysticism and the Modern Museum* (Cambridge, MA: MIT Press, 2010); Martha Schwartz and Emily Waugh, *Recycling Spaces: Curating Urban Evolution—The Work of Martha Schwartz Partners* (San Francisco: ORO, 2012); and Jonny Baker, *Curating Worship* (London: SPCK, 2010).

5
See http://www.netz24.biz/2013/11/curated-shopping-wie-schlaegt-sich-der-e-commerce-trend-in-der-praxis/ (accessed August 9, 2018).

Constellations

The following remarks assume a definition of the curatorial as the context of meaning and action centering on the *becoming-public* of art and culture, which is characterized by distinct relations, conditions, and rules, and which gives rise to different cultures on account of the specific context in any given case.[6] For curatorial practice, then, the focus is on acts of connection with a public dimension, on the role of such acts in

6
Based on this understanding, the MA program "Cultures of the Curatorial" was installed in 2009 at the Academy of Visual Arts Leipzig. For more detail, see Beatrice von Bismarck, "Kulturen des Kuratorischen," in *Handbuch Ausstellungstheorie und -praxis*, ed. ARGE schnittpunkt (Vienna/Cologne/Weimar: Böhlau, 2013), 166. To date, conferences on various research topics attended by

processes of meaning production—or, to put it another way, on shaping the relations generated in and by exhibitions between all those involved. This includes all of the participants (artists and curators, but also gallerists, lenders, critics, and various audiences) yet extends far beyond this circle to include both the exhibits themselves and the displays, spaces, institutions, and discourses.

This sense of the curatorial situation as something temporary comprising both human and nonhuman actors is conveyed by the concept of the constellation. Derived from the Latin *con* (with, together) and *stella* (star), the term denotes the position, as seen from the earth, of changing and unchanging heavenly bodies, and the individual elements being defined by the relations between them. These elements form the framework of the constellation, obtain their meaning relationally, and are less important individually than the resulting whole. They are what they are in the constellation.

In its original scientific context, a constellation is also characterized by a spatiotemporal dynamic. Distinguishing between fixed stars and planets, the heavenly bodies linked in a constellation are assigned a specific mobility that, in turn, influences the constellation. Both as a spatial metaphor that describes the arrangement of bodies in a three-dimensional field and as a characterization of the temporal dimension that mediates between recurring and one-time movements, *constellation* refers to a changeable relational structure between the individual elements, which, in turn, can change in their own right.[7] In this way, it captures a moment in the configuration of elements that is unstable and ephemeral. Instead of a fixed formation, it denotes open-ended stages of assemblage or coming-together.

When applied to the curatorial situation, the concept of the constellation accounts for the dynamic definition of the relations formed between all those involved. On the one hand, it denotes the different contexts in which each obtained their previous meaning and function (which then change as a result of this transfer from other times and places into the

artists, curators, and scho
from disciplines relating
curatorial have produced
publications: Beatrice vo
Bismarck, Jörn Schafaff,
Thomas Weski, eds., *Cul*
the Curatorial (Berlin: St
Press, 2012); and Beatri
Bismarck, Rike Frank,
Benjamin Meyer-Krahn
Schafaff, and Thomas W
eds., *Timing: On the Ten*
Dimensions of Exhibitin
(Berlin: Sternberg Press
Beatrice von Bismarck
Benjamin Meyer-Krah
Hospitality: Hosting Rel
Exhibitions (Berlin: Ste
Press, 2016); and Beatr
Bismarck and Benjami
Meyer-Krahmer, eds.,
Things (Berlin: Sternbe
forthcoming).

7
See Andrea Albrech
"Konstellationen. Zu
kulturwissenschaftli
Karriere eines astrol
astronomischen Kor
Heinrich Rickert, M
Alfred Weber und K
Mannheim," *Scienti*
(2010): 104–49, esp

specific new encounter). On the other hand, it implies that those involved and their participation are also characterized by temporalities of their own—historicity, sequence, duration, timing, rhythm—creating a corresponding dynamic in their interrelations. Understood as a constellation, the curatorial situation is thus less a stable visual presentation and more an arena in which to generate, modify, and rearticulate the relations among all those involved—relations that, in turn, determine the contribution made by each individual participant to the production of meaning in exhibitions.

In this way, the exhibition is permeated by social dynamics not dissimilar to those defined by Pierre Bourdieu for "fields." According to Bourdieu, the structure of fields (meaning both the field of society as a whole and its "sub-fields," such as the economy and art) is defined by the way "agents and institutions constantly struggle, according to the regulations and the rules constitutive of this play (and, in given conjunctures, over those rules themselves), with various degrees of strength and therefore diverse probabilities of success, to appropriate the specific products at stake in the game."[8] To apply this dynamic to the field of the curatorial means expanding the circle of participants to include all components as agents, not in the sense of conflict-free participation, as proposed by Bruno Latour when dealing with nonhuman beings,[9] but rather as influential players in the competitive struggles within the curatorial constellation.[10]

8
Pierre Bourdieu and Loïc J. D. Wacquant, *An Invitation to Reflexive Sociology* (Chicago: Univ. of Chicago Press, 1992), 102.

9
On the omission of conflict in Bruno Latour's theory, see Thomas Lemke, "'Waffen sind an der Garderobe abzugeben.' Bruno Latours Entwurf einer politischen Ökologie," in *Das Politische denken. Zeitgenössische Positionen*, eds. Ulrich Bröckling and Robert Feustel (Bielefeld: transcript Verlag, 2010), 273–93, here 287–9.

10
For an example of a curatorial situation interpreted in this sense, see Beatrice von Bismarck, "The Exhibition as Collective," in *Cultures of the Curatorial*, eds. von Bismarck, Schafaff, and Weski, 289–302.

Transpositions

The characteristic structure of the curatorial constellation is transpositional. This transposition subjects all of an exhibition's component parts to acts of repositioning that, in very general terms, involve a change of relative situatedness. Human and nonhuman actors undergo shifts from one spatial, temporal, social, aesthetic, economic, or cultural context to another, altering their specific meaning, function, and status in the process. All of them, within the framework of the transpositional process, constitute the fabric of the curatorial constellation. Through the relationality of this structure, they create a specific context of meaning, while also being defined by it. Each presentation situation modifies their interrelations, which shape the meaning of each individual element as much as they shape the meaning of the whole. As a result, the processes of recontextualization inseparably tied to exhibiting are undergone not only by the exhibits but also by the exhibition itself, including, for example, every time it is reinstalled during a tour.[11]

By taking those involved out of their previous contexts, such acts of transposition create difference in spatiotemporal terms. This is reflected in etymology, as the Latin *exponere* combines the prefix *ex* (out of) with the verb *ponere* (to place or put). The semantic field of the Latin term—in the sense of to set forth, put out, abandon, subject to, explain, relate, publish, or expose—still resonates in the French *exposition* (exhibition) and *exposé* (brief outline of contents), and in English in relation to literature in *exposition* (text setting forth meaning or purpose) and in the medical field in *exposure* (of living things to damaging environmental impact).[12]

The specific form taken by this spatiotemporal difference determines the meaning, status, functions, and effects of those involved and their relations to one another. Two transpositional procedures of de- and re-contextualization in the curatorial are especially important as politically relevant forms of critical reflexivity: that of *translating* and of *placing outside*.

Both procedures, translating and placing outside, can be described by analogy with Walter Benjamin's definition of montage. According to Benjamin, montage interrupts the structure into which something is cut. The moments of interruption create a distance that allows for appraisal and reevaluation.[13] For viewers to be able to reflect on what is presented and on their individual relation to it, a defamiliarization must take place. Much discussed in connection with practices of collecting and archiving,[14]

11
For more detail on a de
of the curatorial as
a transpositional practi
Beatrice von Bismarck,
"Trans(pos)ition: In the
Language of the Curat
Transfer in the Performi
eds. Susanne Foellmer,
Katharina Schmidt, an
Cornelia Schmitz (Abi
Taylor & Francis/Rout
forthcoming).

12
The English "exhibit,"
other hand, is derived
Latin *exhibere* (to sho
reveal), thus focusing
etymological terms m
strongly on the aspect
deliberately creating
perception.

13
See Walter Benjami
Author as Producer
Walter Benjamin, *S*
Writings: Volume 2,
1931–1934 (Cambr
Harvard Univ. Press
768–82, here 778–

14
A key text in this c
Allan Sekula, "Rea
Archive," in *Blaste*
An Anthology of Wr
Contemporary Artis
Wallis (Cambridge
Press, 1987), 114–
116–8.

montage strips the objects of their former meaning, undressing them and refitting them in relation to the changed environment. The concept of "placing outside," in the sense of being placed outside something or outside oneself, implies this loss of former clothes and wrappings. Beyond the montage context itself, this also causes a break with meanings previously attributed to the exhibits and with the previous contexts within which these meanings were constituted. In this way, the act of exhibiting impacts on different spatiotemporal structures. The interruptions occasioned in any specific case possess a productive force, stimulating reformulation, reappraisal, and reclassification. Suspending, halting, pausing, arresting, putting out of synch, concealing, rendering visible—these are all effects of exhibiting that generate meaning, involving both what is exhibited and all those involved in the process and situation of exhibiting. This production of difference is a prerequisite for the political effects of exhibiting.[15]

Translations

This production of difference can take on the Benjaminian characteristics of translation: always preliminary, transparent, and processual.[16] Both the aspect of ephemeral meaningfulness and that of perpetually starting over can be used in curatorial practice. In the curatorial transposition, the ephemeral character of the meaning, function, and status of curatorial elements comes into play, as past and present relational processes of meaning production are combined while remaining visible within one another, what Benjamin refers to as "transparency."[17] Within this process of survivals, the cultural biography of specific individual elements can be located as it is brought into the curatorial constellation by the exhibit (but also by other elements: vitrine, artist, institution, etc.) as the result of different contexts and modes of usage. In addition, the "social life" of the curatorial elements, in the sense described by cultural anthropologist Arjun Appadurai,

15
For a discussion of the political dimension of curatorial montage, with examples, see Beatrice von Bismarck, "Curatorial Politicity: For instance, Tensta Museum," in *Tensta Museum: Reports from New Sweden*, ed. Maria Lind (Spånga: Tensta Konsthall, forthcoming).

16
Walter Benjamin, "The Task of the Translator" (1921), in Walter Benjamin, *Selected Writings: Volume 1, 1913–1926* (Cambridge, MA: Harvard Univ. Press, 1996), 253–63, here 257–8, 260–1.

17
Ibid., 260.

gains presence as they become representatives of classes and types of such participants, whose meaning, function, and status change over long periods of time as the result of social usages, relations, and conditions.[18] What is essential for the curatorial is that in repeated presentations at different times, the relations that shaped the meaning, function, and status of those involved can themselves be transposed in their transparent, ephemeral quality.

Rather than being synonymous with arbitrary fluidity, these processes of transposition possess a political potential, as stressed by German filmmaker and theorist Hito Steyerl when she underlines the ways Benjamin diverges from conventional notions of translation: rather than locating the act of translating between different languages (and this is central to Steyerl's argument), he sees it taking place within language, integrating people and things and focusing on their interrelations.[19] Steyerl refers here to Benjamin's concept of a language continuum into which the languages of people and of things are embedded. Within this continuum, Benjamin explains, translation takes place as "removal from one language into another via a series of transformations."[20]

For Steyerl's argument, it is crucial that Benjamin focuses less on languages tied by their origin or content to a specific nation or culture,[21] speaking instead of languages of technology, justice, and religion, of sculpture, painting, or poetry.[22] These "languages of practice"[23] mediate between the languages of things and those of humans. The specific form of this translation, with which it either "creates ruling subjects and subordinate objects" or "engages with the energies of the material world,"[24] is what defines the political dimension of these processes. The form decides whether, in the process of translation, things are functionalized for the purpose of representation or whether, in the spirit of rendering present, they "can become creative in the sense of a transformation of the relations which define it."[25] Adding to this juxtaposition of functionalizing fixation versus creative productivity in the translation process, Steyerl also warns of the risk of letting

18
Arjun Appadurai, "Intro Commodities and the P of Value," in *The Social L Things: Commodities in C Perspective*, ed. Arjun A (Cambridge: Cambridg Press, 1986), 3–63, here

19
Hito Steyerl, "The Lan Things," *transversal.eip* (June 2006), http://w net/transversal/0606/s

20
Walter Benjamin, "O Language as Such an Language of Man" (1 Walter Benjamin, *Sel Writings: Volume 1, 1* (Cambridge, MA: H Univ. Press, 1996), 62 70.

21
In this context, Stey Benjamin's understa translation as "a blat declaration of irrelev culturalist approach Steyerl, "The Langu Things."

22
Benjamin, "On Lan Such and on the La Man," 62, 73.

23
Steyerl, "The Langu Things."

24
Ibid.

25
Ibid.

oneself be seduced and overwhelmed by the power of things in the interest of an unreflecting fetishization. Her concern, as she explains, using the documentary form as an example of translation, is with "presencing precarious, risky, at once bold and preposterous articulations of objects and their relations, which still could become models for future types of connection."[26]

26 Ibid.

Viewed in this light, curatorial transposition as translation acquires political potential. Following Steyerl's reading of Benjamin, curatorial translation can be characterized as being not the expression of a power relation created by the language of practice but, rather, something that strengthens the potential for change of the elements it connects, both people and objects, increasing the potentiality of the relations into which they enter. What this form of transposition aims for is the potential of new, different relations.

Placing Outside

In the second political implication of the curatorial shaping of relations that I wish to discuss here, transpositional practice is understood as placing outside. Regardless of whether those involved were previously not public or differently public, the curatorial situation articulates their encounter. In so doing, it creates altered relations on two levels: that of *perception* and of *hospitality*.

Relations of perception are created and shaped insofar as the transfer to being (differently) public alters the conditions in which the exhibits previously found themselves. Putting oneself at the mercy of an unfamiliar and not necessarily favorable outside world, stepping into the public realm, facing the gaze of others and meeting them, exposing oneself but also being exposed and vulnerable—all this describes a central demand of artistic practice and existence since the modern art field took shape in the early nineteenth century. Public visibility became a prerequisite for generating attention, which could, in turn, be converted into what Bourdieu distinguished as types of capital: social, economic, and symbolic.[27] Tensions between passivizing and activating actions characterize the impact of both the aesthetic and the psychological, social, economic, and political dimensions of exhibiting.[28] Exhibiting—in the sense of placing outside—can thus be presented as a state and process of suffering on all these levels.[29] On the other hand, it can also be understood, with Giorgio Agamben's definition of "the face," as a political force integrated into every society. "The face is at once the irreparable being-exposed [essere esposto] of humans and the very opening in which they hide and stay hidden." In this threshold position, instead of expressing any truth about a person, it is pure communicability. Unlike the visage, the face is characterized by its reflexive position with regard to its own becoming-manifest. "There is a face wherever something reaches the level of exposition and tries to grasp its own being exposed."[30] For Agamben, exposition—the face—is the "location of politics," where the power over appearance is contested.[31]

Understood in this way, the modes of producing and shaping the difference resulting from a transfer to (a different) being-public possess a political meaning. They determine the specific modality of visibility and the ensuing hierarchies, power, and status of those involved. Exhibiting something or someone at all, or in a particular way, always means a repositioning within existing orders, but (and this is especially relevant regarding the political potential of the curatorial) it can potentially also participate in changing such orders. It is in the specific shape given to the relations of perception between those involved—a shape defined by the way in which someone or something offers itself up for reception, by whom or what, under which conditions—that the shifts in meaning, value, and the position of people and things are put into effect. Such shifts can lead to modified borders between visibility and invisibility, relating in highly divergent ways to previous orders of visibility. They can cause

27
On the definition of types capital, see, for example, P Bourdieu, "The Forms of Capital" (1983), in *Handb Theory and Research for the Sociology of Education*, ed. G. Richardson (New York Greenwood, 1986), 241–

28
On the activating potenti the passive, see the essays Kathrin Busch and Helm Draxler, eds., *Theorien der Passivität* (Munich: Fink

29
Oskar Bätschmann, *Ausstellungskünstler. Kult Karriere im modernen Kunstsystem* (Cologne: DuMont, 1997). In 197 long after his first retros (1973), Bruce Nauman produced a text piece en *Consummate Mask of Ro* whose last sentence—" die of exposure"—soun a psychological evaluat exhibition conditions. S *Nauman*, exh. cat., Wal Center, Minneapolis, a venues (Basel: Wiese V 1994), 56, 265.

30
See Giorgio Agamben Face," in *Means Witho Notes on Politics* (Minn Univ. of Minnesota Pr 2000), 90–99, here 90

31
Ibid., 92.

hierarchies and attributions of status to become porous, such as those between art and display, high and popular culture, those defined by region, gender, and discipline, or between the roles available within the field. With their self-reflexive structure, such approaches allow the conditions of previous orders of visibility, and their relationship to representation and economization, to be set in motion in an open-ended way. In this context, processes of construction and the underlying interests are revealed as something that can be contested and modified, while the presentation in an exhibition appears as a provisional result, an intermediate state in an ongoing discussion.

Furthermore, the act of curatorial "placing outside" determines the conditions and possibilities of resituating, of taking place and assigning space. In other words, it establishes relations of hospitality. The exhibition is marked as a situation of hospitality not only by the convention of extending invitations (to artists and their works, to independent curators, to various publics) but also by the way it assigns the roles of guest and host, with the latter making an offer.[32] This is by no means always the kind of generous relationship suggested by museum PR materials. It is true that resources are made available for exhibitions (space, funds, time, materials) and that they involve acts of inviting, offering, and welcoming; displays of presence, attention, and recognition; and signals of acceptance and reciprocity. But it is also true that procedures of restriction, control, and surveillance, of refusal and rejection, are inscribed into exhibitions. Hospitality describes the necessary counterweight to the strangeness generated by the curatorial transposition. Transferring people and things from their familiar, habitual surroundings into those of the exhibition may be accompanied by experiences of uncertainty and defenselessness. Looked at this way, exhibiting means a moment of precarious exposedness due to this process and state of displacement. The relations of hospitality in curatorial constellations thus bring into play issues of responsibility and dependence, rules and codes, inclusion and exclusion—clearly

32 For links between the discourse on hospitality, which has resonated strongly in the field of art over the last decade, and the field of the curatorial in particular, see von Bismarck and Meyer-Krahmer, eds., *Hospitality: Hosting Relations in Exhibitions.*

marking the exhibition as something that has been made and that can, in turn, be made differently.

By way of summary, one can say that within the curatorial, constellation and transposition are constitutively related to one another insofar as they facilitate and uphold the dynamic that characterizes its structure. This dynamic marks the way those involved interact as an open-ended and ongoing relational process within which positions change and, with them, the possibilities and forms of participation in the production of meaning. Power, status, tasks, value, and valuation are thus continuously in the process of becoming, both negotiable and subject to redefinition. Translating and placing outside, the modes of transposition, are responsible for the specific shaping of the relations that determine the constellation. Their political dimension makes itself felt in the shaping of relations of perception and hospitality, which, in turn, shape the prerequisites and conditions for participation.

Finally, to conclude with a normative perspective, the relations of perception and hospitality, acting together, link the political dimension of exhibiting to an ethical one: that is, insisting on the responsibility to examine relations of perception in terms of the recognition granted, and relations of hospitality in terms of the protection given. From such a viewpoint, the sense of care contained in the Latin *curare*, on which the curatorial field is conceptually founded, loses its often-criticized paternalistic flavor, being geared less towards people, communities, and objects and more towards the (provisional and dynamic) relationships established between them by curatorial activity.

Translated from German by Nicholas Grindell.

Paul O'Neill is an Irish curator, artist, writer, and educator based in Helsinki and New York. He is the Artistic Director of PUBLICS, a curatorial agency and new art space in Helsinki. Between 2013 and 2017, he was Director of the Graduate Program at the Center for Curatorial Studies (CCS), Bard College. O'Neill is widely regarded as one of the foremost research-oriented curators, and leading scholar of curatorial practice, public art, and exhibition histories. He has held numerous curatorial and research positions over the last twenty years, and he has taught on many curatorial and visual arts programs in Europe and the UK. He has co-curated more than sixty curatorial projects across the world, including *We are the (Epi)center*, P! Gallery, New York (2016), the multifaceted *We are the Center for Curatorial Studies* for the Hessel Museum, Bard College (2016–17), and most recently he was one of the main organizers of the major international symposium *Curating After the Global*, LUMA Foundation, Arles, 2017. His most recent anthologies, *The Curatorial Conundrum: What to Study? What to Research? What to Practice?* and *How Institutions Think: Between Contemporary Art and Curational Discourse,* were co-edited with Lucy Steeds and Mick Wilson and published by the MIT Press in 2016 and 2017, respectively. He is currently working on the co-authored *Durational Aesthetics: Time and Contemporary Art* (London: Bloomsbury, 2018).

Paul O'Neill

Exhibitions as Curatorial Readymade Forms of Escape

Exhibitions as Curatorial Constellations

Let us try to escape together! Before we begin, I would like you to take a moment to imagine and to invoke five things—five sites of contact without prejudice, suggestion, or any persuasion as to what they look or feel like:

1. A small, almost square painting on an orange wall
2. A young child sitting on a colorful chair
3. Pink goo on wood
4. Daffy Duck sitting on a bed
5. A sleeping bag on the floor

In this text, I will try to enact an escape, or at least attempt to invoke its spirit, and what follows is therefore more an exploration than a conclusive statement. Before the enactment, I would like to problematize the term "escape" alongside two other terms—"the curatorial" and "research"—and put them all under the microscope together. I will argue that an understanding of these terms in dialogue with each other is necessary for a more progressive understanding of the "exhibition" as a form of becoming, of togetherness, or of an escape for both the art and the viewer. In doing so, I will navigate through some complexities and contradictions, whilst maintaining steadfastly throughout that the exhibition as form provides an environment where art is transformed through the logic of escape—from being in one state to transforming into another by way of momentarily being public, on show, in the process of being exhibited. Here, escape is a key concept for the curatorial, which defines itself as an act of release—from something, somewhere, someone—accompanied by the wish to be transformed. Escape implicates language itself as being complicit with our need to be able to, at least, imagine ourselves elsewhere. By extending a conception of the curatorial to account for multiple sites of contact, assemblages, and gathering of diverse bodies and subjects, as well as their discursive connections, I wish to open up the exhibition itself as a potential mode of research in its own process of becoming. Conceived as such, different points of contact are made possible in the exhibition, where exhibiting becomes a form of escape for the artwork as much as for the viewer. How can the language of exhibitions therefore enable us to think attentively about escape as a curatorial form?

After more than thirty years of increasingly intense curatorial production and debate, one aspect within curatorial discourse is the continued and even "renewed" contestation of the existence (and legitimacy) of a specifically curatorial field of praxis. In short: It seems that we are experiencing a continuous cycle of consolidation in the discursive arena around curating. In this text, I wish to account for "the curatorial" as constellated forms of emergence, and as a process of "becoming," or "becomingness," and propose that the exhibition as form offers a moment of escape for art.

The exhibition form considered as constellation is

a "bringing and becoming together," whereby the curatorial is aligned with certain conceived practices of "research." This interrelation between the curatorial and research appears to be essential at a moment when there is such a focus on artistic overproduction, and when the discursive field around curating is riddled with attempts to limit (or at least narrowly define) what curating should be (or seeks to be) and to determine which bodies of knowledge shall have enduring consequence. This tendency has been particularly apparent in recent attempts to construct concepts of the curatorial, conceived as forms of practice operating away from, alongside, or supplementary to the main work of curating-as-exhibition-making. This is evident from the briefest of glances at a number of recent attempts at describing the curatorial as somewhat distinct from its historical predecessors—from curatorship (of primarily late-nineteenth- and early-twentieth-century museums), to exhibition-making (in post-Szeemann authored shows), to curating (having manifested itself in coproductive and creative curatorial practices since the 1990s), in that order. For example, Jean-Paul Martinon and Irit Rogoff, in their preface for the recent edited anthology on the curatorial, state that

> If 'curating' is a gamut of professional practices that had to do with setting up exhibitions and other modes of display, then 'the curatorial' operates at a very different level: it explores all that takes place on the stage set-up, both intentionally and unintentionally, by the curator, and views it as an event of knowledge. So to drive home a distinction between 'curating' and 'the curatorial' means to emphasize a shift from the staging of the event to the actual event itself: its enactment, dramatization and performance.[1]

In an earlier text, Rogoff articulates the event of the curatorial as critical thought that does not rush to embody itself, instead raising questions that are to be unraveled over

1 Jean-Paul Martinon, ed., *The Curatorial: A Philosophy of Curating* (London: Bloomsbury, 2013), ix.

time.[2] Whereas Maria Lind's notion of the curatorial is equally temporal, as it involves practicing forms of political agency that try to go beyond the already known,[3] Beatrice von Bismarck's understanding of the curatorial is that of a continuous space of negotiation, contributing to other processes of becoming.[4] Emily Pethick's proposition of the curatorial, in turn, presupposes an unbounded framework, allowing for things, ideas, and outcomes to emerge in the process of being realized.[5] Illustrative of the contested territory around this expanded field of curatorship, these definitions cannot be reduced to a set of positions that exist in opposition to exhibition-making; rather, they support forms of research-based, dialogical practice in which the processual and the serendipitous overlap with speculative actions and open-ended forms of production.

Certainly, these nuanced definitions of "the curatorial" may be read as forms of resistance to the primacy of the practice of curating as resulting in a fixed exhibition form, or to the narrative-oriented authorial model of curation, which might be defined as commissioning new or working with extant artworks for a public manifestation within an exhibitionary frame or organizing principle defined by a curator. I would argue, though, that this is not the primary objective of the curatorial, which prioritizes a type of working with others within a temporary space of cooperation, coproduction, and discursivity that allows ideas to emerge in the process of doing and speaking together. However dissensual, this time spent together can be made public, warts and all. And, in doing so, the discursive aspect of curatorial work is given parity with—rather than being perceived as contingent upon—the main event of staging exhibitions. Similarly, the work of exhibition-making is where processes are set in motion in relation to other activities, actions, and events within the curatorial.

Certain articulations of the curatorial have identified a strand of practice that seeks to resist categorical resolution, preferring to function (in the Adornian sense) as

2
See Irit Rogoff, "Smugg[illegible] Curatorial Model," in *U[illegible] Construction: Perspectives Institutional Practice*, eds Vanessa Joan Müller an[illegible] Nicolaus Schafhausen (Cologne: Walther Kön[illegible] 2006), 132–3.

3
Maria Lind, "The Cura[illegible] *Artforum* 48, no. 2 (200[illegible] 103–5.

4
Beatrice von Bismarck, "Curatorial Criticality: Role of Freelance Cura[illegible] the Field of Contempo[illegible] Art," in *Curating Criti[illegible]* Marianne Eigenheer ([illegible] am Main: Revolver, 20[illegible] 62–69.

5
Emily Pethick, "The D[illegible] Barked at the Elephan[illegible] Room," *The Exhibition[illegible]* (2011): 81–82.

a constellation of activities that do not wish to fully reveal themselves. Instead of conforming to the logic of inside and outside—in terms of the distribution of labor—a constellation of activities exists in which the exhibition, whichever form it takes, can be one of many component parts. Rather than forcing syntheses, this idea of a constellation—as an always-emergent praxis—brings together incommensurable social objects, ideas, and subject relations in order to demonstrate the structural faults and falsities inherent in the notion of the hermetic exhibition as primary curatorial work. Rather than being either contrary to or integrated in, "the curatorial as constellation" of practices proposes a more juxtaposed or simultaneous field of signification, form, content, and critique. The constellation, in this sense, is an ever-shifting and dynamic cluster of elements that are always resisting reduction to a single common denominator. By preserving irreconcilable differences between things, actions, and discourses at the moment of exhibition—in whatever public form this takes—such praxis retains a tension between the universal and the particular, between essentialism and nominalism.

With this in mind, it may be useful to explore how the curatorial and certain understandings of "research" have become more aligned with each other recently, perhaps as a means of moving beyond an understanding of exhibitions as the main outcome of curating-as-production. In relation to the possible conjunctions and divergences between the curatorial and research, the exhibition form may be conceived as a research action in itself as much as a curatorial mode of emergent practice. In this sense, the curatorial "as research"—rather than primarily "as production" or "as authorship"—shifts the emphasis away from the exhibition as spatiotemporal, or as a phenomenologicial encounter with art. Instead, art (as object, concept, or thing, in whatever form it manifests) becomes part of an exploratory process of transformation through being in motion, moving from one state of being towards another, from being art to becoming exhibition as part of the curatorial process. Rather than perceived as static, art is itself changed by this movement, by becoming public, by "being exhibited." Additionally, the eventful experience of art as encounter moves towards a more ontological register, where art is transformed by its own moment of becoming "exhibition." Art stops being art—as it was prior to its showing—and becomes art-in-exhibition, in terms of a temporary moment of being publicly present. At that moment, or in that encounter, art is "becoming" or "being with": a movement and evolution, "changing to something or someone," and a being "in motion"; the *ontic* as (being) real, existence, as living form.

Exhibitions as Readymade Forms of Escape, and How to Describe "THAT WHICH IS NOT HERE"

This "becomingness," from art to exhibition, is perhaps best articulated through an exploration of the phenomenon of *escape*, where art gets to escape from being "just" itself through being "exhibited." In this escape, art moves from private to public, from concept to realization, and into the here and now. It is taken out of its storage and is made public, out of its habitual regulated life as art, as concept, as commodity, as capital, as thing, to become *art-in-exhibition*. This is a difficult idea to explain, especially given that exhibitions are always "somewhere else." They are the "THAT WHICH IS NOT HERE" in still images, in other times, locations, accounts, experiences—in retrospect. I would like to explore this state of THAT WHICH IS NOT HERE through the strange temporality of escape as a way of testing the distinctions between being art (as idea, object, or thing) and being exhibited (becoming public, being shown) and what happens to art when it becomes part of the exhibition form, when it escapes itself and becomes THAT WHICH IS NOT HERE. I will attempt this by simultaneously describing an individual experience of one work of art without naming it, alongside a personal emotional experience related to the artwork, but not limited by it. I will engage in multiple ways of interpreting e concept of escape: in theory, in memory, and in practice. In e meantime, I would like you to do the same. That is, to take moment to evoke a single work of art-in-exhibition you have en transformed by, to reimagine it and bring it into the here d now. At the same time, bring to this memory a feeling, overwhelming sensation even, if possible. This is to remind rselves that when we see or encounter art, we already bring it an a priori emotional state. We already inhabit these elings, and our experiences of the artwork are affected by em.

ANYWAY, HERE GOES, BACK TO THE BEGINNING (TO 1993)

's not me, it's you, babe. Sorry, my apologies, I meant to say, s not you, it's me. Or is that the way it goes? I can never member correctly. It is one of my memory blocks. One of y default settings that always seems to get in the way. Was you facing me, or me facing you when we both stood there, posite each other, and one of us said something like that? hich one of us was looking to find a way out? Neither of would admit to looking to find the door, the exit, quickly ough. Somehow, it was too late before we realized that it s each other, us, you and me, who were getting in each her's way. Where did we come in? How could we get out? eferably separately, without each other's knowing. But, w we knew, we just could not escape each other. Nor from here we were. There was no way around, no way backwards forwards, nor left or right. All sense of direction, even up d down, seemed to be impossible to decipher. Looking ck, I think it was something to do with desire, wanting to sualize ourselves differently.

> If it is this idea of escape—even the mere word itself—that releases us from something, then language is complicit with our need to be able to, at least, imagine ourselves elsewhere.[6]

6 Adam Phillips, *Houdini's Box: On the Arts of Escape* (London: Faber & Faber, 2001), 157.

Linked to a sense of failure and disappointment with the world, the concept of escape is often perceived as an act of release or liberation from something, somewhere, or someone, accompanied by the wish to be transformed. It is a word that makes us grateful. We are thankful that we can escape, because it makes it possible for us to imagine an alternative. The act of escape entails a productive practice of illusory disappearance and the possibility of a displacement of the self. When I think of the phenomenon of escape, it appears to be bound up in our earliest experiences of play, underpinning many of our childhood games, from hide-and-seek to blind man's bluff, or kiss chase. In each scenario, there is an innate tension between the desire to be caught and to get away. There is also an inherent psychological paradox as much as a regulatory modality of escape.

> The skill when hiding is to make it interesting to be found rather than to try to avoid being found altogether. The game fails if the seeker gives up or the hider disappears. These are transgressions of the psychic economy of the game, where everyone is reassuringly found in the end. In a successful game of hide-and-seek everyone is found: no-one, in fact, escapes.[7]

Play is therefore reliant upon our not being too elusive, too good, or too bad. Play should always retain an amateurish or even childish dimension. We must never extract ourselves completely from the game as game, or we will be lost forever. There is a psychology of tentative escapology whereby the practice of avoidance is the condition of preparation, a waiting to be eventually revealed. Elusion, elusiveness, and artful dodgery go hand in hand with an inevitable failure to stay hidden or *out of the game*. When we consider the ontology of play and how it relates to life, our life, then, as Emmanuel Levinas says, "The pleasant game of life ceases to be just a game."[8] The impossibility of getting out of the life-as-reality game, and of giving back to things their toylike "usefulness,"

7
See Mark Hutchinso[n] of Escape," http://ww[w.] markhutchinson.org/ writing%20art%20of[...] html/ (accessed July [...] and Phillips, *Houdin[i's]*

8
Emmanuel Levina[s] trans. Bettina Berg[o] CA: Stanford Uni[versity] 2003), 52.

is bound to the specific moment of one's life when infancy comes to an end and we begin to define the very notion of seriousness as part of growing up. What counts then, in all this experience of being, is the inescapability of life itself, the process of growing up and its very constraints, its social conventions, its realities. The urge to escape is our recognition of this inevitability, where the act of escape or flight from our becoming, from our reality, is a search for refuge. It is not a matter of getting out of life but of going somewhere—so it is therefore a spatial as much as a temporal metaphor. The need to escape is found to be identical at every juncture to which its adventure leads. It is as though the path traveled along could not lessen our dissatisfaction with the reality the adventure tries to lead us away from, towards somewhere else.

Therefore, with our need to escape, being itself appears not only as an obstacle that freethinking has to surmount or overcome but it appears even as an imprisonment from which one must get out. Escaping is when the "I" of existence wants to get out of itself, but does not flee itself as a limited being. Escape therefore puts into question peace with the self as a general entity, since it aspires to break the chains of the I to the self. It is being itself—or the "oneself"—from which escape flees. In escape, the I flees itself, not in opposition to the infinity of what it is not or what it will not become but, rather, due to the very fact that it *is* or that it *becomes*. Escape therefore sits at the very inner structure of our being as a form of self-positing. It is a reminder that the events of our individual lives are masking the inevitability of all life as something that is time-limited, or comes to a certain end. Escape can be a stepping outside of this time limitation, of life-time, but it is always deceptive. Like all immediate pleasure(s), it folds in on itself, it is within a moment of its own experience, but we inevitably fail to escape from ourselves.

So what has this got to do with art and its artistic terms, or when art is exhibited or practiced? If we think back to the idea of play as an important element of this "pleasant game of life," then, by extension, art may be seen as just a game that is played, not in a fictitious or facetious way but really as something we *choose* to play, be part of, and that brings us pleasure, but also as something that *allows* us to escape. I would argue that the concept of escape is perhaps best embodied in the readymade, which—from Duchamp to Koons—has brought about the object's extraction *from* the world, its temporary removal and its reconceptualization, leading to an adjustment of its value *in* the world. The role of the readymade—as that which is adopted from already existing things in the world—proffers an update on the figure of the artist-as-escapologist that is more Houdini (who returns) than Bas Jan Ader (who does not). Simultaneously, the artist as escapologist engages in acts of removal and renewal in which there is a constant slippage between concealing, resurrecting, and being uncovered—performing multiple selves and something to do with fragmented subjectivities as a kind of performed being in many places at once. In enacting this escape, seemingly ordinary, mundane things get away from being themselves without ever losing sight of what they once were. Actors become spectators, we become observers of ourselves, and playing becomes image and form. The room, the gallery, becomes a strange play space, a game becomes a space of display. The temporal dimension of playtime collapses into a multiplicity of time-images: of moments, of body parts, of abstractions of desiring bodies, and of game-times, into a proprioceptive experience. Like the tennis player whose racket becomes part of their body, the images and the games become extensions of each other and us, as viewers and players of the game, as much as they collapse into one another.

Escapology, therefore, provides a sense of melancholic transportation. The artwork engages in a double game, a shifting to and fro of associations. Fear of a world being lost forever is paralleled with an equally persuasive desire to be rediscovered, differently. THAT WHICH IS NOT HERE is therefore not really a game but many games, whilst not being a game at all. We become the things around us, which surround us, whilst they are revealed as both themselves and something more than they once were. The locus of the "end-work" hides in many places—people, things, actions—and times at once, almost getting lost, but always wanting to be found. As a box of tricks invested in an exchange economy of signs, both objects and bodies in action are at once strange and familiar. By employing certain tactics—such as removal, revelation, displacement, or dismantling—there is a reconfiguration; elements are recharged, rethought, and redeployed. There is a reimagining of things and actions as they are, differently, so that the resultant end-work of the curatorial provides an uncanny sense both of its own belonging within and separateness from the world it derives from, and the para-world it has invented. It is neither gallery nor game, neither exhibition nor site. Instead, the gallery plays its own cameo role as the THAT WHICH IS NOT HERE, where the exhibition is a kind of game, and the game becomes a kind of gallery of activities, actions, social interactions, and multiple modes of spectation and consumption.

As a latter-day incarnation of the readymade, there is a withdrawal of the notion of artistic value as a stable form of individual expression embodied in material practice, with the resultant work manifesting itself as a rejection of the mimetic capacity of the artist to reflect social life through their own, singular hand. Instead, based on an understanding of post-autonomous production as the foundation of art after Duchamp, there is a *process* of production in which the delegation of nonartistic labor to others is aligned with the artist's intent. Players become actors or agents of the artist, and vice versa, while the artwork as exhibition becomes a site of potential escape for both. It is perhaps representative of a collapse of the division "between intellectual labour and manual labour as the basis for the future dissolution of art into social praxis" that began with the early avant-garde.[9]

Productive labor and immaterial labor thus dissolve into coproductive practice, so that art can extend itself beyond alienated and alienating aestheticism. Here, the notion of escape is opened up at the point of artistic production, with

9 John Roberts, *The Intangibilities of Form* (London and New York: Verso, 2007), 2–3.

the "dispersal of the artist's hand into forms of heteronymous labour" enabling a dissolution as much as a displacement of the artist from the center of their own authorship.[10]

10 Ibid.

> [This] radical disjunction [is] at the heart of modern practice after the readymade, and as such, is what distinguishes the modern from the pre-modern: the fact that, at the moment of dissolution of its traditional forms, art invites both productive and non-productive labour into its realm as a means of reflecting on the conditions of both art and labour under capitalist relations.[11]

11 Ibid.

The assimilation of the worker into the artist and the artist into worker is a transformation of the alienated character of both, and I would argue a two-way escape from predetermined identities. Whilst there is seemingly rejection of authorship in the traditional sense, there is a diffusion rather than a refusal of authorship. Something is being made—through instruction, construction, invention, rule setting and breaking, alteration, and deception—for although there are multiple actors and agencies at work in the game of THAT WHICH IS NOT HERE, all these elements make up the curatorial work. Additionally, its events make up multiple social relations, which become dissolved into forms of disembodied spectacle, and we primarily experience the making of the exhibition (working with others) and the exhibition itself as part of a group spectacle (rarely alone) where often its narration is constructed in retrospect (after the event).

From this perspective of the THAT WHICH IS NOT HERE, there is a kind of remoteness to this particular experience of escape. We can, therefore, escape in an act of release or liberation from something, somewhere, or someone—from this place and this time—for a moment, which will always be accompanied by some kind of wish to be transformed. But we cannot escape from ourselves. We can become abstracted, we can get out of it, off our heads if we like, out of the game—but not out of our heads or out of ourselves. Escape is therefore also always a site of returning, coming back, coming down—no matter how immersive the experience of getting lost, no matter how high, how removed from the here and now. The act of escape always brings us back to the pre-immersive space, back to where we were, only with a slight din ringing in our ears. Then, afterwards, we remember: It was not you, it was me after all.

THE END

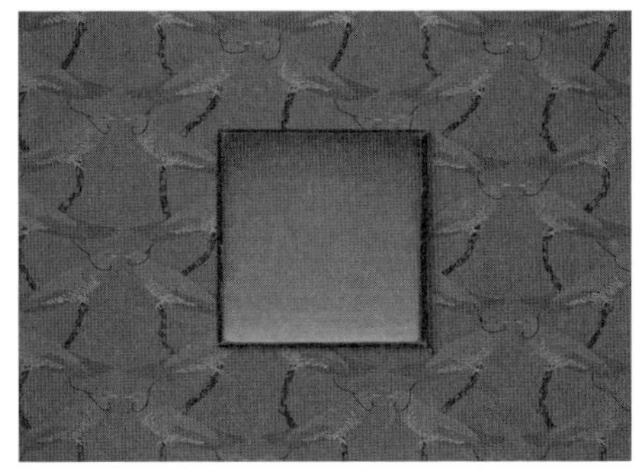

1. A small, almost square painting on an orange wall.

2. A young child sitting on a colorful chair.

3. Pink goo on wood.

4. Daffy Duck sitting on a bed.

A sleeping bag on the floor.

1. *We are the Center for Curatorial Studies*, curated by Paul O'Neill. The Hessel Museum and the Center for Curatorial Studies, Bard College, 2016–17. Installation details showing William McKeown's *Untitled* (2008) on top of his *Cloud Cuckoo Land* (2008–17), wallpaper, dimensions variable. Photo: Chris Kendall.
2. Young child with Mary Heilmann's *Sunny Chair* (Green, 2016) at Whitechapel Gallery, London, shown later as part of *We are the Center for Curatorial Studies*, curated by Paul O'Neill. The Hessel Museum and the Center for Curatorial Studies, Bard College, 2016-17. Photo: Paul O'Neill.
3. *We are the Center for Curatorial Studies*, curated by Paul O'Neill. The Hessel Museum and the Center for Curatorial Studies, Bard College, 2016–17. Installation details with work by artist Nina Canell. Photo: Chris Kendall.
4. Gareth Long, *Work in Progress*, shown as part of *We are the Center for Curatorial Studies*, curated by Paul O'Neill. The Hessel Museum and the Center for Curatorial Studies, Bard College, 2016–17. Courtesy of the artist.
5. *We are the Center for Curatorial Studies*, curated by Paul O'Neill. The Hessel Museum and the Center for Curatorial Studies, Bard College, 2016–17. Installation details with works by artists William McKeown, Eduardo Padilha (sleeping bags, and window) and Falke Pisano. Photo: Paul O'Neill.

Simon Sheikh is a curator and theorist. He is Reader in Art and Program Director of MFA Curating at Goldsmiths, University of London. He is a correspondent for *Springerin*, Vienna, and a columnist for *e-flux journal*, New York. Recent publications include *Former West: Art and the Contemporary After 1989* (2016, with Maria Hlavajova) and *Curating After the Global* (2019, with Paul O'Neill, Lucy Steeds, and Mick Wilson). He is currently a member of the core group for the 3rd Bergen Assembly, *Actually, the Dead are Not Dead* (2019).

Simon Sheikh

Thinking with Exhibitions, Thinking with People

The curatorial always takes place in the middle, between promise (a coming reflection, contemplation, or action) and redemption (intellectual achievement, aesthetic emotion or political resolution). As such, it takes place in a locality that does not know itself: not the museum, the gallery, the exhibition space, the alternative venue, the collector's parlor, the theorist's classroom, the activist battleground, or the virtual environment, but something entirely different. It takes place on an indefinite, but finite horizon.[1]

—Jean-Paul Martinon

1 Jean-Paul Martinon, ed., *The Curatorial: A Philosophy of Curating* (London: Bloomsbury, 2013), 29.

But there is a nastier side of the curator yet to be mentioned, which can be easily grasped if we look at installations, and indeed entire exhibits in the newer postmodern museums, as having their distant and more primitive ancestors in the happenings of the 1960s—artistic phenomena equally spatial, equally ephemeral. The difference lies not only in the absence of humans

> from the installation and, save for the curator, from the newer museums as such. It lies in the very presence of the institution itself: everything is subsumed under it, indeed the curator may be said to be something like its embodiment, its allegorical personification.[2]
>
> —Fredric Jameson

2
Fredric Jameson, "The Aesthetics of Singularit *Left Review*, no. 92 (Ma April 2015): 101–32.

In his recent essay "The Aesthetics of Singularity," Fredric Jameson attempts to construct an ontology of our troubled present, the epoch once known as postmodernism—which by now, in this present moment, surely categorized by any number of designations prefixed with a "post"—through what he terms "an approach to the *cultural logic* of a mode of production,"[3] and thus both a mental and material analysis of the contemporary condition. Interestingly, Jameson does so through a particular cultural practice, or mode of production, and thus through a specific type of producer, namely, the figure of the curator, to which he ascribes both positive and negative attributes, equally characteristic of our actuality. In a possible positive light, he aligns with the figure of the theorist (which may indeed have preceded and spawned the curator), as both are emblematic of the contemporary in their very mode of knowledge production—basically, one of assemblage—and in the sense that they are replacing another, historically modern figure, the avant-garde artist and the universalist philosopher. In both cases, the historical reasons for this shift are fairly straightforward and have, in the first instance, culture, to do with the status of the artwork and its assigned cultural and economic value. Simply put, contemporary art has no formal definition of what an artwork is, nor any logical system of evaluation—its meaning and worth are always inscribed contextually through the institutions of art (academies, galleries, art fairs, magazines, and museums), creating a mesh of possible evaluations and assessments, necessitating the figure of the curator as "the demiurge of those floating and dissolving constellations of strange objects we still call art."[4]

3
Jameson, "The Aesthe Singularity," 101.

4
Ibid., 110.

Standing in the middle of things, the curator creates an assemblage of subjects and objects that is specific and temporal: these things and not those, and at this particular juncture, and exhibitions must just be valued for their *currentness*, which is literally their currency, and not judged aesthetically through universal or even transhistorical criteria from art history. Curating is thus also a form of theory as opposed to philosophy, and the theorist conversely a form of curator: "selecting various bits from our various theoretical and philosophical sources and putting them all together in a kind of conceptual constellation."[5] This is, then, the promise and, if you will, the limits of contemporary critical theory and contemporary exhibition-making, and of curatorial projects in an expanded sense.

5 Ibid.

Does this mean, though, that curating is a form of thinking, and if so, what kind of thinking? This has certainly been the debate within curating and curatorial theory in the last decade or so, particularly in the coinage and contested use of the term *the curatorial*, and its turn from merely being an adjective relating to ways of curating (including curating in the expanded field, such as formats that did away with the exhibition itself) to its current and prominent status as a proper noun. As a notion, the curatorial indicates a specific way of working and thinking that not only stems from curating as a practice but also as something that expands and exceeds it, as a practice in itself, at once stemming from curating and departing from it. It is not without a certain irony, of course, that the strongest and most consistent use of the curatorial presents itself not as a theory but, rather, as "A Philosophy of Curating," which is the subtitle of Jean-Paul Martinon and Irit Rogoff's recent anthology, *The Curatorial*. Here, Martinon and Rogoff famously make a case for the curatorial as separate from curating, with the latter being "a gamut of professional practices that had to do with setting up exhibitions and other modes of display," whereas the curatorial is, succinctly, nothing less than "an event of knowledge."[6]

The use and indeed usefulness of the curatorial is, then, as an analytical tool and a philosophical proposition, and by indication, a separate form of knowledge production that may actually not involve the curating of exhibitions but, rather, the process of producing knowledge and making curatorial constellations that can be drawn from the historical forms and practices of curating. The curatorial could thus be posited as a form of research, not just into exhibition-making but as a specific mode of research that may or may not take on the spatial and temporal form of an exhibition. After the advent of the curatorial and post-research, the exhibition would, so to speak, simply be the designation for any project realized through curating and all that this implies in terms of addressees and research methods. The curatorial is, in this sense, not necessarily something that takes on the form and eventual character of the exhibition but something that employs the thinking involved in exhibition-making and researching.

Like theory, then, the curatorial mode of production conjures a "conceptual installation," whether its point of departure or end goal is the exhibition itself—but unlike theory, though the curatorial gains its specificity and, indeed, its contribution to knowledge and to an overall culture of research from the processes of exhibition-making and the practices of art, and the ways in which these practices correspond to and/or contradict concepts and ideas. Which is to say that objects and subjects can, on occasion, be cumbersome, hesitant, resistant, and even antithetical to the procedures of the project.

Now, this is not to say that there is one guiding principle of curatorial thinking and production of knowledge—far from it—but there are possibly a number of steps undertaken (with various methodologies) within curating that are processual and generative and that lead to the formulation and realization of projects yet in a way that organizes and ultimately presents

6
Jean-Paul Martinon and Rogoff, "Preface," in *The Curatorial*, ed. Martinon

a body of knowledge to a public, no matter how illusive and fictional. Furthermore, from these processes, new ways of collecting, analyzing, and presenting knowledge can be suggested: this is the contribution of the curatorial—no more and no less. Although there is no consensual definition of what curatorial research is, it would seem to encompass varying, and sometimes divergent, ideas of the exhibition as a form of research. The curatorial project is a vehicle for researching into something specific—into a particular field of interest or topic, into a particular cultural location or local artistic practice—or, for cultural research, understood as experimenting with various forms of public address and congregation, building or even antagonizing communities, whether designated and located or universal and unknown, inoperative or becoming. Within exhibitions or otherwise, the curatorial is that which can research into, and onto, an object of study that does not necessarily stem from artistic production and development per se. Rather, the aesthetic and, to a large degree, the art world are here seen as tools for investigating something other than art, for presenting ideas, research results, and project outcomes in a different discourse from other forms, such as politics proper, sociology, science, journalism, and so forth.

Formerizing the West

This is precisely the troubled waters in which a project like *Former West* tries to navigate, cruise, and build up storms within. *Former West* was a multifaceted curatorial project encompassing various modes of presentation, discourse, and research, which ran from 2008 to 2016 and which had both a historical as well as a historicizing aspect attempting to define the contemporary period (in art as well as in politics) as a "former West"—or at least proposing that the West could and certainly should be seen as former, but certainly not defunct. Methodologically, it thus did not offer a thesis in the sense of an idea that could be analyzed and proven or disproven, whether through logic or empery. Rather, it offered a proposition: If we can "formerize" the West, so to speak, then a new space of reflection, and thus of thinking and potentially emancipation and innovation, is opened. It should allow us to think anew, and to imagine something new, but precisely through an assemblage of formats, techniques, and voices, through a conceptual installation, as Jameson suggested.

As curatorial research, *Former West* thus advanced through exhibitions, conferences, and publications as places for research, as well as equally partaking in the development of the concept itself and not just, say, with conferences presenting theory and exhibitions presenting practice. Indeed, art was considered thought, and vice versa, without positing a hierarchy between forms of thinking nor any dialectical relationship between theory and practice. Rather, it was deliberately heterogeneous and contradictory in order to produce the concept of a former West as a tool to navigate and situate the contemporary. Neither in its various iterations and presentations nor in the concluding publication, *Former West: Art and the Contemporary After 1989*, did the project offer a narrative or chronology, and placing contributions on the same horizontal plane is obviously a curatorial gesture, as is the way that these sometimes contradictory positions and arguments are allowed to coexist without prejudice, resolve, or synthesis.

As a construction, though, *Former West* consists of three basic assumptions: that the contemporary as a historical period comes into being with events of 1989, and the end of the bipolar world; but also that contemporary art is a perfect lens through which we can see the contemporary, and is indeed a producer of this very condition of limitless contemporaneity, both subjectively and structurally; and finally, that this contemporary condition has to do with being *former* rather than with presence or futurity. At first glance, it is somewhat counterintuitive to claim a former West as the outcome of the seismic social changes of that overly symbolic historic year 1989, as the end of Communism this heralded has brought the political imagination of a former East to the popular imagination as both a temporal and spatial horizon of possibility. This dominant narrative of 1989 and its aftermath trades in two variations, either as a requiem for Communism and any overarching project for social change (a lament for lost futures) or as a triumphant story about the victory of the West and its values, as in the macho bluster of political thinker Francis Fukuyama's infamous concept of an end to history with the end of Communism.[7]

7
For a cultural analysis of the loss implied by post-Communism, see Charity Scribner's landmark book *Requiem for Communism* (Cambridge, MA: MIT Press, 2003). To understand what I mean by Fukuyama's macho blustering, have a look at this recent interview in *The Guardian* where he not only, somewhat belatedly, laments how neoconservatives misinterpreted his ideas about the end of history but also proudly claims that in what he terms "recently democratized countries," singling out Burma, Indonesia, Poland, and Ukraine, he is "still a rock star." See https://www.theguardian.com/books/2014/dec/27/francis-fukuyama-end-history-books-interview.

Rather than repeat such dead ends, our idea was to posit a former West as the time when the West missed its historical moment, its opportunity to transform and even decolonize itself. The former West can be seen as a contradictory condition coming into clear view after the events of 1989–91, even if its history precedes it, namely, as a twisted mirror to the idea of a former East, and thus as a reconfiguration of the North–South divide. If it is a mirroring of the West's others, then it is twisted in the sense that it names a constitutive asymmetry and epistemological injustice between the West and the rest, that is, the former East and the global South. Talking precisely about a former West rather than just a former East is, then, first and foremost an instrument of criticism. Moreover, employing the term *former*, rather than the more commonplace prefix *post*, is trying to think of a former West not as an "after the West," or an outcome of its greatness and/or demise, but, crucially, as a way of undoing it. In this sense, it is more in tune with the decolonial move, albeit with the caveat that it is always the colonized and not the colonizers that can and must perform this task, raising the question about whether the West in its actuality, as potentially former, can decolonize itself?

Stemming from contemporary art and its myriad practices, *Former West*, as a project, has a specific prism through which it assembles its curatorial constellation, and which, presumably, differentiates the project and its concept from how the contemporary as a condition and historical period emerges out of 1989 and the advent of post-Communism. As stated earlier, the project had a historical aspect, but now it is clear that it does not map the history of the world since 1989 in any linear or thorough socioeconomic fashion—not in terms of social history, political history, or art history—even if it involves elements of all these disciplinary forms. If anything, its approach to the methodologies of history would be that of conceptual history, as described by Reinhart Koselleck and others, though not in order to sort out the source material for a new history but simply to propose a new concept through which such a historical method could be employed. Similarly, it does not write an art history of the period, going through different events and styles, artists and exhibitions, although, again, the concept could potentially be employed for an art-historical periodization.[8]

8
See, for example, the a historian Alexander A 2008 essay "Periodisin Contemporary Art," h www.columbia.edu/cu arthistory/faculty/Alb Periodising-Contemp pdf.

Similarly, as an act of theorizing, it is not akin to the discipline of contemporary political theory (even though the anthology features many such collaborations) but is composed from the practices of contemporary art, in particular, its central activity of curating. This has to do with the first two assumptions previously mentioned, namely, that contemporary art, with its circulation of discourses and objects through an international system of biennials, journals, and art fairs, comes into being as a world system (after 1989) and the end of the Cold War, and thus the ideologies of the two modernities as the goal and evaluation criteria for (modern) art. As such, any ideology in contemporary art is not one of specific aesthetical forms that are possibly, potentially, capable of producing specific political subjectivities but, rather, an ideology of circulation itself (and as such the cultural logic of neoliberal globalism). Secondly, what contemporary art actually produces is the condition of contemporaneity, and it is a perfect place from which to see this condition, which is one of endless circulations and accelerations without resolve or limits, and whose only potential ending seems to be the end of the world itself.

The composition of the *Former West* anthology from 2016, then, not only aims at art and culture, and an understanding of culture as both cultural politics and political culture, but it also employs curatorial thinking in its way of composing and comparing positions. Rather than creating a narrative arc, and a synthesis of thinking, it is deliberately contradictory and inconclusive as a curatorial assemblage, where meaning is created in how things are placed next to each other, in sequence and in dialogue, as well as in contestation and contrast. What is implied here, and also what is at stake in a more general and political sense, is the curatorial as a specific system of knowledge production and its relation to other forms of research and an overall research culture—thus the relationship between knowledge and power. Moreover, the curatorial mediates between knowing and unknowing, encompassing all this means in relation to empowering subjects, groups, and movements, which is not simply a question of art and its audiences but of its alignments and constituencies.

From Assemblages to Assemblies

If *Former West* can be seen as an example of how curating can contribute to knowledge, it also places its production of knowledge and its research trajectory outside of the designated nstitutional settings for this work, such as the museum and he university. It is in this way that it is interdisciplinary, and can present its ideas not only in the form of texts but also hrough exhibitions as research tools. Now, in the museal model, the exhibition tends towards being the *outcome* of research process, however meticulous or superficial, however roundbreaking or solidifying, and so on. *Former West* proposed another model, perhaps even two models, that are nonetheless interconnected. As outlined above, *Former West*, as research project, dealt in curatorial knowledge and, as such, with an expanded practice for curating, not only in the form of xhibition-making but also in terms of theory. Secondly, there was the model of the exhibition itself within the project, not as its outcome or conclusion but as one of its research tools. The exhibition was seen as a representational space, as well as a place for experimentation and research. In other words, the exhibition, and the curatorial method employed, could be thought of not only as a form of mediation of research but also as a site for carrying out this research, as a venue for *enacted research*.

Research, here, is not only that which comes before realization but also that which is realized throughout actualization. That which would otherwise be thought of as a formal means of transmitting knowledge—such as design structures, display models, and perceptual experiments—is here an integral part of the curatorial mode of address, its content production, its proposition. In a historical sense, institutions of art mediate, and are as such educational platforms, and curators can therefore not be distinguished from educators in any principal sense. The museum, and by extension curatorial processes, inscribes both subjects and objects in specific relations of power and knowledge—of the nation-state, of Western civilization, etc.—in a transfer of knowledge and direction of desires and agencies that are educational, entertaining, narrative, and/or informative, such traits that are as often complementary as they are conflicting.

Can we thus think of transposing the knowledge production of curatorial research and thinking onto institutional formats? Can we, so to speak, begin to institute differently? One such effort to implement new curatorial research methods into instituting and institution-making is the Bergen Assembly, a triennial established in 2011 in Bergen, Norway, as "an initiative for Art and Research." The name itself indicates an attempt to change the mode of address of the international biennial format, with its circulation of the contemporary, into something that is also a political form of gathering. This is mostly associated with grassroots politics particularly after the rise and fall of the Occupy movement and its close relations to the cultural sphere, and especially cultural producers. In itself, this creates an inbuilt contradiction, namely, how can an institution of art—established by government and renowned professionals from the art world—become an *assembly*? This form is usually understood to be transient rather than solid and recurring, and, crucially, emerging from the ground up, from the gathering and self-organization of people, as *a* people, if not *the* people.

As formulated by Judith Butler,[9] popular assemblies form unexpectedly and dissolve under voluntary or involuntary conditions, and this transience is, I would suggest, bound up with their "critical" function. As much as collective expressions of the popular will call into question the legitimacy of a government that claims to represent the people, they can also lose themselves in the forms of government that they support and institute.

9 Judith Butler, *Notes Toward a Performative Theory of Assembly* (Cambridge, MA: Harvard Univ. Press, 2015), 7.

Any institution that tries to facilitate such democratic forms, including institutions of art, would do well to carefully heed these cautionary words. On the one hand, it is clear that any instituting from the top down that deals in audiences and publics cannot be an assembly proper, while, on the other hand, as Butler goes on to observe, the very "conditions for acting together are devastated or falling away." Could the solid foundations of the art biennial and triennial perhaps offer precisely the kind of support structure popular assemblies need in our time of increasingly de-democratized democracies in the former West and beyond? Such questions cannot be answered easily, and it would certainly be a much bigger task than the parameters of this essay allow.

But let us merely propose two aspects that must, for now, remain subjects for further research. First of all, it would need an analysis of art institutions (like the all-pervasive biennials) as not just places for representation but also as places of governance, a move that the art world, so far, has been drastically resistant to embrace. But we also need to ask ourselves how we govern. Secondly, it must imply the way in which we imagine and implement the interaction, the meeting and the conversation with art and artworks that we want to engage audiences, communities, constituencies, and, possibly, assemblies with—a curatorial methodology that is not only engaged with assemblage but also with forms of assembly.

If an art event is not yet an assembly, and maybe never can be, or never should be, depending on your politics of aesthetics, it can certainly implement a different encounter with the artwork, and with the ideas and methods of contemporary art and theory. As a curatorial method, the current core group for the Bergen Assembly (including this author) is considering how to move from a thematic approach of the grand exhibition towards a methodological approach, specifically in letting artists and the various communities of Bergen have conversations about artistic methods and politics *before* rather than only *after* (or perhaps during) the exhibition itself. A concrete way of doing this is to work with artists on new works that are produced not for specific communities but, rather, in dialogue and in discussion with a variety of communities. This will enable them not only to embed the work in the context and fabric of the city but also strengthen the works themselves, allowing for different competences and knowledges to influence each other, even when they do not end in resolution, consensus, and agreement. The idea is to bring the magnificent but often quite complex ideas and thought processes of contemporary art and political theory closer to people's everyday lives and struggles—something we find in certain urban and LGBTQ+ movements, to name but a few, and something that we would have found, historically, in the workers movement. These are the connections that need to be made, and remade, from and *for* the spaces of art. In our times of uncertainty and urgency, it is not only that the people need art and its institutions but also, and perhaps more so, that the institutions and discourses of contemporary art need the people.

Kim Seong Eun, DPhil, is an anthropologist specializing in museology and contemporary art, and her research interest lies in the agency of media art for the body and sensorial experiences in museums and the modality of combining the curatorial and the commons. Kim was a curator at Nam June Paik Art Center (2011–14), and is currently in charge of Education and Public Programs, Leeum, Samsung Museum of Art (2014–). Among her recent works are the exhibition *Common Front, Affectively* (NJPAC, 2018), study and research project *Senses± Thesaurus* (*c-lab, Coreana Museum of Art, 2018), publication *Between Doing and Knowing* (Stage for Learning, Arko Art Center, 2017), and the transdisciplinary public program series *Intermedia Theater: World Citizenship, Constellation of Things* (Leeum, 2015–16).

Kim Seong Eun

A Critical Muscle, a Choreographic Terrain

"I am a cultural anthropologist. In conducting research on contemporary art and curating exhibitions and public programs in the art museum, I explore multiple possibilities to theorize the curatorial." What typically follows my "elevator speech," or self-introduction, are rather predictable questions: Why does an anthropologist work in an art museum in the first place? (Because the art museum is not among the frequent fields that anthropologists seek out.) Why does the anthropologist in the field, not in academia, mention theory first rather than practice? (Because there are few things that you can do only at your desk in the museum.) Whenever confronted with these curious responses, I am compelled to question myself even further. Above all, why is it so scarce (especially in Korea) to look at the curatorial of contemporary art through the lens of anthropology? This is something akin to an admission of alienation, accompanied by the seeming marginality of research of this kind. However, a recent and growing tendency among curators around the globe to vigorously work on projects combined with anthropology is active enough to assuage such scholarly loneliness. For example, Marcelo Rezende discusses ways of reconstituting the history of exhibitions not in art-historical terms but by ethnographic methodology,[1] and Wiebke Gronemeyer proposes the idea of the "curatorial complex" in the "material turn" resorting to anthropological theories on material agency to create and mediate social relations.[2] Paul O'Neill, Lucy Steeds, and Mick Wilson organized a symposium and published a book theoretically derived from Mary Douglas's *How Institutions Think* (1986) to rethink art institutions from within.[3]

Another question to myself: What is it like to carry out research in the museum? This fundamental and rather self-reflexive question is perhaps, in itself, a subject for research. There is a need to research into the museum itself as well as what the museum deals with. In other words, what must research on the museum, done in the museum, be like? To start, it should be open to a symphonic collaboration with other disciplinary fields; but, having its own theoretical realm, it cannot be reduced to any of the disciplines in particular. Curating in the museum should become research in itself, which can give rise to a matrix of new theories on practices. Further, the museum is not a medium of interpretation and dissemination but, rather, the active agent to cause a theoretical event to take place, and therefore theories about the museum can only be born out of the spatiotemporal context of the museum. "A theory is absolutely fundamental not to the analysis of current conditions but to the positing of a set of alternatives and then to the kind of plotting out of how they might come into being."[4] Theories whose primary task consists in questioning are firmly grounded on bodily realities (unlike the implications of when we call something such as an armchair argument "a theory"). If we designate it a theory to inquire about alternative possibilities to the homogenizing practices of the museum, then the dynamics of theories may thus reinvigorate museums by unfolding questions in sensory and performative ways, always in a state of "becoming."

1
In a public seminar held Oslo National Academy Arts in 2016, Rezende t about a form of exhibiti making that interweaves contemporary art and co history, referring to the ethnographies of French anthropologist Michel and Brazilian anthropol Darcy Ribeiro. Marcelo Rezende, "An Ethnogra a Method, an Exhibitio a Fiction," in *Of(f) Our The Aftermath of the Ep and Other Curatorial A* (Kunsthøgskolen i Osl http://www.khio.no/er events/154/ (accessed 31, 2018).

2
The curatorial comple a concept derived fron Bennett's "exhibitiona complex." Here, the "r points to the material conditions and relatio enable actors to perfo a connected network. Gronemeyer, *The Cur Complex: Social Dimen Knowledge Production* (Paderborn: Willheln Verlag, 2018).

3
Paul O'Neill, Lucy Steeds, and Mick W *How Institutions Thin Contemporary Art an Discourse* (Cambridg MIT Press, 2017).

4
Irit Rogoff, "About Study: Infrastructur Education," in *Reth Education: A 12 Hou Encounter*, CreArt Network of Cities f Creation (Kristians 2015).

The power of theories lies in their functions that disperse a sense of linguistic utterance, unsettle the mechanism of understanding, and shake up the division between doing and knowing. All of these series of operations get started by "conceptualization." What emerged remarkably from the 2010s is the notion of "the curatorial." Quite a few publications came out in this period asserting "the curatorial" as a noun in their titles, such as *Performing the Curatorial: Within and Beyond Art* (2012), *Cultures of the Curatorial* (2012/2014/2016), and *The Curatorial: A Philosophy of Curating* (2013). In line with this research turn and discursive turn in the related fields of museology and curatorial studies, the concept of the curatorial was forged by research- or theory-oriented curators based on their own curating experiences in different platforms. For example, Maria Lind sees the curatorial as having a viral presence and as being analogous to "the political" conceived by Chantal Mouffe, in that it is concerned with political acts that try to go beyond what is already known.[5] For another conceptualization, Jean-Paul Martinon, in his *Theses in the Philosophy of Curating*, establishes the curatorial as a "gift"—evoking Marcel Mauss's *The Gift*—whose structure is that of absolute heteronomy and generosity prior to any contractual agreement of reciprocity.[6]

Originally an adjective but now obtaining the status of a noun, the curatorial has come to mean a practice-based work of research and a mode of knowledge production; a processual event of knowledge that occurs in the space created for this or through this; and the whole spectrum of its theorization, historicization, and politicization. The curatorial research, more often than not, meets with art history and art criticism, but the impetus toward an evolving theoretical concept for a transdisciplinary yet self-contained domain of research is given by the tenacious elaboration of curators in the field.[7] Another term that has arisen in the discourse is "the para-curatorial," which indicates the curating of talks, lectures, conversations, workshops, symposia, performances, screenings, and publications as well as exhibitions.[8] The para-curatorial

5
Maria Lind, "Active Cultures: On the Curatorial," *Artforum* 48, no. 2 (October 2009): 103–4; "An Introduction," in *Performing the Curatorial: Within and Beyond Art*, ed. Maria Lind (Berlin: Sternberg Press, 2012), 20.

6
Jean-Paul Martinon, "Theses in the Philosophy of Curating," in *The Curatorial: A Philosophy of Curating*, ed. Jean-Paul Martinon (London: Bloomsbury, 2013), 25–26.

7
Terry Smith, *Thinking Contemporary Curating*, ICI Perspectives in Curating, no. 1 (New York: Independent Curators International, 2012), 38–47.

8
Jens Hoffmann in conversation with Maria Lind, "To Show or Not to Show," *Mousse*, no. 31 (November 2011), http://moussemagazine.it/jens-hoffmann-maria-lind-2011/ (accessed August 31, 2018). Lívia Páldi, "Notes on the Paracuartorial," *The Exhibitionist*, no. 4 (June 2011): 291–6.

was advanced first by independent curators working in a temporary platform, like biennials, who realized a necessity for drastic changes to the production of artists and curators in a time of crisis where bureaucracies, institutional policies, and commercializing forces regulate and standardize art. The para-curatorial has grown from an awareness that, as much as art-making and exhibition-making, it is vitally important to think about the conceptual and theoretical frameworks for these activities and to circulate those ideas.[9] So, this new emphasis is often called the "curatorialization of education" or "educational turn." Not dependent on—and, actually, parallel to—exhibitions, these curatorial activities may comment on the hegemony and protocol of exhibitions in producing and mediating bodies of enacted, embodied, and situated knowledge.

The idea of the para-curatorial has been embraced by the museum enough now to be institutionalized. For those who might misapprehend the "educational" implied in the para-curatorial, these programs may look like something devised to make the exhibition more accessible for the public—to teach them about it—thus being supplementary and secondary to the exhibition. However, the para-curatorial is different from curating education programs in the traditional museum approach, that is, one presupposed to promote the visitor's understanding of artworks and exhibitions on the basis of institutionally approved knowledge. Rather, working as a single organism with the exhibition, para-curatorial programs do not presume a schematic teaching-learning relationship but instead put emphasis more on crafting a context of time and space where different relationships among participants are shaped and shifted. In this respect, a work by the scholar Fred Myers from an anthropological perspective is noteworthy.[10] The increase of programming beyond exhibitions is partly for the sake of bringing more people into the museum, and, in this vein, Myers borrows what the performance anthropologist Barbara Kirshenblatt-Gimblett phrases as museums being made "eventful." Programs such as lectures, symposia, and

9
Paul O'Neill and Mick eds., *Curating and the Educational Turn* (Lon Amsterdam: Open Edi De Appel, 2010), 19.

10
Fred Myers, "The C Cultural Productio Contingencies of P in Globalizing Mus Practices," in *Muse Public Cultures / Gl Transformations*, ed et al. (Durham, NC Univ. Press, 2006),

performances are "fast" events that punctuate exhibitions, considered a "slow" event. The exhibition, with a narrow amplitude and a scattered rhythm, can be interspersed with the disruptive and intensive pulsation of these events in a condensed time frame.

Myers analyzes a symposium in conjunction with the exhibition *Dreamings: The Art of Aboriginal Australia* held at the Asia Society in New York in 1988. He sees it as an "exhibitionary complex" for cultural production, and his detailed ethnography of the public symposium as a kind of scholarly performance reenacts each actor's performativity, including the curator, the critic, the artists, and himself as an academic. Despite the confidence of their immediate possession of knowledge, respectively, anxieties and tensions were inevitably betrayed as they brought up the exhibition and discussed it in the public setting. This is because such performances staged in the museum defamiliarize the transparency of the exhibition presumed to be apparent to all, and allude to the likelihood of unfamiliar knowledge emerging. For Myers, here is where the symposium's performativity comes into play. The renewed recognition of performativity is also what has theoretically consolidated the notions of the curatorial and the para-curatorial. The performativity spelled out in contemporary art evolved from the pursuit for participatory ethics in relational aesthetics, to the public manifestation of conflict and resistance in political relations, and to the ntervention in communities through dialogical interactions.[11] n tandem with this genealogy of performativity, there are ncreasing attempts in the museum to create a communal and ommon space to encourage social participation and exchange, nd this is expanded into the conditions and structures f knowledge before and after (and inside and outside) xhibitions. In a conversation between Irit Rogoff and Beatrice on Bismarck on compatibility and discrepancy between urating and the curatorial, these writers place a stress on nowledge production when different fields come together, in rms of producing not only transdisciplinary but "unframed"

11
Katya Garcia-Anton, "Slaves to the Rhythm: Performing Sociability in the Exhibitionary Complex," *OnCurating—Performing the Exhibition*, no. 15 (2012): 24–34.

knowledge, so as to "constitute new subjects in the world."[12]

When a practice first suggested as an "alternative" to the canon infiltrates the museum, it goes through a process of institutionalization wherein it is likely to be framed by the institution and then again canonized. Such buzzwords as "participation" and "encounter" have become clichés in the museum, and are now fetishized uncritically and even romantically. A call for social solidarity and political correctness, which is often deceptive and hollowed out, has degenerated into merely an administrative yardstick for institutional decision-makers and funding bodies. It is therefore imperative to invent new forms, ones that gather people together and allow them to express themselves to each other, to materialize this in different bodies of knowledge and turn what used to be seen as individual activities into something common and collective. The curatorial has to not only articulate a subject matter but formulate a formal configuration, and with a view to this, the curatorial research is undertaken in such a way that form and content are commensurable, or more radically speaking, form gives birth to content.[13] What is needed, as proposed by Charles Esche, is to work out a format that can engender a small community, if temporary, through educational links with the audience,[14] and bring about their action and contemplation, in concord or in collision, in theatrical and performative ways.[15]

Exercises for Critical Muscle

This idea is reflected in two programs called *The Critic's Club* from 2015. The first was held in Seoul at Leeum, Samsung Museum of Art, as part of *Unlearning Workshop*, in conjunction with the exhibition *Haegue Yang: Shooting the Elephant 象 Thinking the Elephant*. The exhibition title was inspired by two literary works: George Orwell's *Shooting an Elephant* and Romain Gary's *The Roots of Heaven*. The workshop was named for the concept "unlearn," which Yang

12
A conversation between Rogoff and Beatrice von Bismarck, "Curating/Curatorial," in *Cultures o[f the] Curatorial*, eds. Beatrice [von] Bismarck, Jörn Schafaff, [and] Thomas Weski (Berlin: Sternberg Press, 2012),

13
Mélanie Bouteloup, "[...] Reading that Counts[...]" *Curatorial Conundru[ms: What to] Study? What to Resea[rch? What] to Practice?*, eds. Paul [O'Neill,] Mick Wilson, and L[ucy Steeds] (Cambridge, MA: M[IT Press,] 2016), 121.

14
Esche argues that in [...] institutionalism, wh[at he] calls experimental institutionalism, it is [...] to work with a smal[l group of] committed people r[ather than] a broader audience, [...] them from a passive [...] into active collabora[tors...] Charles Esche, "W[...] Leaning by Doing: [...] Interview," *OnCura[ting]* (New) Institution(a[lism] (December 2013): [...]

15
Part of the progra[m ...] Shanghai Biennale [...] *Opera* is a case in p[oint ...] this perspective. L[...] "Theory Opera: W[hen Theory] Gets to Work, It S[...] *Not Ask Again: M[...] 11th Shanghai Bie[nnale]*, Raqs Media Colle[ctive] (Shanghai: Power [Station of] Art, 2016), 280.

often draws upon, meaning to make an effort to forget and erase what one has already learned. To unlearn, to revert to an uninformed state, is made possible paradoxically by learning, since one can discard only when there is something to discard. To give viewers access to multilayered references made in Yang's works, *Unlearning Workshop* was equipped with the works and materials of different figures, such as Sol LeWitt, Oskar Schlemmer, and Sophie Taeuber-Arp, as well as Orwell and Émile Ajar (aka Romain Gary). Viewers were led to explore for themselves what the artist sought to unlearn—how she wants to escape from the already learned in the transition between visual art and literature, and how this is embodied in the exhibition.

In the final week of the exhibition, students who were enrolled in an art criticism course led by Prof. Chung Sukyung, Seoul National University, assembled for *Unlearning Workshop*. Beforehand, they read Orwell's essay and viewed the exhibition as many times as they liked. Although the class was part of the academic curriculum and guided by the lecturer, the museum activity was more of an exercise to share the exhibition's vocabulary and learn it as embodied knowledge. Joining them for the discussion, this author posed two questions on behalf of the statement of *The Critic's Club*. First, Orwell and Yang as both artists and intellectuals, reflect deeply on the society they live in, and cope with the contradictions between domination and subordination, and between the universal and the singular. Would Yang's multilayered references to a broad range of humanities—"anachronistic referencing" in her own terms—be effective as a consequence of her reflections? Secondly, in a corner of *Unlearning Workshop*, participants were invited to create their own anthropomorphic sculptures using multifarious objects in a way similar to Yang's and, while handling the everyday materials and chatting together, to feel a sense of community, however loose. Referring to *The Unavowable Community* (Maurice Blanchot), *The Confronted Community* (Jean-Luc Nancy), and *The Coming Community* (Giorgio Agamben), what communal sense would Yang mean to nourish?

Revolving around these two questions, students spun different threads into the discussion. They came from various disciplines, including literature, economics, psychology, and biology, as well as art history, aesthetics, and painting, and thus their views varied significantly—from those of the general public who feel alienated from contemporary art, to those of artists who have a keen perceptiveness. A personal experience in Laos prompted one student to read clearly the everydayness of shamanistic acts contained in Yang's work. Another student contemplated on "our" culture and positioned the discussion differently in terms of multiculturalism and towards other cultures. There was a student who, as a viewer of the exhibition, felt identified with the narrator in Orwell's text in that both are forced to make a certain choice and judgment. For some students, the fact that the word "elephant" is used twice in the title pressed viewers into relying on outside references to discover what the elephant is, and they ended up confined within those frames of reference. For others, the fact that Yang's sculptures are commingled in the exhibition space without partitions is comparable to the nature of their meanings, which seem to be emerging but, soon after, halted and spread out into the air: that is, being in-between, or intermediate, as such terms are used in the titles of Yang's works.

Another session of *The Critic's Club* was held as part of *Aesthetic Schools at the Airport* in conjunction with the exhibition *Elmgreen & Dragset: Aéroport Mille Plateaux* at PLATEAU. Led by Prof. Lim Shan from the Department of Curatorial Studies at Dongduk Women's University, participants were graduate students enrolled in a class titled Introduction to Aesthetics and Exhibition-Making at Dongduk, and another class called Cultural Theories at Ewha Womans University. The solo show by Elmgreen & Dragset, based on *A Thousand Plateaus: Capitalism and Schizophrenia* by Gilles Deleuze and Félix Guattari and *Non-Places: An Introduction to Supermodernity* by Marc Augé, transformed the entire museum into an airport. There were waiting and boarding areas, check-in counters, security checkpoints, a baggage-claim carousel, and a duty-free shop. While these were true-to-life creations, there were also some features embedded that betray or make absurd the characteristics of the place, demonstrating that the airport itself is realistic and unrealistic at the same time. The qualities of the airport as a place that temporarily nullifies different borders—to pass through, rather than stay in—are superimposed by the exhibition on the museum as a space and institution.

The Critic's Club took place in the waiting area. The professor as moderator proposed the following subject matters: the airport as a place and a concept, the background of fusing the name of the museum with the exhibition's title, and the unison of airport and museum. He then encouraged members of the general public to join the students and the museum staff for a discussion. In this exhibition that constantly evoked complicated philosophical notions, some students felt that these were beyond the limits of their shallow knowledge, but at the same time, due to the very superficiality of their knowing, the exhibition's layers could be absorbed in a more clear-cut way. Talking about how such notions from Deleuze and Guattari as "deterritorialization" and "rhizome" were embodied in the exhibition, others saw that the show was neither about the airport nor the museum but, instead, suggested the nondescriptness of the place. Individual works were also analyzed: *I Am Thinking of You*, an outdoor installation in the form of a phone booth, was presented too straightforwardly without offering time to "think" about "what it is to think"; *Powerless Structures* strongly reminded viewers of their helplessness as exhibition viewers who do not belong to the context of the scene.

One of the heated debates concerned scenography. Drawing on Henri Lefebvre's theory on the social production of space, what some of the participants pointed out is that we are all too familiar with the visibility of space only as images produced by media, but the estrangement effect that the airport overlapped with the museum produced highlights the not easily recognized social aspects of space. According to the analysis of one student, artistic works and practical props seemed to be on the same footing, not necessarily one starring and the other supporting, and museum ushers and guards looked like they were acting in "theatrical" displays, where the movements of viewers played a certain part in the (empty) stage. Other exhibition-related programs of *Aesthetic Schools at the Airport* were touched upon, including lectures by Deleuzian philosophers and especially the reading program. Just as people in airports spend their waiting time mostly reading, visitors to this exhibition were invited to read aloud Alain de Botton's *A Week at the Airport*: Each reader began where the previous participant stopped, and each was allowed to read as many paragraphs as they wished. This reading program, and *The Critic's Club* too, seized upon the performativity of reading aloud, speaking out in a way that could bring the exhibition alive.

Participants in both installments of *The Critic's Club* talked about the relationship between reading books and viewing exhibitions—which should come first?—and confessed difficulty in rendering in critical language such works as Yang's and Elmgreen & Dragset's, whose critiques often entail endless footnotes. Nonetheless, many of them seemed to affirm the vitality and potency that the words poured out of and into the exhibition (and their reciprocal movements) could generate. This means that the critical ability towards contemporary art can become robust like a bodily muscle, built up over time through exercises in utterance and enunciation and without any hierarchies between knowledge and ignorance. Programs like *The Critic's Club* do not aim at a coherent flow of academic discussion with a great wealth of knowledge but, rather, as an exercise to "think together." It is to cultivate a willingness to let awkward and even frictional moments occur, to let it be seen and heard. Running into these junctures, the participants themselves reconcile how to think together and act together.

In order not to be complicit with the supposed attitude of the museum to instruct and enlighten audiences, what is necessary—more than telling museum visitors what to take in, and how, and why—is to give audiences a chance to strengthen their critical muscle, and to grant them a right to produce the unexpected learning for themselves.[16] This implies the mediation not of perfect understanding but of incomprehensibility, the art of organizing "an unruly, aberrant gaze" and "a postponed knowing."[17] *The Critic's Club* apparently takes the form of a typical seminar, but when it is brought to the museum context and staged like a performance, its curatorial prioritizes "not knowing." Among the entities assembled there, human or nonhuman, there are certain movements taking place in which the influences of one body upon another are transferred and transformed. Resonant with different intensities depending on the experience, the sensory bodies are continuously affecting and being affected by other bodies. Their agencies enter into a stage that can bolster up a collective body, which includes a process of understanding, and also a moment of repossessing one's own subjectivity by acting based on self-determination. This is why performances are taking an increasingly important role in the museum.[18]

There is a thread of connection between choreography to produce such performances and the curatorial as creating a spatiotemporal situation where language and image, subject and body, are mediated and modified. The structure of the curatorial is always dualistic, with cognition and sensation, with presentation and representation, and with materiality and textuality. It is choreographic in that it generates immediate sensory experience through bodily arrangement and scenography, and weaves highly dense discourses with open seams. Key to the curatorial (putting elaborative and provocative acts in unison) is how to write in the spatiotemporal coordinate, with predetermined interpretations and narratives, on the one hand, and bodily and emotional

16 Clémentine Deliss, "Explore or Educate," in *Curating Subjects*, ed. Paul O'Neill (London: Open Editions, 2007), 87.

17 Gabriele Brandstetter, "Written on Water: Choreographies of the Curatorial," in *Cultures of the Curatorial*, eds. von Bismarck, Schafaff, and Weski, 125.

18 Dorothea von Hantelmann, *How to Do Things with Art: The Meaning of Art's Performativity* (Zürich: JRP/Ringier, 2010), 190–2.

movements that are sometimes spontaneous, on the other, simultaneously.[19] The curatorial is thus choreographic: bodies moving together (choreo-) to be written (-graphy). "Choreography is the term that presides over a class of ideas: an idea is perhaps in this case a thought or suggestion as to a possible course of action. … Choreography elicits action upon action: an environment of grammatical rule governed by exception, the contradiction of absolute proof visibly in agreement with the demonstration of its own failure."[20] The curatorial that corresponds to the choreographic is itself the initiative of moving and writing the body behind which a driving force is the unknown, the uncertain.

In terms of inventing a form by which questions about contemporary art and exhibitions can be performatively written, it might be an interesting possibility to combine choreographic properties of the curatorial with a choreography for performances. In 2015, *Intermedia Theater*, a cross-disciplinary series at Leeum, was given the theme "Constellation of Things" and invited choreographer Ro Kyung Ae to work with one of the programs. This called attention to a tendency in the field of performing arts, as exemplified in William Forsythe's idea of "choreographic objects," where objects are not merely backdrops but their movements are turned into new choreographic work. Ro, together with performers Kang Jin An, Kong Young Sun, and Song Myung Kyu, carried out a three-month research into the ceramic collection on permanent display at the museum. In the early stage, they read essays on the formation principle of Chinese compound ideographs, the Japanese poetry of Haiku, and a theory of montage film in order to study the ways that discrete words are merged to produce a new meaning and bodies of abstract knowledge can be shaped visually.

Next, they visited the permanent displays several times. Unlike contemporary art, they found it difficult to connect with traditional art in choreographic terms, but as these face-to-face encounters with the works grew over time, their sensory experience came to reveal itself to inform

19 Gabriele Brandstetter, "Transcription–Materiali[…] Signature: Dancing and […] between Resistance and […] in *Emerging Bodies: The Performance of Worldmak[…] Dance and Choreography*, […] Gabriele Klein and San[…] Noeth (Bielefeld: transc[…] Verlag, 2011), 119–36. S[…] to the curatorial, the adj[…] "choreographic" has bee[…] theorized to the point o[…] status as a noun. Jenn Jo[…] *Choreographic* (Cambric[…] MIT Press, 2014).

20 William Forsythe, "Choreographic Objec[…] *William Forsythe and th[…] of Choreography: It Star[…] Any Point*, ed. Steven S[…] (Abingdon: Routledge[…] 90.

choreographic contours. Although the special exhibition *Exquisite and Precious: The Splendor of Korean Art*, held in the same period of time, helped them with information about the patterns, forms, and brushwork of traditional art, what they concentrated on more was letting their bodies explore the works viscerally by being there repeatedly, without being framed by art-historical knowledge. Among the objects, they were attracted to Buncheong ware and white porcelain—works that are simple but modern, and that contain wit and humor from everyday life. Their choreography sought to condense objects into extremely ephemeral moments of human bodily movements, making them manifest through three modalities: imagery, narrative, and association. Their research was presented as a performance entitled *Dance into the Exhibit* held at the Leeum auditorium.

The designer, Ahn Mano, extracted patterns from the ceramics and turned them into moving images as a stage backdrop; and some pieces of traditional Korean music, both vocal and instrumental, were selected as a soundtrack. These are typical elements one might expect in a staged performance. However, contrary to expectations, the three dancers were not on the stage. Instead, they presented themselves outside of the auditorium, specifically, in the lounge next to it. From inside the auditorium, one could see the lounge space only when the window shade was lifted from the floor-to-ceiling glass wall on the left-hand side. Due to the fixed seating in the auditorium, the audience was forced to position themselves awkwardly, looking at the moving images onstage and at the moving performers behind the glass wall from the side, watching each separately in an unsynchronized way. The bodies of the performers and those of the audience were in motion, at different angles, and the field of vision normally converging in one direction was broken apart. The primordial actions and motions behind the window glass began with silence and became more active and explosive along with the escalating beats of music. This overlapped with the audience's experience, in essence, of looking at artworks inside a glass vitrine in a typical museum situation. A performance having a fleeting dimension of time can meet ancient works that have survived a long period of time. The spatiality of the museum—where objects, be they traditional or modern, are anchored—requires viewers "to think in several tenses simultaneously," which can accord the museum contemporaneity through a "disjunctive relationship to temporality."[21]

Instead of emphasis laid on a final outcome, the performance reflected a concern with forms through which to make the research process public. This is derived from an awareness that the museum needs to break away from the convention of simply commissioning artists to produce works. Having been symbolized by certainty and stability, the museum as an institution today has to think about its changing roles: how to disclose itself as flexible and vulnerable; how to understand itself as being producer, collaborator, and convener.[22] Mindful of this, the performance programs in conjunction with Olafur Eliasson's solo show at Leeum, *The parliament of possibilities*, were organized. The use of the word "parliament," with its political implications, recalls philosopher and anthropologist Bruno Latour's "the parliament of things."[23] From the work of an artist of Icelandic descent, Latour describes the Icelandic "Althing," the oldest parliament in Europe, meaning "a space for all things." He takes notice of the ancient word for "thing" in the Old English, which meant an "assembly" or "forum" as well as nonhuman things. Latour finds that Eliasson's work ignores "the tired old divisions between wild and domesticated, private and public, technical and organic," to be replaced "by a set of experimentations on the conditions that nurture our collective lives."[24]

The subjectivity of "I" is enabled by other beings, whether they are humans, things, animals, or the natural environment, and Eliasson's works invite one to rethink relationships with others by arranging the notion of assembly in a multifaceted sense. This is the case in *Rainbow assembly*, too: Fine mist and shimmering rainbows are created artificially, to which the sound of spraying rain and the

21
Bishop argues that "the permanent collection ca a museum's greatest wea breaking the stasis of presentism. This is beca requires us to think in s tenses simultaneously." Bishop, *Radical Museolo What's 'Contemporary' in Museums of Contempora* (London: Koenig Book 19–20, 23–24. Mark Fr also states that "bringin a museum to life throu performance assumes a life in the collection ar of the collection an environment." Mark F "Museum, Artifact, Ac *und Archiv* 5 (2014): 1

22
In one of the program *Intermedia Theater: Co of Things* in 2015, Dor Willsdon, then Leanr George Roberts Cura Education and Public San Francisco Museu Modern Art, gave a t "Museum as Event." notes that art museur becoming more and a venue for live art ev because many artists working with forms pedagogy, dialogue, a practice that can be as performances.

23
Bruno Latour, *We H Been Modern*, trans. Porter (Cambridge, Harvard Univ. Press 142–5.

24
Bruno Latour, "Atm Atmosphere," in *Ol The Weather Project*, ed. Susan May (Lo Modern, 2003), 30,

surrounding muttering and mumbling are amalgamated into a tactile feeling. In this work, choreographer Jung Young Doo led an impromptu workshop drawing on animal movements. Eliasson himself ran around in the event *Life is space 4* held in the Institut für Raumexperimente in 2011, in a session of "Lion Exercise." Not just mimicking animal moves, this activity was meant to train the human body by relocating it in a new set of sensorial relations. From choreographer Xavier Le Roy's research project on the movements of animals and machines, dancer Christine De Smedt took the lion's movements and performed these together with program participants, an activity in which "the eyes are not dominant anymore" and the perception gained from what one hears and senses "becomes a three-dimensional experience."[25]

25 Anna Engberg-Pedersen, ed., *Olafur Eliasson: Life is space 4; 17 June 2011* (Berlin: Studio Olafur Eliasson, 2012).

Jung chose to restore the very bodily senses of human beings that have disappeared as mankind has lost a communal lifestyle. Animals have special sensorial functions that humans do not. Most of these are indispensable for survival, and those of fish or birds, among others, are necessary to live gregariously in large flocks. Humans used to lead a communal life centered upon a certain unit of community, but present-day life is much more individual and thereby we end up with many of our bodily senses degraded. Inspired by animal movements, the different exercises of Jung's workshop seek to find what humans have lost by prompting participants with drills in the sensorial experiences of space and distance, location and direction, and sound, smell, and energy. After the workshop, the participants staged an improvisational performance in *Rainbow assembly*. There was no prior scenario, and the only guiding principle was to follow the animal-like senses that were somewhat restored in their own bodies. To sounds made by traditional musician Jeong Songhee using various nonmusical tools, somewhere between music and ambient noise, their movements naturally took on a gathering form. As their movements intermingled with other spectators, they created a parallel scene, hidden or fictional, alongside the artist's intentions and the exhibition's context—to bring up the parameters of what is already there in the museum and to let those gathered experience sensorially through the dialectics between the premediated ways of reenactment and the spontaneity of participating bodies.[26] This is a form of learning performed in a bodily manner in which the curatorial meets with the choreographic.

26
Boris Charmatz and Cat
Wood, "If Tate Modern
Musée de la danse?," in
*Experience, Re-Live: BM
Live Programme*, ed. Cec
Wee (London: Tate Pub
Programmes, 2016), 19

Beyond and Within, At Once

As institutional critique has severely pointed out, the museum was collapsing into ruins, in the words of Douglas Crimp. And it is "through its crevices, cracks, and usually dormant spaces" that the bodily gestures of performances have intervened.[27] Without a doubt, performances have become what the museum wants, what the museum needs. And we have also reached a stage where belief in the critical power of performance brought to the museum should be accompanied by a keen awareness of the dangers that come when performance is appropriated and institutionalized by the museum. Will performance let us reimagine and reanimate the museum enough? This is the reason why the aforementioned projects theorized and curatorialized the notion of performance itself, not in a narrow sense of dance or theater but more broadly including the workings of all moving bodies. The curatorial projects dealt with the physical characteristics of the body, the relationship of its movements in time and space, and the interactions between bodies; and also with the process and structure of dialogue and exchange in which social bodies get together and move. All these are intended to form a choreographic terrain for performance in the museum. If we try to assemble performative activities that can shed light on the contingencies of specific bodily acts in a given spatiotemporal context, then the institutional changes that the bodily assembly can bring to the museum may perhaps be more powerful than anticipated.

27
Mark Franko and And
Lepecki, "Dance in the
Museum," *Dance Resea
Journal* 46, no. 3 (Dece
2014): 1–4.

What forms and functions does a curatorial model have

to perform, not only as a means to present a research outcome but also as a place of enacted research itself?[28] To inhabit this question might be a guiding principle for doing theory in the museum. We need to take a critical and timely look at whether the many discursive activities of the museum resulting from attempts to construct a new matrix of theory and practice remain arbitrary and abstruse, only producing fatigue and repulsion from the public. Some institutions maintain a patronizing and self-enlightened attitude that pushes the public into an extremely passive position, while simply shifting the responsibility to the public, saying things like "everything is up to you" or "everything is open to your interpretations." It is often the case, as if there were only two possible options for the museum—to be either for the public or for professionals—that museums neglect research into who the public is, or what the public means, because this information is not easy to capture or take in.

It is therefore urgent to think theoretically out of practices for how the transition and transformation of unstable and indeterminate knowledge can take place. By refining the performative ability of the public, whose members have different concepts and senses, theories can plot out how alternatives might come into being in the midst of translating and experimenting different ways of knowing. These theoretical curatorial praxes can be a route through which to find a new grammar and syntax to the museum, and also be a criticism and research into the museum grounded in social, cultural, and political conditions. Institutionalized museums were, and still are, an object of continued criticism, but it is that very never-ending critique that is the raison d'être for the museum. For the performativity of the institution may always conceive of something that cannot be exhausted by institutionalization, something yet to come.[29] The critical performativity of institutions lies in the endeavor to find the uncommon in what is regarded as common, to articulate political relations manifested through participants relying on and refuting each other, and to draw new and different acts

28
Simon Sheikh, "Towards the Exhibition as Research," in *Curating Research*, eds. Paul O'Neill and Mick Wilson (Amsterdam, New York: Open Editions, 2014), 33, 40.

29
Athena Athanasiou, "Performing the Institution 'As If It Were Possible,'" in *Former West: Art and the Contemporary After 1989*, eds. Maria Hlavajova and Simon Sheikh (Cambridge, MA: MIT Press, 2016), 680, 685.

from it. It is none other than the museum as an institution that can secure time, in physical and chemical senses, to freeze and solidify theories—and hence, it is the museum's theoretical responsibility to explore what lies beyond the institution, with the institution, and within the institution.

James Voorhies is a curator and art historian of modern and contemporary art. He is Chair of the Graduate Program in Curatorial Practice and Associate Professor of Contemporary Art at California College of the Arts in San Francisco. He is also Director of Curatorial Research Bureau, a bookshop, learning site, exhibition, and public program located at Yerba Buena Center for the Arts. He holds a PhD in modern and contemporary art history from The Ohio State University and is the founder of Bureau for Open Culture. His book *Beyond Objecthood: The Exhibition as a Critical Form since 1968* was published by the MIT Press in 2017. Research for his new book *Binding Agents: Toward an Aesthetic of the Postcolonial in Contemporary Exhibition* received support from the Graham Foundation and Etant donnés Contemporary Art.

James Voorhies

I Call This Work Research

Monday, August 13, 2018
Curatorial Research Bureau
Yerba Buena Center for the Arts
San Francisco, California

The eleven-foot gold-velour panel curtains arrive. The storefront space with a wall of windows facing a busy downtown San Francisco street and spotted with movable wood tables and book displays, which only a week earlier had settled into a momentary organized-disorganized stasis, is again thrown into disarray. Installation of the curtains, plus long aluminum suspension rods and scaffolding, is accompanied by the sound of drilling and hammering. The bookshop manager (in their third week on the job) steadily proceeds amid the chaos, writing artists and publishers to inquire about consigning their publications. A friend and patron stops in for coffee. She looks at books and journals, walks around the space, talks with me about providing support. Soothing notes from a Max Richter CD, at times barely audible above the noise of construction, coat the space: my relentless insistence on calmness, however one can have it, even when it's obviously unachievable. Another visitor, a curator friend at the institution across the street, stops over with a handful of books for us to review and potentially consign. Do they want coffee? No. I'm making cappuccinos. Emails continue to pour across the screen about an overdue press release, followed by quick calls to marketing and communications teams to discuss the language used (incorrectly) to describe this bookshop/vitrine/exhibition/ public program/sometime "Open Seminar"/ sometime private seminar platform-space. Indeed, the slashes, hybridity, and shape-shifting—both conceptual and literal— of the Curatorial Research Bureau are difficult to communicate in 250 words. But, oddly, aren't the slashes, hybridity, shape-shifting, and illegibility what make the CRB attractive as a thing, precisely because its combination of activities, peoples, and functions is not easily discernible?

Curatorial Research Bureau (CRB) is complex: a consumer space selling books, an academic site hosting graduate seminars, the location of an array of public and private programs, and the new home of the California College of the Arts (CCA) Graduate Program in Curatorial Practice. CRB sits administratively within two institutions dedicated to the contemporary arts, CCA and Yerba Buena Center for the Arts (YBCA), both in San Francisco. It is administered by the curatorial practice program in partnership with YBCA and Bureau for Open Culture (BOC), a curatorial initiative that I lead in collaboration with my partner, the illustrator and designer Nate Padavick. As BOC, we have repeatedly nestled into various institutional contexts since the inception of BOC at Columbus College of Art & Design, Ohio, in 2007, attempting to forge intersections among art, design, education, public space, and consumer culture—all while pushing against and, as the entangled and enmeshed position of CRB demonstrates, asking institutions to confront their engrained characteristics in order to offer new ways to engage audiences with art and its ideas.

The typographical slashes, while not easy to relay in a press release, do in fact communicate something. The multipronged quality of CRB is responsive to (and a product of) the hyper-hybridization of our contemporary moment, where a "bookshop/screening" or a "coffee bar/artist talk" conflate the consumption of material and immaterial culture as equally valuable modes of experience and cultural exchange. Recognizing the fuzzy line between audiences and consumers, the CRB bookshop as a consumerist form will provide programmatic possibilities for curating art and cultural presentations. It will seek to transform that familiar consumer bookshop site into a learning site, leveraging the platform for social connectivity and education *as exhibition*. Audiences (/consumers) know how to engage with the retail situation of shopping (fig. 1). Here, at CRB, distinctions between the arts and entertainment, even between a club and the general public, or between art and academic institutions, will become increasingly blurred, in both public and private scenes, all in the pursuit of audience-building, in pursuit of connecting ideas to people, and people to people, through the lens of contemporary art and culture.

How do I talk about this work as part of my research as a curator?

February 26, 2016
Consumer Research Center/
Carpenter Center for the Visual Arts
Harvard University
Cambridge, Massachusetts

Curatorial Research Bureau is, one could say, version 2.0 of a program I launched in February 2016 at Harvard's Carpenter Center for the Visual Arts (CCVA), where I was the John R. and Barbara Robinson Family Director (fig. 2). The program was called Consumer Research Center/ (CRC/). The "/" was built right into the title for that project, and CRC/ also engaged in activities exploring the hybrid consumer form as a viable mode for high-touch social connectivity in a twenty-first-century arts organization. CRC/ posed similar questions about the influence and value of consumer points of sale (POS) for building publics (audiences) around an arts institution. Comparable to CRB, it was a partnership with Berlin-based publisher and international distributor Motto Books, where Motto supplied titles from around the globe with direction from me about specific content pertinent to upcoming programs and exhibitions. In Cambridge, my team at CCVA gathered publications by faculty at Harvard and nearby academic institutions, such as MIT and Northeastern University, to complement the global offerings by Motto. And, again comparable to CRB, we strove to create a platform where the immediate surrounding public would feel they had something at stake in what we offered.

As part of the programming at CCVA, I organized a series of "Open Seminars" inside the space of the CRC/. The faculty in the Visual and Environmental Studies department, Harvard's undergraduate arts program housed at the Carpenter Center, often invited artists and writers to engage with their students, mostly in the private arena of seminars and studios. I was interested in how to invert that activity, make it public and available to broader audiences. In coordination with faculty, we identified artists and writers, such as Nina Beier, Natalie Czech, Karel Martens, Simon Dybbroe Møller, Gloria Sutton, and Ulla von Brandenburg, whose visits to Harvard could step into the public realm through the Open Seminar format.

That spring, I taught a seminar course and organized an exhibition, both under the title *Phil Collins: A Learning Site*. The course had twelve students—undergraduate and graduate—mostly from Harvard but also from Brown University and MIT. The multilayered practice of British artist Phil Collins was the focus of a constellation of public curatorial and private academic activities that transpired in their respective precincts of the Carpenter Center. Over the course of three months, the exhibition and seminar combined into a singular thing dedicated to presenting, experiencing, studying, and analyzing the work of one of contemporary art's most engaging voices. As a community, we experienced from different analytic perspectives the provocations that Collins presents in his work. This occurred through a variety of channels. In a traditional seminar, my students discussed texts by Claire Bishop, Mai Abu ElDahab, Anton Vidokle, Maria Lind, Fulvia Carnevale, Judith Butler, Nicolas Bourriaud, and others. We looked at a history of spectatorship, participation, and social engagement in contemporary art over the past forty years through the lens of Collins's practice. We read about artist Robert Smithson. We viewed work by artist and choreographer Yvonne Rainer. We discussed the writings of critic Michael Fried. We used case studies of exhibitions, artworks, and institutions to create a kind of knowledge toolbox that would allow us to think about and analyze the changing role of the spectator—from indifferent viewer to integrated participant—and the artists promulgating this shift. Among them, we considered the work of Group Material, Carsten Höller, Oda Projesi, Liam Gillick, Andrea Fraser, Walid Raad, Martha Rosler, Elmgreen

& Dragset, and Bik Van der Pol. The course was also a critical reflection on curatorial strategies in exhibitions at museums and biennials in the United States and Europe, including Tate Modern, Kunstverein München, Moderna Museet, the 2009 Venice Biennale, New Museum, Skulptur Projekte Münster, and documenta.

The exhibition component was another channel. Collins's video *the meaning of style* (2011) was installed during the entire run of the program. That installation space transformed twice into the site of two Open Seminars. As part of the course requirements, students (under my direction) collectively hosted two Open Seminars dedicated to subjects in contemporary art related to Collins's practice: spectatorship, participation, critique (fig. 3). Each seminar drew about forty attendees from the general public. In addition to analyzing *the meaning of style*, we watched clips from *the louder you scream, the faster we go* (2005), *they shoot horses* (2004), and *how to make a refugee* (1999). We analyzed Collins's films as a group with the unpredictable contributions of public audiences, providing students with valuable insight and exposure to addressing in real time the often wide-ranging questions and comments posed by people who attend public programs.

In a third channel, the Open Seminars were complemented by a program I organized for Harvard Film Archive (the Carpenter Center's cinema) to present feature films by Collins. Free and open to the public, visitors watched on successive evenings *the world won't listen* (2004–11) and *This Unfortunate Thing Between Us* (2011). Collins then spent a week at Harvard leading a seminar with my students and a separate workshop involving Harvard Radio Broadcasting, the campus radio station (fig. 4). The week was capped off with a screening of his film *Tomorrow Is Always Too Long* (2014) followed by a public conversation with Collins and me. In order to test these different channels of engagement, Collins and his work were threaded throughout every facet of CCVA's programmatic mission that spring.

Slashes and hybridity. Public and private. Orchestrated

connections and coordinated mediations. This is what my curatorial research practice looks like.

Tuesday, August 14, 2018
Curatorial Research Bureau
Yerba Buena Center for the Arts
San Francisco, California

Today, more drilling and measuring; metal tracks for the curtains installed; more boxes of books arrive from Motto; budget meetings to discuss how to account expenses and submit requests to the college for reimbursements. I walk over to SFMOMA to meet with a curator about an upcoming visit by the Rotterdam-based duo Bik Van der Pol to discuss how they might intersect with CCA graduate students. That afternoon at CRB: I meet with another SFMOMA curator and CCA's dean of design to discuss the museum's forthcoming exhibition about Sea Ranch, the famed housing development envisioned by Lawrence Halprin three hours north of San Francisco. How can CCA be involved? That's often the question. I pursue making something out of context. I prioritize context—of art, ideas, people, places, and things—as an active ingredient in the practice of curatorial research. The late-afternoon meeting concludes abruptly; we need to move the modular table to make room for the scaffolding needed to install another track for the curtain. Next: a discussion with the bookshop manager about advancement in our organization (and we're not even open yet!) then continued reflections with marketing and communications about the language used in the press release. Also: the website—almost finished, completing headshots of people at both institutions who help administer this project while fielding more photographs of the CCA Curatorial Practice alumni. I make more cappuccinos. I offer espressos to visitors. I walk to the hardware store to return light bulbs that were too bright. I pick up L brackets.

What about this work is research?

May 26, 2011
Bureau for Open Culture >Beer Garden
MASS MoCA
North Adams, Massachusetts

Bureau for Open Culture >Beer Garden opened Memorial Day weekend in 2011. This project was an element of *I Am Searching for Field Character*, a four-month program I organized at the invitation of MASS MoCA curator Susan Cross. *I Am Searching for Field Character*, itself, was part of Cross's exhibition *The Workers: Precarity/Invisibility/Mobility*. *Field Character* was another hybrid animal, an exhibition/residency/public program/publication studio/workshop/learning site/archival research and interview project/store, and—slash—beer garden. *Field Character* explored the economic and social qualities of the cultural worker, staged within MASS MoCA's massive arts complex, a sprawling former factory campus. The overarching focus on labor was central to *The Workers*, installed in the museum's main building. Cross's exhibition examined the conflating characteristics of material and immaterial workers, taking a cue partially from the changing socioeconomics of the rural, mountainous region of the Berkshires where MASS MoCA is located. Western

Massachusetts is known for its sprawling brick industrial complexes of the nineteenth and twentieth century. Many were water-powered mills and originally produced textiles. In MASS MoCA's case, the textile factory eventually became the home of Sprague, a company that made capacitors and other electronic components until closing in 1985. The Berkshires today is populated with small-scale industries, colleges, tourism, and arts organizations, along with many artists, academics, writers, and culture producers who call it home and collectively contribute to the lifestyle of the region. *Field Character* examined this workforce by engaging with it, selling products such as leather goods, books, butter, and yogurt in a store run by the artist collaborative Red76 led by Sam Gould (fig. 5). BOC hosted a weekly beer garden sited at MASS MoCA next to the Hoosic River where occasional readings took place but mostly just casual gatherings of locals and tourists to drink beer and talk (fig. 6). BOC programs were free of charge, although we did charge for beer. BOC was located in a small building behind the museum. Through my insistence (and persistence), I negotiated with museum officials to allow visitors to arrive at the beer garden by walking across an exterior bridge and thus circumventing the interior of the museum. North Adams residents and tourists, therefore, engaged with BOC on their own terms, not the museum's.

Part exhibition, part performance, part studio, part unclassifiable—*I Am Searching for Field Character* identified and shaped a portrait of the cultural worker with an emphasis on their precarious economic existence. Our daily presence in the space, working as shopkeepers, bartenders, curators, writers, tour guides, community organizers, and educators, intentionally gave visitors more than they expected after walking into our small building. Our simultaneous roles had hybridity built into them. The shop and beer garden were thresholds, equalizers that allowed the most introverted and unsure museum visitor to engage with the space through the well-worn and understandable cultural form of shopping. Goods with prices could be found at the entrance. Once inside, however, visitors wandered around and looked longer, talked with us, and learned about our programs, upcoming exhibitions, and the *Field Character* project. We conflated and purposely obscured notions of labor and the immaterial touristic, service, and culture industries transpiring inside architecture built originally for workers who made material goods. We were there to serve. Our performance was research to better understand how to address audiences.

Wednesday, August 15, 2018
Curatorial Research Bureau
Yerba Buena Center for the Arts
San Francisco, California

A FedEx packet of materials—zines, collages, and posters—by ALBUM arrives. The Norwegian artist duo Eline Mugaas and Elise Storsveen based in Oslo and known as ALBUM periodically makes zines sourced from advertising and popular culture. Since 2008, Mugaas and Storsveen have been sifting through printed material found in Scandinavian households from the 1960s through the 1980s, then combining the visual matter into a fanzine, or limited-edition, saddle-stitched publications. Photographs and illustrations printed in a range of media—from cookbooks, travel journals, and etiquette manuals to fashion magazines, sex-ed manuals, and gardening and science journals—are taken from original sources, juxtaposed, and reproduced in the ongoing zine. The publications are free of text. Each issue of *ALBUM* is dedicated to particular themes, such as the lonely man, femininity, architecture, family, outer space, and nature. In these fanzines, consumerism, popular culture, and domesticity seamlessly converge, reinforcing the fluidity and exchange among everyday life and the onslaught of advertising and news media images.

I had calls today with the college's development team about fundraising and meetings with YBCA about the opening party on September 27, 2018. We also talked with YBCA about the integration of our curatorial practice students into upcoming YBCA meetings in order to provide students with opportunities to bear witness to the complexities and even mundane points of operating an institution and organizing exhibitions. We purchased houseplants from a nearby nursery and collected vinyl text panels from the manufacturer. The website http://www.curatorialresearchbureau.org was uploaded to the World Wide Web.

At Curatorial Research Bureau, I'm presenting the ALBUM collages and posters as part of the assembly and display of materials for the exhibition *Marianne Wex: 'Let's Take Back Our Space.'* The display is first in a series of modest presentations alled "Case Studies." Each month, Case Studies will identify book to unfurl into an exhibition of archival materials, hotographic reproductions, periodicals, ephemera, sound, and ext that amplify ideas explored by the featured publication, sing the inventory of the CRB bookshop as a launching point or assembling the materials. Wex's 1979 publication *'Let's ake Back Our Space'* led us to compile a collection of visual ocumentation, reproductions, books, and writing related to LBUM, Jérôme Saint-Loubert Bié, Caravaggio, Hal Fischer, ndré Malraux, Martine Syms, and Wolfgang Tillmans.

Marianne Wex: In the early 1970s, this German artist

shifted her practice from painting to photography. She began surreptitiously photographing men and women in public spaces around Hamburg (where she lived), systematically capturing their body language. More than posturing, she was interested in "involuntary and unconscious" gestures, the natural states of behavior caught unawares. She photographed people sitting on benches at train stations or standing at crosswalks (fig. 7). She documented people lying on the beach, sitting on the grass in parks, leaning against doorways and automobiles, or standing with arms akimbo. Taking stock of her immediate context in Hamburg, she eventually amassed a staggering collection of more than five thousand photographs as part of her artistic research. She organized and sorted this collection, separating images of men and women and then arranging the photographs into different categories, such as "leg and feet position" and "arms and hand positions," and then various subcategories such as "standing persons," "seated persons," and "walking persons."

Not unlike how Wex looked at her immediate, rich, and resourceful context as a palette for making work, Case Studies demonstrates (especially for students) how to look around, to take notice—in this instance, of publications—and make something of something, of the materials at hand. Identify the overlaps, make them legible through the tactics of display and juxtaposition. Think curatorially.

Three bookshops and a beer garden. I call these things exhibitions. I call this work research.

Thursday, August 16, 2018
Curatorial Research Bureau
Yerba Buena Center for the Arts
San Francisco, California

Today, after months of planning, meetings, emails, and even more meetings and emails about Curatorial Research Bureau, the space at YBCA suddenly came together (as things do with exhibitions). The ripple-folded curtains, with their magisterial height, velour fiber, and gold color, have a commanding and calming presence. They will serve to dampen sound and provide privacy for students and professors in the CCA Curatorial Practice program, who will hold their seminars in the space enclosed by the curtains. A few classes during the fall term will occur while the bookshop is open. The problem, therefore, was how to allow the space to be bookshop/graduate seminar accommodating our consumers/audiences/students. The problem was how to provide privacy while the bookshop is accessible to the public. After considering several scenarios, including building walls or even relocating seminars to other parts of the YBCA office complex, the curtain arrived as a viable solution. The iconic ripple fold is intended as a visual cue that we own the curtain, we acknowledge the recognizable and familiar theatrical aesthetic and, in turn, we own the performance embedded in the daily operation of Curatorial Research Bureau. Indeed, it is a theatrical stage for students and professors, for guests, artists, and the visiting public. The curtain, too, will frame the space for public events: talks, readings, screenings, and, of course, the overtly recognizable performances. Today, we installed the vinyl text panels and continued pursuing publications by nearby colleagues, artists, and writers as we build up inventory that is global/local.

Teaching, administering, directing, chairing, traveling, writing, hiking, dinners, vacations. My social media, exhibitions, and books. These all amount to my curatorial practice. The multiplicity of this activity is my research for thinking about the curation of scenes and orchestration of experiences and people in the fields of contemporary art and education. By assembling pieces and parts, gathering people and resources, combining objects and ideas, I create things that are composed of a constellation of many characteristics. This work becomes discernible and operates under names like Curatorial Research Bureau and Bureau for Open Culture. It also comes together in larger research projects such as my book *Beyond Objecthood: The Exhibition as a Critical Form since 1968*, published by the MIT Press in 2017. And while this work is responsive to context, it hardly accepts it without a challenge. If anything, context is viewed as valuable fodder and an amicable adversary to push against in order to create something else, something more, for audiences near and far. That's why physical and online spaces are, since 2007 when we founded BOC, essential. These are the conditions that I work through with Padavick. I'm interested in taking familiar contexts and forms—the bookshop and beer garden, the curtain and the seminar, the academy and the museum—as a means for curatorial performance in the public realm (fig. 8). I'm attracted to forms as modes for curatorial research, as means for thinking curatorially in order to learn and understand better how to foster a scene, create an audience for the space, concept, and institution.

Friday, August 17, 2018
Curatorial Research Bureau
Yerba Buena Center for the Arts
San Francisco, California
A quiet day installing Case Studies; construction is over; Max Richter is clearly audible; the sun filters into the space on the final day of a busy week and,

coincidentally, Nate's birthday. We work alone in calmness, assembling and finessing the space, uploading more books to the CRB website, designing the newsletter (fig. 9). I finish this essay and assemble the accompanying images. Curatorial Research Bureau will open its doors on September 4, 2018, the first day of class at California College of the Arts.

I call this work research.

Fig. 1. Curatorial Research Bureau, Yerba Buena Center for the Arts, San Francisco, California.

Fig. 2. Consumer Research Center/, Carpenter Center for the Visual Arts, Harvard University, Cambridge, Massachusetts.

Fig. 3. Open Seminar—*Phil Collins: A Learning Site*, Carpenter Center for the Visual Arts, Harvard University, Cambridge, Massachusetts.

Fig. 4. Phil Collins visits seminar in Visual and Environmental Studies, Carpenter Center for the Visual Arts, Harvard University, Cambridge, Massachusetts.

Fig. 5. Red76's *Bartleby's Pen* as part of *I Am Searching for Field Character*, MASS MoCA, North Adams, Massachusetts.

Fig. 6. Bureau for Open Culture >Beer Garden, as part of *I A Searching for Field Character*, MASS MoCA, North Adams, Massachusetts.

ig. 8. Curatorial Research Bureau, Yerba Buena Center for the rts, San Francisco, California.

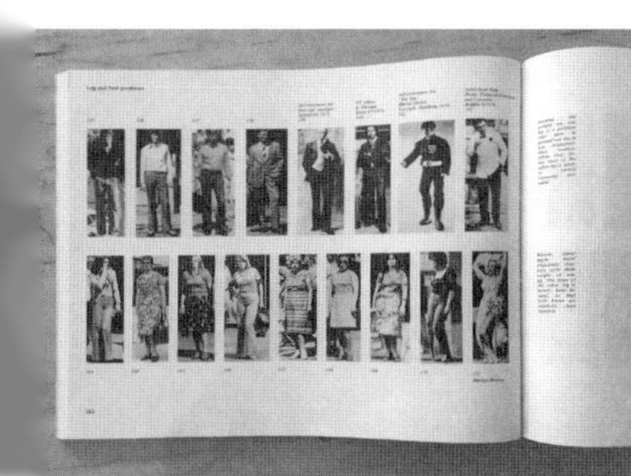

. 7. Page from *'Let's Take Back Our Space': "Female" and "Male" ly Language as a Result of Patriarchal Structure* (1979).

Fig. 9.

The Imaginary of Institutions

Annette Jael Lehmann has studied Comparative Literature, Art History, American Studies, and Philosophy in Berlin, Oxford, and Berkeley. She was Assistant Research Professor at the DFG-Collaborative Research Centre *SFB 447: Kulturen des Performativen* (1999–2005) and obtained her habilitation in Visual Culture at the Freie Universität Berlin (2005). Since 2007, she has been Professor of Contemporary Art, Visual Culture, and Theater at the Freie Universität Berlin. She is also PI at Einstein Center Digital Future (ECDF) Berlin and PR at *Excellence Cluster Temporal Communities* at the Freie Universität Berlin. Her publications include: *Mediale Performanzen. Historische Konzepte und Perspektiven* (Freiburg, 2002); *Kunst und Neue Medien* (Tübingen, 2008); *Exposures: Visual Culture, Discourse and Performance* (Tübingen, 2009); *Black Mountain Research* (Bielefeld, 2016). http://www.annette-jael-lehmann.de/

Annette Jael Lehmann

Mind the Gap: Insights into Practice-Based Research on Performance Art and Media between Universities and Museums

Even though performance art, its significance, and influence have been subject to a large amount of both research and exhibitions in the past decades, most approaches presenting and communicating performative arts and media were and still are largely bound to representational forms of knowledge production and traditional, object-centered exhibition formats. With the aim to expand such approaches, the collaborative and interdisciplinary research project with the working title "Mind the Gap: Performance Art and Media—Practice-Based Research between Universities and Museums" pursues collaborative international practice-based research on new strategies of exhibiting and collecting performance art in a globalized world. The project, thereby, seems to be haunted by a call of duty from a declaration by artist Allan Kaprow in 1967, with a ghostlike presence today, more than fifty years later:

> I am put off by museums in general; they reek of a holy death which offends my sense of reality. Moreover, apart from my personal view, most advanced art of the

> last half-dozen years is, in my view, inappropriate for museum display. It is an art of the world: enormous scale, environmental scope, mixed media, spectator participation, technology, themes drawn from the daily milieu, and so forth. Museums do more than isolate such work from life, they subtly sanctify it and thus kill it.[1]

1 Allan Kaprow, *An Exhi[...] sponsored by the Art Allia[...] the Pasadena Art Museu[...]* cat. (Pasadena, CA: Pas[...] Art Museum, 1967). Q[...] from http://schichtwec[...] li/?p=2295&lang=de/ ([...] June 25, 2018).

In his catalogue statement, Kaprow gave some unusual credit for the presentation of his work at the Pasadena Art Museum, a retrospective exhibition that later traveled to Washington University, St. Louis, and University of Texas, Austin, for a few weeks:

> The collaborating institutions have shown unusual understanding and willingness to accommodate the problem, because being sensitive to the broad issues it calls up today, they are trying to make a step in the direction of solving it. That issue is not so much the abolition of all museums—they are entirely proper for the art of the past—; it is rather the extension of the museum function into the domain of contemporary needs, in which it can act as a force for innovations lying outside of its physical limits. Eventually, in this way, the modern museum may gradually lose that cloying association of holiness that it presently inherits from another age. Hopefully, it will become an educational institute, a computerized bank of cultural history, and an agency for action.[2]

2 Ibid.

Mind the Gap readdresses a key problem and possible solutions for the current research of performance art: Although a substantial amount of research analyzing the impact of performance art in the twentieth and twenty-first century is being done, this research requires a stronger collaborative connection with the professional practices of curating performance art and media in an expanded field of exhibition-making and disseminating cultural knowledge.

The project builds upon the recognition that contemporary practice-based research and curatorial practice in performative art and media are resolutely challenged by profound changes in the production and experience of knowledge and contemporary culture. Prevailing accounts and concepts of performance art are still essentially based on representational systems and forms, which were predominantly developed along traditional research and exhibition formats for images and objects in a specific disposition of space and architecture, and in a context of analog technologies. The relevance of revisiting and revitalizing performative art from the twentieth and twenty-first century, particularly in exhibitions over the last decade, thus requires a profound shift in new models and methods of telling histories of (performance) art, as well as developing more experiential knowledge and learning practices in inter-institutional collaborations.

Testing the potentials of collaboration between universities and museums, the research and education project *Black Mountain Research* (2013–15) was a forerunner and best-practice model in a joint endeavor between Hamburger Bahnhof–Museum für Gegenwart–Berlin and Freie Universität Berlin. As a continuous work in progress, we developed a multifaceted kaleidoscope of contributions, negotiating both Black Mountain College's historical and current dimensions along the museum exhibition *Black Mountain. Ein interdisziplinäres Experiment 1933–1957* (May 6–September 27, 2015).[3] Our digital platform (http://black-mountain-research.com/) served as an experimental, accessible forum in which students, scholars, artists, and curators from different institutions and participating projects were working, writing, archiving, and exchanging ideas collaboratively.[4] These forms of exchange and cooperation seek to give impetus to new research questions, collaboration, and educational practices of the participating educational facilities. Moreover, this former project aimed to approach the problem of both the limits of representational thinking and the separation of its modes of knowledge production in

Black Mountain Research team meeting: Annette Jael Lehmann, Verena Kittel, and Anna-Lena Werner at the exhibition *Black Mountain. An Interdisciplinary Experiment 1933–1957* at Hamburger Bahnhof–Museum für Gegenwart–Berlin. Photo: Freie Universität Berlin / Juliane Küppers.

Summer Arts Institute Faculty, Black Mountain College, 1946. Left to right: Leo Amino, Jacob Lawrence, Leo Lionni, Ted Dreier, Nora Lionni, Beaumont Newhall, Gwendolyn Lawrence, Ise Gropius, Jean Varda (in tree), Nancy Newhall (sitting), Walter Gropius, Mary "Molly" Gregory, Josef Albers, Anni Albers. Courtesy of the Western Regional Archives, State Archives of North Carolina.

3 See Annette Jael Lehmann, *Black Mountain Research* (Bielefeld: Kerber Verlag, 2016).

4 See http://www.black-mountain-research.com/ (accessed June 25, 2018).

relationship to analog and digital art cultures by a practice-led inquiry.

Generally, the project *Mind the Gap* is dedicated to research-driven and even experimental collection presentations as collaborations between universities and museums in the public realm. It will continue to experiment in the field of practice-based research with dialogic and interdisciplinary modeling of new knowledge by bringing together practitioners, theorists, and exhibition makers who are interconnected through specific fields and scopes of interest and by collaborative institutional practices and partnerships. The project currently has a thematic focus on the possibilities of new forms of narration, scenography, audience involvement, education, and digital knowledge design for performance art and media in a global perspective. Thereby, embracing a notion of a knowledge that is liquid and temporary, we pose questions rather than present fixed solutions, carrying out best-practice examples and sounding out possibilities of cooperation in order to develop new approaches.[5]

Discussions with our partners unfolded in two joint international workshops at the Hamburger Bahnhof–Museum für Gegenwart–Berlin in 2016 and recently at the Freie Universität Berlin in 2017–18. The first workshop as part of our collaborative network was entitled "Joint Adventures: Practice-Based Research between Universities and Museums." Against the background of our collaborative and interdisciplinary research project, the workshop addressed questions on the significance of performance art and the possibilities of exhibiting it in view of key aesthetic questions of the past, present, and future. Curators and researchers from significant museums and universities—namely, Gabriele Knapstein and Anna-Catharina Gebbers from Hamburger Bahnhof–Museum für Gegenwart–Berlin, Emily Pringle from Tate in London, Margriet Schavemaker from the Stedelijk Museum in Amsterdam, and Marie Laurberg and Irene Campolmi from the Louisiana Museum of Modern Art in Copenhagen—were invited to present case studies of their

Josef Albers's drawing c
1939–40. Left to right:
Jalowetz, Bela Martin,
Stone, Betty Brett, Alb
(kneeling), Robert de N
Martha McMillan, Eu
Shifris. Courtesy of the
Regional Archives, Sta
Archives of North Car

5
This is in close contex
Rogoff's claim of
a paradigmatic shift c
traditional relations b
that goes into making
that goes into viewin
objects of visual cultu
attention. Irit Rogoff
Away: Participations
Culture," in *After Cr*
Responses to Art and
ed. Gavin Butt (Mal
Wiley-Blackwell, 20
117–34.

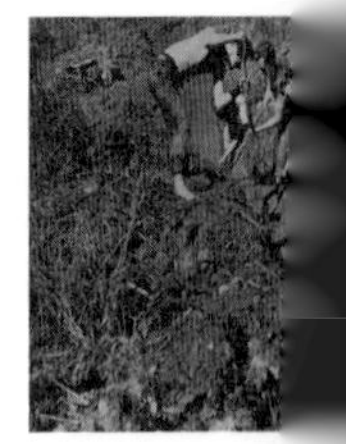

Students working
ditch for the Studi
Lake Eden Camp
Mountain College
Courtesy of the W
Regional Archives
Archives of North

uratorial and research work. Moreover, we jointly discussed ew practice-based research in the context of exhibition-aking and the dissemination of knowledge that does not uild upon representational systems but, rather, is connected a network culture. Our discussions revolved around a wide nge of topics and concepts, subsumed under the following eywords: Archive, Collaboration, Documentation, Exhibition, istories, Involvement of the Audience, Museum, Original, erformance Art, Performativity, Research, and Scenography. Vith its mind-map-like structure, these can be understood as assemblage structurally mirroring the project's aim of an pen, fluid, dynamic, and process-based approach towards the roduction of knowledge. I will summarize some arguments ong the following three monumental topics: Archive, xhibition, and Museum.

Happening and conversations on July 17, 2015 about Black Mountain College, at Hamburger Bahnhof–Museum für Gegenwart–Berlin. Photo: *Black Mountain Research*.

Archive (and Collections)

erformance is widely regarded as that which cannot be chived—its presentness is at odds with the archive's quest r permanence, its disappearing acts resisting the desire to bel, stack, and store. Performance and performative arts anscend their radical ephemerality, and, at the same time, e demand for documenting and archiving their practices behalf of performance research and historiography has own. What then is the relationship between performance d the archive?[6] The project explores and challenges this lationship in all its facets, including the role of performance the culture of museum collections and the role of the chive in conceptualizations of performance. Additional nsiderations include the cultural histories and ideologies of chival practices, the future of performance and the archive in e digital age,[7] performance as an archive of its own history, d performative interventions into archival culture. And ill other facets to consider are the role of forgeries, rumors, d lies in the development of performance history; the role

6
Here are my three most important references from a complex and ongoing debate over the last decade: Jacques Derrida, "Archive Fever: A Freudian Impression," *Diacritics* 25, no. 2 (Summer 1995): 9–63; Hal Foster, "An Archival Impulse," *October*, no. 110 (2004): 3–22; Rebecca Schneider, "Archives: Performance Remains," *Performance Research* 6, no. 2 (2001): 100–8; and Diana Taylor, *The Archive and the Repertoire: Performing Cultural Memory in the Americas* (Durham, NC: Duke Univ. Press, 2003).

7
This is a field within a large research agenda that we in the first workshop only touched upon briefly. It was the subject of the second workshop, *In*

of the document in performance research; the practices of performance archives; and performers' archives.[8]

Some of the most ambitious initiatives in recent years have been the projects re.act.feminism #1: performance art of the 1960s and 1970s today; and re.act.feminism #2: a performing archive. These projects formed a continually expanding, temporary, and living performance archive that traveled through six European countries from 2011 to 2013. Artists, in particular, were critically addressing the history of performance using the most diverse methods and formats, while also exploring its current potentials for resistance and subversion in continually new and experimental ways.

The core of the projects was a mobile archive and workstation with a growing collection of videos, photographs, and other documents of feminist, gender-critical, and queer performance art. It was a transnational and cross-generational endeavor featuring works by artists and artist collectives from the 1960s to the beginning of the 1980s, as well as contemporary positions from Eastern and Western Europe, the Mediterranean and Middle East, the United States, and in Latin America. On its journey through Europe—starting in Spain and continuing through Poland, Croatia, Denmark, Estonia, and ending in Germany—this temporary archive continued to expand through local research and cooperation with art institutions, academies, and universities. It was also "activated" through exhibitions, screenings, performances, and discussions along the way.[9]

In our discussions at the first workshop, we identified the central problem of archiving performance art as a persistent question of materiality: What is and can be actually collected? On the one hand, the selection of artworks demonstrates the huge responsibility for museums, but also their potential to step outside of the canon.[10] On the other hand, the collection of documents and photographs from the performative event also poses a question of whether the archiving of such material might act against the initial impulse, the "liveness," of the performance.[11] One step would

Flux—Browsing t
at the Freie Unive
in collaboration w
(at) Harvard Univ
2017. For the gen
see, for example: N
Museum 2.0 blog (
CA: 2010). Nancy
"Digital: Museum
Curator as Champ
Age of Social Me
53, no. 1 (2010): 3

8
See a recent confe
contribution from
Museum in Harle
"Archiving Perfor
the Future: A Dis
Lorraine O'Grady
by Glenn Wharto
Darms, Thomas J.
Lorraine O'Grady
in conjunction wi
International Net
Conservation of C
Art (INCCA-NA
cosponsored by N
University's Depa
Museum Studies,
youtube.com/watc
XseB9AzbmGU/,
October 15, 2013
25, 2018).

9
Quoted from http
reactfeminism.org
(accessed June 25,

10
A few of the many
difficulties in work
collections, docum
performances in th
well as documenta
exhibitions of perf
found at the Muse
Boston: http://ww
programs/perform
joan-jonas-reanim
www.mfa.org/colle
contemporary-art/
art/; or at the Mus
Art, New York: htt
org/interactives/ex
marinaabramovic/
June 25, 2018).

be to accept that performance, documentation, and archiving are artifacts, each with its own authorial and medium-specific characteristics, resulting in the question: What strategies offer a nonhierarchical relationship, a relationship that allows this supposed opposition to be overcome? This moves beyond debates about the relationship between the live and the mediated to consider the processes of making and experiencing performance. Techniques from visual art are especially informative in this context, where exhibitions with performative themes treat document and performance in a complementary way. Another initial step in finding a solution for this difficulty could be to include experts like conservators or the artists themselves and to jointly decide which objects and documents may remain in the collection. Thus, we suggested including the process of categorizing performance art as part of the storage, in order to show that it is not fixed but, instead, a living archive that could show examples from different periods. Another idea discussed was the archiving of the curatorial work itself, for example, the email correspondence between the individuals and institutions involved. Further difficulties that must be dealt with include the problem of digitization, which leads to an enormous quantity of documentation, but also the question of how the digitized information can be accessed in the future.

For a long time, documentation has been a substantial aspect of performance art. This fact has not only been central to a large discourse of and within the genre, but it was also a key point of our discussions during the workshop. Starting with the question of whether it is in any way possible to document an experience authentically, we soon agreed that the term "documentation" should generally be questioned and that the myth of performance art being resistant to recordings should be criticized. Contrarily, the recording and its devices are from the beginning part of the piece, of the experience, and they are not separate from it. Moreover, we cannot access many events and, thus, perceive lots of performances only digitally, for example, through photographs, allowing only an

11
This addresses, however, the persistent problem concerning collections and collecting, which has been discussed over the last two decades. Consider again the early debates, such as Susan M. Pearce, *Interpreting Objects and Collections* (London and New York: Routledge, 1994), 193–204.

imaginary approach towards the performance pieces.[12] For these reasons, the transformation of the event into a film or an installation is really at the center of our inquiry. Likewise, the documentation and representation of events is, therefore, gaining more and more power. As we tried to put it, "there is no such thing as no documentation," or, in other words: Even a blank page is not nothing; the question is not whether to document or not but how to bring the material together. Additionally, we foregrounded the limits of the archive, as, by archiving performance art, we always run the danger of formatting it for the art market and thereby transforming it into a pure commodity. More basically, we need to reflect further on the notion of the original, in particular, by posing three questions: Is there a collection without originals? Can a performance art archive only work in joint and collaborative initiatives?[13] And how can a visitor to an exhibition have an experience of objects that communicate an event?

Exhibition (of Performance Art and Media)

The term "performance art" itself bears certain difficulties concerning its translation but also its definition.[14] Indeed, this circumstance is part of the genre, which is in itself live and productive but is similarly challenging concerning its methodology and research. We thus proposed that the ontology of the artwork should consequently be left open. The question of the role of the archive, collection, and documentation of the performance is immediately followed by questions of its exhibition. For example, when exhibiting performance art, is interaction the central point? Why would we want to exhibit performance art, and what does it mean for the museum? Consequentially, the aspect of responsibility comes into play, as the museum must make a choice on what is important to be memorialized, instead of instrumentalizing performance art to activate the museum. As proposed in this discussion, it is exactly this curatorial decision, hence not

12
There have been new atte in this direction over the years, largely with video documentation, for exam the publisher Routledge: *Routledge Performance Ar* a developing resource pr access to a wide range of audio-visual material fro and present practitioners performance. This const growing online collectio to deliver these resource directly to the classroom theater, and library. The consists of streamed vid audio footage with criti commentary, is fully sea and cross-referenced, ar updated every three mo includes unique materi the Victoria & Albert M National Video Archiv Performance Recordin specially commissioned by leading experts to a each video, http://www routledgeperformance com/browse/subjects/ June 25, 2018).

13
An example of this is effort by Asia Art Arc (AAA) and the Intern Institute of Social His (Amsterdam, Netherl project aimed to rema Malaysian-American Langenbach's private of video documentati (originally in DV and format) spanning ove years of performance Southeast Asia from the present. Langenb archive documents a sociopolitical events Southeast Asia, focu predominantly on Si Malaysia, Indonesia, Vietnam, Cambodia Burma. The entire a comprised of over 1 of video and several 35 mm slides of doc ranging from perfor installation, and str performances to his through the region. is part of AAA's Pe Art Archive Initiat to locate and digiti of collections docu performance art in Other aspects of th include the digitiz key personal archi

only the process of the piece but also the curatorial process that should be communicated publicly, enabling a more democratic position of the audience.[15] We therefore suggested to materialize, for instance, the curator's fascination, the background that draws curators to the exhibited objects, but also to include problematic questions and topics, such as the reasons why a certain artwork has been excluded from the exhibition. Furthermore, we need to develop new methods and tools for considering the experience of issues and contents difficult to endorse and unfold as a possibility of the production of knowledge that impacts society—an experience that activates reflective learning processes that impact our frame of reference. Another difficulty of exhibiting performance art is, more generally, the transportation of a dynamic situation, such as a performance, into a fixed and static environment, such as the rooms of a museum. Alternative practice-based strategies confronting this difficulty certainly exist: One particularly outstanding method was unfolded in the exhibition *Art—Music—Dance: Staging the Derra de Moroda Dance Archives* at the Museum der Moderne Salzburg in 2016. Ten artists were invited to do research in the archives and to produce artworks based on their reflections on the archival materials, ranging from painting and drawing to video and sound installations and performance art. By collaborating with contemporary artists, the museum thus provided an alternative way of presenting and reframing the presentation of historical archives of dance and performance. Whereas in the exhibition *2053: A Living Museum* at Tate Liverpool in 2015, the museum nvited professional and nonprofessional performance and dance artists, as well as Liverpool citizens, to perform the works displayed earlier in the exhibition *An Imagined Museum*, and to reenact them with the use of their senses and bodies. Performance art was thus used as a means of providing lternative sensorial interpretations of artworks.

When exhibiting performance art, questions about the arration of its history also come into play.[16] We particularly ighlighted the importance of not telling a global art

of Hong Kong artist Frog King's ongoing documentation of regional performance art festivals, interviews, and *Action Script: Symposium on Performance Art Practice and Documentation in Asia* held in 2010. The digitization phase of this project was completed in 2011. The archive of video documentation is now accessible online at the AAA Library, http://www.aaa.org.hk/ (accessed June 25, 2018).

14
This can reopen an entire debate in itself, which is only touched upon briefly in this context. However, it is until today not appropriate to redefine performance from an ontological point of view because of its flexible and permeable boundaries. This is historically in line with Richard Schechner's basic perspective on performance, which is broad and inclusive. He sees it as including much more than theater, tracking along an entire spectrum that ranges from everyday life to rituals and art. See Richard Schechner, *Performance Theory* (London and New York: Routledge Classics, 2003).

15
In Germany, one key example of this is the Humboldt Lab, Museum as Laboratory, Staatliche Museen zu Berlin, http://www.smb.museum/en/museums-institutions/humboldt-forum/about-the-humboldt-forum/humboldt-lab.html/ (accessed June 25, 2018).

16
The most prestigious exhibition on performance art history thus far has been *100 Years: A History of Performance Art* at the Museum of Modern Art, New York, in 2010. The exhibition led viewers chronologically through the galleries and was conceived as a "living exhibition" of documentation that was supposed to continue to grow exponentially into the

history but, rather, histories rooted in cultural practices of different regions in the world, further stressing global artistic networks. Moreover, we proposed, instead of focusing on the reconstruction of things, to approach them from different angles, even problematize and display conflicting stories, and mark things and names we potentially leave out like the memory of the audience, thereby creating a space of imagination. On that note, another key point of our workshop was the involvement of spectators. We reflected on alternative possibilities beyond the cognitive way of transmitting artworks, which could be a socioemotional interaction, as well as a conversation with the audience starting before and after the exhibition, even on social media or in seminars. Moreover, we also emphasized a stronger importance of the audience experience, considered a creative contribution in its own right. The staging, display, and scenography of ephemeral arts in the museum are not without difficulties either. How are ephemeral arts applied in the museum? Reenact the performance? Display the documents related to the performance, and show a video of it? How are artists involved in that process? Each of these questions has to be answered when organizing an exhibition about performance art. One example of a rather unconventional approach concerning this issue could be the already-mentioned exhibitions in Salzburg and Liverpool. And still other important related questions one should think about when organizing an exhibition: What is always on display and what is not and why? What do we know about the art that is not on display? The exhibition *The Stedelijk Museum & the Second World War*, curated by Schavemaker in 2015, which also presented and communicated the provenance research, may be an approach to encountering this difficulty.

future. *100 Years* aims to s[...] the extraordinary variety [...] "live" performance over t[...] ten decades, http://www.[...]org/explore/inside_out/2010/04/05/100-yea[...]history-of-performance-[...] (accessed June 25, 2018). [...] exhibition strategy may [...] analyzed through the framework of a much ea[...] publication by Mary An[...] Staniszewski, *The Power [of] Display: A History of Ex[...] Installations at the Muse[...] Modern Art* (Cambridge[...] MIT Press, 1998).

Museum (as Specific Site of Collaborative Research)

While aware of the risks of a cross-disciplinary practice, like the co-opting by the museum of democratic processes, one consensus of the workshop was that a stronger collaboration between experts from different fields and institutions should be targeted. Cross-disciplinary collaboration could not only help in judging the quality of artworks but also in bridging the still-existing gap between theory and practice. It could, therefore, also signify a new way of knowledge production and, thus, help to find ways to go beyond the conventional—beyond conventional ways of knowledge production and beyond the canon of individual fields, creating new connections in between them. As reflected in the exhibition project "Museum Global," organized by Knapstein and Gebbers of the Museum Hamburger Bahnhof, among others, a joint desire of workshop participants was to reread the collections of museums from a global perspective.[17] The museum, instead of functioning as an institution of containment representing static knowledge, could rather question, open up, and challenge its own canon and collection history and connect it to histories and artistic networks from other contexts, thereby acknowledging its own narration as one amongst others. In this sense, the notion of the museum as *lieu de mémoire* emerges—the museum as a place in which objects that were previously dislocated and decontextualized are presented, consequently located, and thus experienced by spectators in a certain situation creating a special memory.[18]

One particular difficulty of performance research pointed out in the workshop is that we look at what it is, rather than what it does. There is increasing interest among art historians, especially concerning dance, but in their investigations an important point is often missing: how to look at movement, how to move. How is it done? One answer to this problem may be the notion of research through practice, as realized in the 2014 Tate research project "The Experience and Value of Live Art: What can making and editing film tell us?" organized by Pringle and education professor Pat Thomson of the University of Nottingham. In this project, fifteen participants aged fifteen to twenty-five

17
For a project description, see http://www.kulturstiftung-des-bundes.de/cms/en/projekte/bild_und_raum/museum_global.html/ (accessed June 25, 2018).

18
This is in line with accepting political conflicts in the process. Accordingly, Chantal Mouffe rejects the idea that consensus should be the end product of every democratic process. Politics of artistic practices and theories of multiple modernities, she argues, are in favor of a multipolar world with real cultural and political pluralism. Chantal Mouffe, *Agonistics: Thinking the World Politically* (London and New York: Verso, 2013).

were developing their own dance pieces based on key elements of *Trio A* (1966) by Yvonne Rainer, previously introduced to them by a contemporary dance educator and artist, which were presented to an invited audience at the end of the first workshop. A professional filmmaker filmed the entire workshop. In a second step, the participants edited the film footage and produced their own films, aiming to represent their individual experiences. The students, becoming co-curators or teachers, performed actions and developed skills, especially in view of the different layers of interpretation and translation included in the process. Conceptually, this approach may be a more effective way of producing knowledge. A similar practice-based way of knowledge production can also be ascribed to the exhibition at the Museum der Moderne in Salzburg, mentioned previously.

Even though most exhibition practices in museums have overcome the focus on displaying materials, the physical presence of objects in installations or the containing of large amounts of archival materials shows that the problem of exhibiting performance art and media prevails. Throughout the mid-twentieth century, performance has been closely tied to the search for alternatives to established art forms, which many artists felt had become fetishized as objects of economic and cultural value. Consequently, several institutions and artists now stage reenactments of earlier performances in order to recapture the experience of a live event. Additionally, a set of new strategies, elaborately described as situations, relational aesthetics, interventions and, in particular, various modes of participation of diverse audiences, are currently in practice.[19] These approaches often touch upon the core aesthetics of performativity in past and present. They still struggle, however, to come to terms with performative aesthetics in various art forms, not because of their lack of liveness but, rather, their displacement from a specific, sociohistorical and/or cultural-political environment in which the art took place. Thus, the central question would be how to build new communities in specific cultural environments for practice-based inquiry

19
I thereby share the
critique of an ideolo
participation: Mark
and Shumon Basar,
Someone Say Partici
(Cambridge, MA:
2006); Markus Mie
Nightmare of Partic
(Berlin: Sternberg
or, for example, the
The Participatory In
Museum of Conte
Zagreb, May 13–1

of performance art and media with the goal of negotiating a relocation in new contexts.[20] More generally, as Claire Bishop has pointed out in *Radical Museology* (2014):

20
Currently debated, for example, is Sheila Watson, ed., *Museums and their Communities* (London and New York: Routledge, 2007).

> This present-minded approach to history produces an understanding of today which sightlines on the future, and reimagines the museum as an active, historical agent that speaks in the name not of national pride or hegemony but of creative questioning and dissent. It suggests a spectator no longer focused on the auratic contemplation of individual works, but one who is aware of being presented with arguments and positions to read or contest. Finally, it defetishizes objects by continually juxtaposing works of art with documentary materials, copies, and reconstructions. The contemporary becomes less a question of periodization or discourse than a *method* or practice, potentially applicable to all historical periods.[21]

21
Claire Bishop, *Radical Museology: or, What's 'Contemporary' in Museums of Contemporary Art?* (Cologne: Walther König, 2014), 59.

Along these few lines out of our ongoing glossary, which we use as a scrapbook for relevant categories of reflection in theory and practice for the project, I here try to give some snapshots and temporary insights into the current state of the explorations of our collaborative network. More generally, the interest in (un)doing the history of performance art is nourished not only by art-historical curiosity but also by the observation that the fundamental innovations introduced by the performative aesthetics in institutions—universities and museums alike—initiate a paradigm shift in a certain thought pattern. This can be recognized beyond the narrow confines of the art context, in almost all aspects of knowledge production in contemporary life. We strongly believe that the uncoupling of knowledge production from specific places or materials can be observed not only in the sphere of art but also in various other spheres of life, thus producing a series of new questions in relation to it. There, we locate the fundament of future potentials and challenges of this practice-based research project between universities and museums. Although it is our focus to develop innovative practice-based research and curatorial strategies to understand, present, and pass on performance, performative arts, and media in a global culture, this collaborative project is exemplary for practice-as-research in various interdisciplinary constellations, such as art history, contemporary art, curatorial research, museum studies, or visual and digital culture today. The key questions in collaborations between museums and universities generally are as follows: What are the central concepts, methods, and case studies of applied knowledge to be developed together? How do we find a common language to implement certain practices? What is translatable, and what does not work at all? How do we overcome bureaucratic borders? Do we need a stable, institutionalized relationship between the institutions, or should we just establish temporary joint platforms and teams? It is important, however, to mention that this form of collaboration does not merely indicate a temporary fusion of two institutions. Instead of emphasizing the disappearance of the difference between the two, practice-based research highlights their shared research practices, which are integrated into the specific conditions of the places (or non-places), working methods, and reflections of this collaborative knowledge production in particular ways.[22] The processes of collaborative research thus prove to be directly related to the respective architectural, environmental, urban, social, and economic fields and are influenced in relation to these in an open-ended way.

What has hitherto been relatively ignored in this context is that the emergence of the performative arts and aesthetics was also paralleled by the development of art as research and new forms of artistic knowledge production since the 1970s. The process of collaboration in the project *Mind the Gap* will therefore also reflect on the question of how various performative practices established new teaching and research methods in the arts, initiating a paradigm shift for boundary-pushing art and exhibition practices as collective forms of knowledge whose effects have persisted to this day. The

22
This marks the nece to spatial thinking a as inherent in the p collaboration. See H Lefebvre, *The Produ* (Malden, MA: Wil Blackwell, 1991/20 Nick Kaye, *Site-Spe Performance, Place a Documentation* (Lo New York: Routled

focus on the idea of tacit knowledge is especially important within the research's framework, since artistic research practices are often characterized by a specific entanglement of cognitive and (habitual) bodily forms of knowledge. This is particularly significant in relation to the social efficacy of these artistic processes in diverse cultural contexts, since a shift in traditional knowledge systems can be established here. This also corresponds to an artistic culture of knowledge that doesn't base research, education, and learning on a corpus of objective truths but, rather, contributes to their development through social and performative contexts of action. Accordingly, this is linked to the insight that the apprehension of the world and the construction of knowledge cannot be described purely in terms of cognition and that it additionally always requires bodily forms of cultural practice. This shift in the concept of knowledge is to be situated within the context of the performative turn in the boundary-pushing art practices of the twentieth century that moved away from text and focused on the processes of bringing forth, making, and doing. In 1949, the American philosopher Gilbert Ryle distinguished between two forms of knowledge: knowing how and knowing that. While the first refers to an everyday knowledge of how to do things that people apply without needing to have any necessary familiarity with the rules governing their actions, the second primarily refers to a theoretical form of knowledge that can be described as such and expressed by rules. Ryle does not construct a hierarchy between both forms of knowledge and juxtaposes them as equals. The peculiar potential of art consists in being a site where both forms of knowledge meet and overlap. In this context, we reflect on the particular performativity of knowledge, not as a standardized form of knowledge but, rather, in terms of its specific dynamics, relationality, and subjectivity. Michael Polanyi described in the late 1960s just such a conception of knowledge that is bound up with dynamic structures and actions as "tacit knowledge,"[23] which, as a knowledge of rules and experiences, is also bound in a special way to (bodily) actions.[24]

23
Michael Polanyi, *The Tacit Dimension* (Chicago: Univ. of Chicago Press, 1966).

24
This certainly includes an interdependency of analog and digital media in the discussions. Here, I would follow the approach of Brian Massumi. In *Parables for the Virtual*, Massumi views the body and media, such as television, film, and the internet, as cultural formations that operate on multiple

Moreover, we will emphasize that performance art was deployed by the neo-avant-garde of the twentieth century as an investigatory instrument for the transformation of the *lifeworld* in general and, in the process, focused primarily on its own conditions. This offers significant links to contemporary debates surrounding the expansion of creativity and the generation of innovative forms of labor in which, however, the distinction between work in an economic field and artistic practice has been completely dissolved. This co-optation of artistic self-determination into the framework of neoliberal teleology is to be critically examined. Against this backdrop, performativity as the conceptual core of *Mind the Gap* is apprehended as an aesthetically and socially effective formula for boundary-pushing research productivity from historical and contemporary perspectives. It will thus be interrogated in terms of its particular learning methods, forms of knowledge, and modes of constituting reality. At the same time, our project aims to give impetus to a revision and expansion of art and cultural history, which asserts that the boundary-pushing art practices since the end of the 1970s cannot be understood without reference to the performative turn in the arts, and that the decisive premises are borne out by a consideration of the transformed spaces for and respective processes of artistic productivity. At the same time, a central question emerges surrounding the performativity of art practices in general: How can such art be understood from the perspective of acts and actions? The performative concepts and practices involved in the various art forms have primarily been decisive in the development of new aesthetic procedures, categories, and their social mediation. They have also exerted a considerable influence on global tendencies towards increasing multimediality, performativity, and hybridization in art.

In an economic and cultural context in which publicly funded cultural and educational institutions such as universities and museums are widely under threat, the collaborative project *Mind the Gap* seeks to give tangible evidence of the diverse interrelations between research and

registers of sensation bey the reach of the reading techniques founded on t standard rhetorical and s models. Although the bo been the focus of much contemporary cultural t models that are typically neglect the most salient characteristics of embod existence, especially mo affect, and sensation. Re and assessing William J radical empiricism and Bergson's philosophy of perception through the the postwar French phi of Deleuze, Guattari, a Foucault, Massumi link a cultural logic of varia questions of movemen and sensation. Replaci traditional opposition and figural with new distinctions between s motion (and between virtual) tackles related theoretical issues by a them to cultural medi diverse as architecture or the digital art of St Brian Massumi, *Para Virtual: Movement, A Sensation* (Durham, N Univ. Press, 2002).

practice, which reveal both types of institutions as dynamic, shifting, and contested spaces of creativity, subversion, refuge, labor, testimony, imagination, choreography, repetition, invitation, inhabitation, solitude, and conviviality. In other words, both institutions seek to establish alive and dynamic sites of experiential and fluid knowledge production. Including transnational contributions from Europe, America, and non-Western countries, the project foregrounds the performative and multidimensional aspects of these research practices themselves, including approaches that display and disrupt representational exhibition forms, rituals, and technologies; research which acknowledges and takes sustenance from the university as ideal and the myth of safe space for reflection and intellectual pursuit; research which responds to and even benefits from the lost materiality and immediate presence of its subjects and objects, most particularly performative arts and their para-traces, including marginalia or large, difficult collections, excavating potentials of transformative social engagements in the future. Then, hopefully, new ways of practice-based research on performance art and media between universities and museums in *Mind the Gap* may offer one lens through which to approach the question: What are museums and universities for in the twenty-first century?

Dorothee Richter is Professor in Contemporary Curating at the Zürich University of the Arts. Since 2005, she has been head of the Postgraduate Program in Curating (MAS/CAS), http://www.curating.org. She also founded the "Research Platform for Curating, Practice-Based Doctoral Program," a collaboration of the Postgraduate Program in Curating and the Department of Fine Arts, University of Reading, now the "PhD in Practice in Curating," which is funded by "Swissuniversities." Therefore, she holds also a professorship at the University of Reading, UK. From 1999 to the end of 2003, Richter was artistic director of the Künstlerhaus Bremen, where she curated a discursive program based on feminist issues, urban situations, power relation issues, and institutional critique. She has worked as a curator ever since. Her curatorial projects are *New Social Sculptures* (Kunstmuseum Thun, 2012), *Speculative Curating, Performative Interventions* (Migros Museum, Zürich, 2016–17) and now she is directing the OnCurating Project Space. Also, she is the publisher of *OnCurating* (http://www.OnCurating.org/), an online and print magazine on curatorial practice and theory. Her own PhD dealt with Fluxus, *Fluxus: Art—Synonymous with Life? Myths about Authorship, Production, Gender and Community.*

Dorothee Richter

From (Un)learning Curating to Teaching to Transgress

Our web journal *OnCurating* (http://www.OnCurating.org/) was developed out of the urgency to make available worldwide a public critical discussion of curatorial practice and theory, but in order to arrive at the now preliminary conclusion of that shared platform, I worked in different collaborations and formats on these questions. This meandering between formats and institutions became xtremely interesting and fruitful, hopefully not just to me nd my colleagues and students but also to our surprisingly iverse and truly international readership and, in some cases, also co-curators. Today, *OnCurating* materializes as an online journal, as a printed publication, as projects with museums and institutions, and as the OnCurating project space. In ddition, *OnCurating* is closely related to the Postgraduate Program in Curating (http://www.curating.org) offered by ürich University of the Arts (ZHdK) as well as to the PhD ogram, a collaboration between ZHdK and the University Reading, UK. But let me start with an early project that based on this notion of meandering between educational

Curating Degree Zero Archive in Geneva, Centre d'Art Contemporain Genève, installation concept CCC Programme, sound Mental Groove Records, Geneva. Courtesy of Curating Degree Zero Archive.

Curating Degree Zero Archive in Edinburgh College of Art, display system by Duncan Brenner. Courtesy of Curating Degree Zero Archive.

situations and curating, a project that was also presented and reinterpreted in Korea.

The Story's First Step—Curating Degree Zero Archive

We started Curating Degree Zero Archive (co-initiated with Barnaby Drabble) with forty-five different critical and experimental curatorial positions by contemporary art curators in 2003—and we ended with over a hundred positions in 2008. Each curatorial position was represented by catalogues, CDs, DVDs, documentation, and so forth. At every venue, additional material was included and new discussions were organized. Curating Degree Zero Archive was invited to Seoul by Insa Art Space and reinterpreted by Sasa[44] and MeeNa Park from December 2006 to January 2007; the centerpiece was an unusual world map. This area-accurate map—originally proposed in 1974 by German historian Arno Peters[1]— was published by Chilean-born artist, architect, and filmmaker Alfredo Jaar as an edition. It functioned as a visual node around a critical postcolonial discourse, which, of course, also questions the underlying paradigms of a Western art world. The map ended up in the archive as part of the project *Do All Oceans Have Walls?* curated by Eva Schmidt and Horst Griese in Bremen, where Peters had worked and lived. His world map shows that European countries are very small compared to their usually represented size, and thus allows us to see how multi-authorial discursive practices in art proceed, namely, as processes involving resignification and various authors. The "world map" was reperformed at Insa Art Space in Seoul, where its reperformance clearly revealed that "critique" and signifying processes may be linked to become a joint practice, resulting in a *Temporary Archive of Shared Interests*, as formulated by the De Geuzen artist group.

In my view, self-critique is part of a critical practice. Thus, we became increasingly aware of the limitations of an actual existing archive that, due to our network, contained

1
From the website: "T Projection World M the most stimulating, controversial, images world. When this ma introduced by histori cartographer Dr. Arr a Press Conference i in 1974 it generated of debate. The first E version of the map w published in 1983, a continues to have pa fans as well as staun detractors. The eartl The challenge of an is to represent a rou a flat surface. There thousands of map p Each has certain str corresponding weal Choosing among t exercise in values c you have to decide important to you. T generally determin you intend to use t Peters Projection i accurate map." See petersmap.com/ (a August 25, 2018).

an interesting amount of Western curatorial positions but was missing those that could be associated with a "Global South" or postcolonial voices—and it became difficult to move physically because its weight also increased substantially. In that regard, the presentation in Seoul was especially important. If Curating Degree Zero Archive's strength was to present a certain amount of books, DVDs, videos, and websites, and its possibilities were about inventing new discursive formats in local contexts, then its shortcomings were its clumsiness, limited outreach, and limited perspectives. One has to remember that we started out with forty-five positions and ended up with over a hundred, so the increase in weight was enormous. What was interesting was the crossover of spatial events and digital resources: We listed all curatorial positions with links to their projects, but it became clear that we had missed out on the more democratic possibilities of the World Wide Web. In the end, we gave the material to the ZHdK library, where it is currently available.

Curating Degree Zero Archive in Seoul, Insa Art Space, reinterpreted by Sasa[44] and MeeNa Park. Courtesy of Curating Degree Zero.

The Next Step—How OnCurating.org Came to Be

I founded the web platform OnCurating.org with students of the MAS in Curating program in 2008 as a new stage of the traveling archive and discussion platform Curating Degree Zero Archive. The first issues exist only in PDF format, but subsequently we changed to a content management system that allows everything to be read online; we still produce a PDF for each issue and installed a print-on-demand service to offer the glossy, nice-looking printed magazine versions as well. From the beginning, we focused on different aspects of curating, and we invited guest editors to produce issues alongside a conference or specific topics. Additionally, we receive a lot of proposals, which we welcome. This means that different interests, research projects, and viewpoints are able to use this platform to publish, with the general direction of having a critical perspective on curating. And, unlike other publications that concentrate on reviewing museum exhibitions, we consider curating to be connected to the politics of site, display, transfer, and translation. Of course, we see ourselves in the tradition of avant-garde and neo-avant-garde attempts to fundamentally question paradigms of the arts, the discourse having become more important than materiality, and we wanted to initiate something in which different authors had the possibility of having a voice (production by a multitude). We were very engaged in having a maximum of availability (distribution as a democratic possibility), and we always wanted to anchor the archive or texts in the present, to connect events and other novel formats to the written part of the discourse.

Screenshot *OnCurating*. Courtesy of OnCurating.

OnCurating's Spaces of Appearance

Especially for the PhDs, we have formulated our programmatic understanding more precisely, but the following outline explains what we understand as "Critical Curating": The PhD in Practice in Curating program understands curating or the curatorial not as a philosophical concept but as a practice that is deeply involved in the politics of site, display, transfer, and translation, and regimes of visibility. It is based on a concept of critical research that takes as its starting point the investigation of what is often the overly simplistic understanding of the curator as a new agent in the fields of art and culture. The program understands the curatorial as a multi-authored approach to the production of meaning, which is intrinsically linked to transformations of contemporary societies, the reorganization of labor, cultural policies, politics of inclusion/exclusion, and issues poised on points of intersection.

The program has been developed in the context of cultural analysis, theories of power, and theories of communities based on feminist, queer, postcolonial, ecological, post-Marxist, and other political and emancipatory positions. Many of these emerge out of political struggles or social movements. The practice-based PhD program sees curatorial knowledge production as a space for the negotiation of social, political, cultural, and economic conflicts. It understands curating as agency from which new constellations emerge. These could be represented in the format of an exhibition but also equally in other forms of meaning production through a context-related media conglomerate. This involves a critical review of contemporary curatorial practices and theories, and critical reflection on the rise of a so-called curatorial class. By engaging with these trajectories, the conditions and foundations of knowledge production in the curatorial field become the subject of critical research leading to their repositioning.[2]

To give an example of the formats in which *OnCurating* can intervene, besides functioning as a critical journal on curatorial issues, I would like to mention a project that we did with students of the Postgraduate Program in Curating following an invitation by Kunsthalle Zürich. The Kunsthalle showed two extensive collections of printed material, one from Christoph Schifferli and another from Kunsthalle director Daniel Baumann. We wanted to add new editions by artists and also the ability to print them out for visitors to take with them, then and there, in the exhibition space. The student population is extremely diverse and proposed artists from their networks and respective countries, and, of course, we as lecturers at the program (Ronald Kolb and I) also proposed artists. This was decided in a collective process, with the precondition that the lecturers would have final say, if necessary. Two scientific researchers, Maja Widmer and Barbara Preisig, curated a symposium during the show. These texts, as well as the invited new editions by artists, then went into Issue 27 of *OnCurating* with the title "Ephemera: Invitation cards, press releases, inserts, and other forms of artistic (self-)marketing." In the exhibition, all visitors could print out the new editions and, in this way, put together a new collection or a new exhibition.

Among our new editions—by such artists as AES+F,

2 For programmatic thoughts for the PhD in Practice in Curating, a cooperative program between the University of Reading, UK, and Zürich University of the Arts (ZHdK), see http://www.curating.org/.

åyr, Peter Aerschmann, Beni Bischof, Maja Cule, Critical Art Ensemble, DullTech™, Karl Holmqvist, Marcus Kraft, Juan López, Michael Meier and Christoph Franz, Modeling Agency (Janus Høm and Martyn Reynolds), Helena Hernández and Rafael Koller (aka The Niñxs), Sarah Ortmeyer, Angki Purbandono, PUNK IS DADA, Rosalie Schweiker and Maria Guggenbichler, Stipan Tadić, Britta Thie, Valentin Hauri, Valerio Pellegrini, and Eva Vuillemin and Ruth Erdt—some found their way into the existing collections of Schifferli and Baumann.

Ephemeral production by artists occurred beginning in the 1960s and 1970s—suddenly, all formats of exhibition-making, of the arts, of the distribution and production of invitation cards, press releases, inserts, and other forms of artistic (self-)marketing became part of the reorganization of the art field. From my perspective, this reformulation was embedded in a radical institutional critique. Ephemera, editions, and invitation cards were seen as specific, interesting objects; they not only offered a space of self-representation but also made art available to everybody. This was meant as a critique of power relations and was part of a reevaluation of artistic paradigms as well as value systems and hierarchies. It is in this light that historically ephemeral products started to circulate. Ironically, through the consecration of these new products as art (through presenting them in a *Kunsthalle*), the "junk got value"—as Fluxus artist/poet Emmett Williams once muttered, somewhat disappointedly.

From its revolutionary beginnings to its (problematic) acceptance as a new genre, this kind of work is endangered today. Invitation cards are vanishing; they are being replaced by email, Facebook invitations, Twitter, and other fluid digital news. In answer to this, we started work on a project to accompany the exhibition *They printed it!* at Kunsthalle Zürich with a hybrid form of digital, endlessly reproducible self-marketing editions—which, of course, you (the reader) are also able to print out from the PDF of the issue.

As always, we see the working group of students as

They printed it! wit
station of *OnCura*
Courtesy of OnCu

intrinsically valuable. Knowledge from different cultural and professional backgrounds comes together to be confronted, to mingle, to struggle, and to come to new conclusions.

Teaching to Transgress in Curating

Let me develop here some thoughts that inspire my work more generally. I must confess there is something in curating, and similarly in teaching, that makes me passionate: a "teaching to transgress," as bell hooks formulated in the title of her publication. "The academy is not paradise," hooks writes, "But learning is a place where paradise can be created. The classroom, with all its limitations, remains a location of possibility. In that field of possibility we have the opportunity to labor for an openness of mind and heart that allows us to face reality even as we collectively imagine ways to move beyond boundaries, to transgress. This is education as the practice of freedom."[3]

The theoretical connection to addressing people through curating (or any other form of cultural utterance) is, of course, the notion of interpellation that was described by Louis Althusser.[4] Interpellation means that with an utterance, one also constitutes the subjectivity of the addressee. And rereading this slightly rigid concept through the notion of a screen, wherein interpersonal processes (as proposed by Jacques Lacan) position subjectivity as the ongoing projection of an image towards the imagined other, one could understand the urgency in cultural and pedagogical processes. In short, it means that any subject is involved in producing versions of themselves according to the imagined desire of the other. "Being with" could be understood as a permanent involvement with the other or, to be precise, with the imagined desire of the other. Or, to use the concept of hegemony and counter-hegemony by Antonio Gramsci, cultural utterances produce narrations of either affirmative or dissident attitudes towards the regime in which they appear.

3 bell hooks, *Teaching to Transgress: Education as the Practice of Freedom* (London and New York: Routledge, 1994), 207.

4 Louis Althusser, "Ideology and Ideological State Apparatuses," in *On the Reproduction of Capitalism: Ideology and Ideological State Apparatuses* (1971), trans. G. M. Goshgarian (London and New York: Verso, 2014).

The drive and urgency I feel in teaching is related to what Jacques Derrida once formulated as a "university without conditions," a model he positioned against contemporary universities that work hand in hand with industries, be it in connection with technical innovations or, I take the liberty to add, anything that might be called creative industries. Derrida demands that the university position itself against "economic powers (to corporations and to national and international capital), to the powers of the media, ideological, religious, and cultural powers, and so forth—in short, to all the powers that limit democracy to come."[5] It is important to claim the free space that the university can provide. Democracy as a concept is, from Derrida's perspective, always something that is in suspense; it is an inherent state of tension between a governmental institution that has only to be installed far enough that it allows the possibility of open processes. A contradiction in itself. Democracy oscillates between being too vague and being too rigid. Again, I am aware that I am shortening this argument to the extreme. But from this perspective, an educational turn in curating is unnecessary to claim (or perhaps only emphasize) the unavoidable, more-obviously educational part of curating—that any exhibition positions visitors as subjects, and any exhibition, in so far, makes proposals or demands on developing a specific subjectivity, specific communities, and specific attitudes towards a greater society.

5
Jacques Derrida, "The [...] the Profession or the U[...] without Condition (Th[...] the 'Humanities,' Wha[...] Take Place Tomorrow)[...] *Jacques Derrida and the Humanities: A Critical* [...] ed. Tom Cohen (Cam[...] Cambridge Univ. Pres[...] 26. "Consequence of t[...] such an unconditional[...] could oppose the univ[...] a great number of pov[...] example to state pow[...] thus to the power of [...] nation-state and to it[...] of indivisible sovereig[...] indicates how the un[...] might be in advance [...] cosmopolitan, but un[...] extending beyond w[...] citizenship and the n[...] in general), to econo[...] (to corporations and [...] and international ca[...] powers of the media[...] ideological, religious[...] cultural powers, and [...] in short, to all the p[...] limit democracy to [...]

Intervention into a Collection

Here, I will discuss a collaborative work with artist Christian Falsnaes, which was part of the series *Speculative Curating* that I organized following an invitation by the Migros Museum of Contemporary Art, Zürich, to work with its collection. Students and museumgoers participated, as Falsnaes often works with the moment of seducing a group of people (in this case, members of the public) to follow his command—or, as in this project, initiating a learning process with a group to explore how each member might be able to give orders to a group of others (akin to, for example, an aerobic workout or other contemporary social behavior). In this project, participants were encouraged to speak to an artwork, and so forth, where the behavior patterns in the formal exhibition space are perhaps a bit ridiculous, as was reflected by the performance. The performance itself was recorded and later cut into a video that plays with a songlike, repetitive structure.

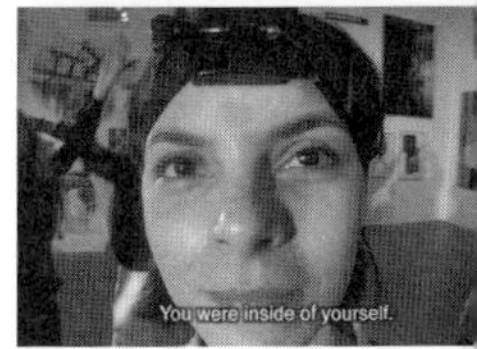

Christian Falsnaes, *Speculative Curating* (with the Postgraduate Program in Curating, Zürich), Migros Museum, Zürich, 2016. Courtesy of MAS in Curating.

One could argue that this work deals with producing subjectivity in the digital area of modern disciplinary societies; here, the digital space functions as a tool to reproduce behavior patterns in an intensified way: The gaze regimes of a central viewpoint are abandoned, and the hallucinatory moment of the digital is shown. As demonstrated in this piece, I think it is important to involve students at all levels of the production of an artwork. In this case, students acted as the protagonists in an artist video, reflecting the collection of the Migros Museum. To come really close is the agenda behind it.

My Position as a Professor

To think more intensively about my position as a professor, Derrida's text proved quite valuable. He insists on a specific attitude on the part of the professor. For him, the word *profess*, with its Latin origin, means to declare openly, to declare publicly: "The declaration of the one who professes is a *performative* declaration in some way. It pledges like an act of sworn faith, an oath, a testimony, a manifestation, an attestation, or a promise, a commitment. To profess is to make a pledge while committing one's responsibility. 'To make profession of' is to declare out loud what one is, what one believes, what one wants to be, while asking another to take one's word and believe this declaration."[6] In a way, this only works if one is able to take risks—personal risks, that

6
Derrida, "The Future of the Profession or the University without Condition," 31–32.

is—the risk not to please and the risk to formulate within the university hierarchy a certain standpoint. It means transgressing the boundaries of any institutional system and to find your own formats—of course, together with others. It often also means choosing a complicated pathway. For me, this means not ordering students to do something; it means showing possibilities and theories, opening up spaces to discuss what we read and do together. This also means that I am dedicated to opening up possibilities for students to be part of a curatorial group that develops projects together. In my understanding, this means, of course, showing and discussing my own position. I am a feminist, and I am, for example, firmly against the boycott movement of Israeli art and artists; I am interested in other knowledges (as opposed to knowledge systems of Western origin) and theories around structural violence, which might be more precise than the notion of the Anthropocene.

Because we (which, in this case, means me working with different project partners) meander between practical and theoretical approaches, between the classroom and the art museum, between the digital space and the architectural space of an institution, I got the impression that these forms of intensive investigation—textual, spatial, with artists, alongside scientific parameters—helped to create a kaleidoscope of knowledges, which amend each other and build upon one another. This is a process that does not, of course, develop without friction and gaps. Producing limitless editions in an exhibition (again, with an additional worldwide access) could also be seen as a critique of the new collections of printed material. We installed a moment of mimicry of a collection, but we also were obviously opposed to the production of art market value, which functions through the shortage of the product.

A narrow understanding of curating would be to see it just as a new creative profession, where the genius artist is now overstepped by the genius curator, a view that I have argued against in detail in previous articles on curatorial and artistic authorship. This narrow view would also reject the position of curator as a capable and powerful cultural author in post-Fordism. In actuality, the dependencies are more subtle and, just as for any freelancer, should be taken seriously. Dependencies exist—on institutions, on policies, on funding bodies, and on the politics at large of networks. In this respect, one could argue that the curator is a paradigmatic post-Fordist cultural worker, a situation my students will understand not only through reading and discussing but also by being involved and part of the process of producing projects and exhibitions.

Indeed, processes of unlearning and learning are most needed in curating. Suffice it to say that if learning/unlearning is not thought of as a mutual process, it will not function. It is a mutual process for all involved—students, artists, lecturers, and sometimes the institutionalized museum curators. This learning and unlearning is taking place at the intersection of the university, the museum, and the political sphere. And it is my conviction that one is only able to do something meaningful as a curator (or educator or political activist) if one joins a shared goal, a communal mission that moves beyond a self-centered position.

Lim Shan received his PhD in Media Aesthetics and Cultural Theory at Lancaster University and is currently Assistant Professor in the Department of Curatorial Studies and Art Management at Dongduk Women's University. He was a curator of the Alternative Space Loop (Seoul) and Art Center Nabi (Seoul) and worked as a reporter of *Monthly Art*. He curated exhibitions including *Art Meets Architecture: An Investigation on 'In-between'* (2002) and *Sound Community* (2015). He is the author of *Context in Curating* (2016), *A Young Man—Nam June Paik: Aesthetics of Integration in His Early Art* (2012). Lim translated Arlene Goldbard's *New Creative Community*, Charlie Gere's *Digital Culture*, and Erwin Panofsky's *Meaning in the Visual Arts*.

Lim Shan

Art as Strategy for Social Transformation and Community Pedagogy: Lessons from Institutional Critique and Critical Pedagogy*

Many art sociologists, including Janet Wolff, agree that he institution of art is like a "gatekeeper" that functions s a mediator between art and the public. It is within the apacity of the institution of art to decide who is an artist, ow to become one, how the artist is to practice their art, vhere and how the public encounters art, and so on. In other vords, the gatekeeper that is the institution of art holds oth power and authority within a given context while also aintaining itself through pertinent operational mechanisms nd functionalities. In response to this privileged status, stitutional critique has generated diverse attitudes of social iticism that resist the impositions of such power relations. hese attitudes demand a conscious "action" that would defy nplicit subordination to a certain set of conventionalized les or to authoritative dictums that arise from power. The stinct feature of criticism—which obliges it to adhere to ndependent" thinking—is often mentioned when arguing oth the unfeasibility and futility of institutional critique thin the art world. The artist's critical practice concerning

essay includes parts of a lecture ented in Seoul at "Perigee Art School," ed by the nonprofit exhibition space gee Gallery, August 3–24, 2017. The of the lecture was "Community, Art, Curating."

the art world cannot stand as art "outside" the institution of art, thus defeating the practical purpose of institutional critique. This line of thought stems from the view that the (in)validity of critiques can be discussed based on the distance between the critic and the object of critique. But are we not aware of the inevitable relation between critique and institutions—that they coexist in a symbiotic relationship? Institutional critique is neither wholly within nor entirely outside the institution of art. Rather, it possesses a duality of in and out, deconstruction and construction.

Institutional critique creates a disputatious rupture on the public's conventional perception of such contexts as the artist, artworks, or structures of exhibition within a given institution. It was in 1985 that artist Andrea Fraser coined the term "institutional critique" in an article discussing the works of Louise Lawler.[1] Lawler aimed to give herself and other artists a different status, such as that of a curator, designer, or facilitator. Her exhibitions brought attention not only to the production of artworks but also to collecting, sales, and display. In such ways, Lawler examined the normality of art conventions. From the 1980s, Lawler employed different practices in an effort to critically examine the role of the artist in the production and acculturation of art. She put other artists' works within her own exhibitionary space, and photographed the works of others that have occupied parts of the institutional space or the private houses of collectors. She also experimented with submitting and curating those works in her own exhibitions. Lawler's critical works on the functionalities within the context of traditional galleries were described by Fraser as "symbolic" strategies. Meanwhile, Lawler took what is considered supplementary, and not primary, to exhibitions—such as brochures, invitations, matchbooks, and souvenirs—and replicated them to function as art objects. She also parodied promotional material commonly found within the art system. Fraser referred to these projects as "subversive" critical strategies that aim at the mechanisms of institutional "presentation." Lawler's subversive

1 Andrea Fraser, "In an Place," *Art in America* 1985): 122–9.

strategies still remain within the traditional idea of the artist who is placed within the relations of interchangeability. Yet, while engaging elements belonging to the art system, she does not rely on the institution of art to bring about its critical efficacy. Perhaps it is for this reason that her works can be more disruptive than the critiques taking place within the institution.

While Lawler presented a critique of the institution from within and without the institution during the 1980s, twenty years prior to this were the early practitioners of institutional critique, who more or less responded to institutional authority. The symbolic or subversive strategies of institutional critique were largely regarded by certain scholars as momentous and also very political practices that lie within the boundaries of conceptual art. As these researchers analyzed a series of artists who associated themselves with institutional critique and conceptual art, they peered into the will and yearning that drove these artists to transform the institutional apparatus of art. Benjamin Buchloh has noted, however, that the purpose of conceptual art is not limited to changing the artistic apparatus. For him, conceptual art is a genre that replaces the aesthetics of industrial production and consumption with the aesthetics of administration and nstitutional validation.[2] In other words, rather than attempt o change its own status within the institution, conceptual rt is strictly dependent on the status conferred upon it by he institution. At the same time, Buchloh points out that institutional critique" is one of three core issues of conceptual rt, mentioning European artists such as Marcel Broodthaers, aniel Buren, and Hans Haacke as belonging to the first eneration of institutional critique. They are largely known have cast their doubts on institutional ideologies, exposing em and directly criticizing the entities that execute them.

Broodthaers constructed fictional museums to turn aditional institutional practices into travesties. His *Musée Art Moderne, Département des Aigles, Section XIXème Siècle* 968) moved away from relying on the historical course

2 Benjamin H. D. Buchloh, "Conceptual Art 1962–1969: From the Aesthetic of Administration to the Critique of Institutions," *October*, no. 55 (Winter 1990): 119.

firmly determined by modern museums and instead critiqued its decontextualizing power. And for this, he employed a system of classification usually employed by museums to establish a hierarchy of knowledge. Broodthaers mimicked the role of the curator, who determines the idea of the exhibition, decides on the placement of works, and selects works to be displayed. While Lawler parodied the museum's institutional authority, Broodthaers carried out the "fictional" duties of the institutional authority. Bringing in large wooden containers, postcards, replicas, and labels as display objects so as to transform them into functions fitting to the museum, he called into question the museum's political and economic status by presenting installations that were at once delicate and ironic. Rosalind Krauss read Broodthaers's work as a kind of critical practice that deconstructs the modernist's conception of medium-specificity, but also as part of an acute critical strategy against the museum as an established art institution that confers value and determines categories.[3] According to Hal Foster, Broodthaers demystified the myth of the art museum by "exposing its alibis" in such manners.[4]

Through his *in situ* works, Buren demonstrated how artists can experiment with the physical space of the gallery. His work dealt with the difference between the interior and the exterior of a space, constructing a visual form through which the interior "art space" and the exterior "ordinary world" were to be connected. He never presented the institution of art as a discursive space but argued, rather, that any critical intervention in institutions can only be limited to a specific time and place. Buren's early works summoned the architectural and ideological boundaries of institutions that defined objects as "fine art." There is a comparison to be drawn between Buren's practice, which revealed the hidden structures that justified painting as high art, and Broodthaers's, which studied the context of the museum. Buren's politics of space later reverberated through curatorial strategies that concerned site-specific art. Identifying the conditions by which something functions as art and is categorized as art

3 Rosalind Krauss, *A V[...] North Sea: Art in the [...] Post-Medium Conditi[...]* Neurath Memorial L[...] vol. 31 (New York: T[...] Hudson, 2000).

4 Hal Foster, "Subvers[...] in Foster, *Recodings: [...] Spectacle, Cultural Po[...]* (Seattle: Bay Press, [...]

within institutional and ideological spaces, Buren focused not only on the formal aspects of art institutions but also on how such institutions frame art.

Haacke's institutional critique consisted of examining how museums, corporations, politicians, and collectors utilized art, either sociopolitically or economically. Haacke self-reflectively recognized the problems inherent in the institution and in existing systems. His works that explain the relation between economic power and cultural power attest to this fact. For instance, in an article titled "Museums: Managers of Consciousness," Haacke argues that the leaflet "The Business Behind Art Knows the Art of Good Business," published by the Metropolitan Museum of Art in 1984, manifests the realistic importance of corporate sponsorship in art exhibition. For Haacke, the museum is a site for a vast interplay of interests. While being a cultural space of compromise where artistic functions are implemented, it is also a place of critique where the confluence of private capital and invasive mass media gives rise to controversial issues. With sufficient understanding of the realm of mutual play between the interior and exterior of the artistic sphere, Haacke also embodied it. He expressed in different ways the difficulty of upholding an independent stance and maintaining a critical distance within expanded art institutions.

Institutional critique, and the writings and works of the aforementioned artists who have theorized the concept, has been discussed and anthologized by many writers[5] in addition to Buchloh, such as Peter Osborne[6] and Foster. From the late 1960s through the 1970s, these writers gradually expanded the function of institutional critique in their art practices. It may have been triggered by the realization that the critique belonging to the modernist discourse—which relies on the autonomy of the artwork—was inadequate to respond to the "new" art that set out to intervene in the institutional framework by engaging site-specific, contingent, and situational events. Another factor may have been the rising awareness that the role of the artist should be broadened

5
Alexander Alberro and Blake Stimson, eds., *Institutional Critique: An Anthology of Artists' Writings* (Cambridge, MA: MIT Press, 2009).

6
Peter Osborne, *Conceptual Art* (London: Phaidon, 2002).

beyond merely moving one's artwork from the studio to the exhibition, and start to include a more critical and responsive practice that deals with the overall context of the institution. These artists gradually placed institutional critique as a genre and also strived to set it apart from the historically avant-garde methodologies such as Dadaism and Surrealism. This effort has been described as expanding the conceptual possibilities of institutional critique without consigning it to a certain kind of artistic act. Broodthaers and Buren worked from within and without the physical spaces of art institutions. Haacke demonstrated through his research projects—by way of acceding to museum and gallery invitations—the political and economic relations present in the status of art institutions, thereby shedding light on the importance of exhibitions' intermediary role. Such pioneering activities by these artists began with a critical interest in the institutions of art of the time and soon brought the multidimensional encounter among space, the public, and the artwork into a larger discourse.

The form of critique expanded into a curatorial practice as critical art started to focus on tackling institutional frames. The traditional role of artists shifted. Moving away from the object-based practice, artists began to display artworks, non-artworks, and readymades all to reflect curatorial concepts. The exhibition space and the "situation" of the artwork are thus inextricably connected.[7] Maria Lind, director-curator of Kunstverein München from 2002 to 2004, and Manuel Borja-Villel, director of the Museu d'Art Contemporani de Barcelona from 1988 to 2008, are two of the representative critical practitioners who contributed to understanding the institution of art museums as more than just a space where artworks could be viewed. In their involvement in planning and heading museum projects, they emphasized the awareness that art institutions should function as a site where shared social concerns must be articulated. By delving into the deeper layers of the institution, they also helped enrich the discussion on what sort of alternative critical strategies may be possible and practical. And in the process, they utilized

7
See Paul O'Neill, *The Curating and the Cur Culture(s)* (Cambrid MIT Press, 2012), a Hans-Dieter Huber, Curators—Curators in *Men in Black: Har Curatorial Practice*, e Christoph Tannert Tischler (Frankfurt Revolver, 2004), 12

international curatorial networks and collaborated with other art institutions, universities, and activist groups.

Some museums are no longer atemporal spaces for the display of aesthetic objects; they have made the shift to becoming sites where social issues are examined through the sharing of political consciousness and where they are intimately interconnected with the realities of communities. Many artists and curators are cooperating to use institutions as a platform where issues of the everyday world are explored. As is well known, political art (or the political use of art) is no longer unfamiliar territory, nor is it still exclusive to the early artists and curators associated with institutional critique. The practice of institutional critique is always ready to enter into a different paradigm. Irit Rogoff, who has offered a new way of thought regarding various forms of the critical attitude, provides an interesting insight into the matter.[8] For Rogoff, criticality has a duality. First, it operates through the form of criticism embodied in the individual subject laboring within the art institution, presenting a new perceptual model by which the form can be reframed or analyzed. At the same time, it is also one that can be formed by examining, through critical participants of a broader category, the performative and participatory conditions of current art institutions. This idea is worth noting in conceiving a new concept of critique that would cater to the practice of institutional critique.

Institutional critique, now converted into and expressed hrough curatorial practice, still refutes the hegemonic ower of the capitalist art system. Since the practice of onceptual art, which was conscious of its own institutional rame, institutional critique has reflected on the relation etween the "method" that is critique and the "object" that s art institutions. It sometimes stood in as another name or "political" art that, far from representing political issues, uestioned its own productive framework. These various ractices of institutional critique recognize the existence and ecessity of the art system, yet persistently question its very atus and undermine its authority. Thus, as an attempt at

8 Irit Rogoff, "From Criticism to Critique to Criticality" (2003), with link to PDF of "'Smuggling'—An Embodied Criticality" (2006), European Institute for Progressive Cultural Policies, http://eipcp.net/transversal/0806/rogoff1/en/ (accessed July 12, 2018).

social change, these communicative acts surrounding art give rise to a discourse of resistance. As a liberation paradigm, the practice is grounded in the philosophy of resistance against the fundamentally oppressive and hegemonic apparatus. Here, we agree that there is a need to build a social praxis to create a utopia. The critical consciousness responding to the social circumstance is no longer new, yet there is no denying that the philosophy of institutional critique along with progressive thought, both of which stand against conservative thought within the institution to aim for revolutionary change, remains valid both in its presence and agenda.

In order to identify how artistic processes are wrested by the agenda of dehumanization, the oppressive system germinated by its substructure must be identified. And this work requires a concerted effort to bring critical reflection and the spirit of resistance, which arose from institutional critique, into the ideological matrix of actual power. The significance of such critical attitudes that were the focus of institutional critique in art is deeply related to the practice of pedagogy, which started from another kind of critical awareness of the realities of communities during the same period (1960s–1970s). Brazilian educator and philosopher Paulo Freire embraced art, art education, and cultural research as methodologies for his pedagogy, presenting a structure of community change that would practice reflective introspection. Here, the "dialogical" education between educator and "educatee" carries out the will of human beings as "conscious" entities that aspire to freedom. Freire developed a program that would foster the ability to critically approach knowledge and power for the purpose of changing both oneself and community life. Critical pedagogy, as his methodology was called, argues for the mutual intervention of the educator and educatee in the democratic process of dialogue, introspection, and action. Through such a concept of mutual dialogue, both subjects perceive the various processes happening in their place of growth with a sense of shared responsibility. And by this, they are able to look at the world not as a stable entity but as a reality of change where domination and struggle are dynamically intertwined.[9]

Drawing from Freire's concept of liberation pedagogy and extending it through the 1980s and up to today, American social critic Henry Giroux developed a critical paradigm that focused on the institution of education as a place of oppression, noting the layered contradictions in the rhetoric of education. His liberation theory is for the politics of "difference" and stands against the rigid dichotomy of conventional social categories. His political practice involves the desire to deconstruct and construct "boundaries" in ordinary public life and the consciousness of the citizen. In this sense, a conceptual link can be made with the practice of institutional critique in the realm of art. According to Giroux, this process allows the educator to analyze the way in which dominant cultures set boundaries, in turn giving the educatee the opportunity to think of the possibility of their deconstruction. And when new forms of culture and identity intersect, a progressive pedagogy can be constructed in the place of "difference."[10] And for those educatees who desire to be liberated from certain dominating settings, by understanding how cultural hegemony is generated and maintained both historically and socially, they can acquire the significance of inquiring into power.

In Giroux's emancipatory thought, institutions reproduce knowledge. One of the greatest contributions of Giroux is that by presenting a critical view of the institution of public education and its future, he helped develop the understanding of power operating within society. For Giroux, ideological analysis is a core instrument in pedagogy. It is a meaningful way in which one can critically intervene in the issues that problematize the relations between authority and freedom, ethics and knowledge, language and experience.[11] In other words, ideology as a mechanism that allows one to question institutional settings of domination and subjection, centralization and marginalization, raises awareness of the theoretical point of departure required by the conditions of

9
Paulo Freire, *Pedagogy of the Oppressed* (New York: Continuum, 1970), 61.

10
Henry A. Giroux, "Critical Theory and the Politics of Culture and Voice: Rethinking the Discourse of Educational Research," in *Qualitative Research in Education: Focus and Methods*, eds. Robert Sherman and Rodman Webb (New York: Falmer, 1988), 193.

11
Henry A. Giroux, "When Schools Become Dead Zones of the Imagination: A Critical Pedagogy Manifesto," *The High School Journal* 99, no. 4 (Summer 2016): 358.

critical learning and behavior. In this sense, hegemony as a dominant ideology is closely connected to the institutional frame that interferes in the formation of relations within social classes, including our everyday experiences. Giroux's critical pedagogy demands from the educator the practice of institutional critique, one that would persistently decode the policies and practices of the ideological hegemony in which our educational system is deeply steeped.

In *Popular Culture, Schooling and Everyday Life*, written and edited with Roger Simon, Giroux emphasizes that pedagogy is characterized by the cultural production and exchange that take place within citizens' everyday lives and their communities. He also argued that one must pay attention to how knowledge is produced, mediated, rejected, or even represented through power relations both in and out of the educational institution.[12] Critical pedagogy, therefore, cannot be limited to an *a priori* discourse. It is rather assuredly a shared process of interaction and mutual introspection that is not confined to a fixed political and ethical structure. This is why critical pedagogy for Giroux is a core driving force in creating a democratic public space within educational institutions. In light of these perceptions, and as Giroux himself has identified, critical pedagogy takes on the form of a kind of "cultural politics."[13] It is a realm that demands the active participation of cultural activists who can seriously rethink the relations among subjects within the educational institution in order to rupture the boundaries of knowledge and methods of learning that have long secured themselves within the cultural context—and, in the process, create anew a necessary language. Through this process, critical pedagogy affirms that knowledge is a product of a "social construct," constructed by dialectical and relational processes.

In Giroux's theory of critical pedagogy, the educator as cultural activist becomes a "transformative intellectual" to rethink the nature of the educator and to present ways in which the role could be revised.[14] The task of the educator practicing critical pedagogy is to define their activity as

12 Henry A. Giroux and Simon, "Popular Cultu Pedagogy of Pleasure a Meaning," in *Popular Schooling and Everyday* Giroux and Simon (G MA: Bergin & Garvey 2.

13 Henry A. Giroux, *Bor Crossings: Cultural W the Politics of Educatio* and New York: Rout 2005), 142.

14 Henry A. Giroux, " Transformative Int *Social Education* 49 1985): 377.

an intellectual labor separate from mere instrumental acts, articulate the ideological conditions and practical environment of reality, and clearly recognize the role of bringing various political and economic concerns into the public agenda. The individual, the community, and the purpose of social change are placed in a more expanded frame of critical pedagogy. Thus, community pedagogy that uses art for social transformation extends its roots by drawing from the theory and practice of critical pedagogy. In other words, by sharing the background and will of critical pedagogy, the educator-artist of community pedagogy must be trained as a public intellectual and have an activist's responsibility to pose earnest questions regarding one's own method, content, and purpose of education.

This change of perception—that is, considering the function of art as social action—is the first step for community pedagogy to overcome the artistic practice of institutional critique. Marked by its performativity and social participation, community pedagogy also calls for a fundamental change in the idea of the artist's role. Rather than the autonomous and self-sufficient individual who operates on aesthetic intentions such as self-expression, the artist is now to foster a critical consciousness for social change by aiming for a "dialogical" structure through interdependent processes, and it is this artist who can lead the artistic practice of community pedagogy. Artists must carry out the "dialogue" with the hegemony of existing institutions. While responding to the tensions that arise from the deployment of various powers of the institution, artists must also attempt to subvert such articulated forms. This is necessary to resist the power and charm of the structures of art labor—which forces incorporation into the mainstream—and to bring about a common alternative that would overcome mainstream beliefs and values. Despite knowing that temporary interventions and micro-political gestures will do little to shake the giant hegemonic system, community pedagogy must still organize artistic curatorial programs that can relentlessly search for new critical standpoints. All this is predicated on recognizing that, instead of artistic creation that fits the mold of practical achievements pressed by the capitalist market and ideological demands steered by the culture of canons, there is a need to prepare for a transformation into an aesthetic community that would uncover, and subsequently renounce, those hierarchies and conventions produced by knowledge and power and placed within social relations.

This conscious mutual process in community pedagogy may come in contact with participants in a way where all understand a common set of "shared values"[15] at some historical moment. Here, they discover a critical frame that encompasses the epistemological direction of the aesthetic act of participation and resistance, and also experience dialogue as social practice based on the shared values. The dialogical metaphor reminiscent of the works of Russian scholar Mikhail Bakhtin is not limited to the ontology of the artwork itself. It is an essential value in the constitution of the cooperative function of community pedagogy as strategic practice for social change. It implies that the practice of art within community pedagogy must be performed as ordinary interactions among humans,[16] and that this is predicated on the creative collaboration of dialogue beyond the institutional boundaries of galleries, museums, or schools. It is wary of the posture that induces passive contemplation and learning from the public by presenting objects and information in their finished forms. Pablo Helguera, a New York–based artist whose social practice intersects with his institutional role as a museum educational programmer at MoMA, has used the term "transpedagogy." It is to describe the project of converging educational methods and artistic production in a way that does not conform to the institutional conventions of existing art education and museums.[17] The projects that concern Helguera operate beyond the traditional polarity of artist/museum. The artists of such projects embrace their own "institutionality" by thoroughly comprehending and analyzing from every possible angle the many hidden implications of the art world's social and economic components.[18] Seeking

15
Claire Bishop, *Artificial Participatory Art and the of Spectatorship* (London 2012), 8.

16
Grant Kester, *Convers Pieces: Community and Communication in Mo* (Berkeley: Univ. of Ca Press, 2004), 123.

17
Pablo Helguera, "N a Transpedagogy," in *Architecture, Pedagog Experiments in Lear* Ken Ehrlich (San F Blurb, 2010), 99.

18
Ibid., 103–4.

to break away from these exclusive discourses, they see the possibility to initiate a kind of self-reflection by projecting their institutionality onto the museum's hierarchical inertia. Their attempts at deconstructing institutional frames have presented ways in which a new kind of transparency can be experienced.

A program of critical action that can carry out the agenda of community pedagogy requires an ethical responsibility in the process of exchanging meaning with the other, for it can generate a discourse that guides the imagination of reality and utopia. Traditional thinking relied on the idea of the autonomy of art that would free the artist from ethical accountability. But when the dignity of human existence is made part of artistic production and socially critical strategies, and when, by justifying it, the responsibility to forge relations of dialogical experience with others within the community is imposed on community pedagogy, then community pedagogy is inevitably ethical in its nature. This hould be distinguished, however, from an ethical standpoint hat holds the authority of value judgments of right and wrong egarding critical acts. Community pedagogy is rather closer o a kind of aesthetic and political ethos that allows critical nd creative thought to respond to social inequality, and also rompts one to ruminate on—and sympathize with—the easons that dialogical art and pedagogy intervene in social ransformation.

Inherent within community pedagogy is a continuous nd fluid interchange free from fixed procedures within ie cooperative curatorial program. Here, as a catalyst for ie change of consciousness of participants, dialogue is fundamental ground on which the dynamics of social ange may operate. But the formation of the individual and oups that relate to the ethos for social cooperation does not op at the ideal of building communities based on common lues. Hence, one may come closer to hostile strategies in e process of practical discourses that foster social change. is is because of the overarching dichotomy that affects the many ways in which political activism is understood. Focused on context and situations, institutional critique attempted to connect space, the public, and artworks; and the subject of critical consciousness has thereupon expanded the category of practicing subjects from individual artists to collective communities. The common attempt to further audience participation in critical practice—so as to deconstruct the dominant system involved with cultural systematization and to share political, economic, and ideological concerns—is now gradually removing the auteurism of the artist and the curator, as well as Enlightenment values, from the realm of art appreciation and the aesthetic formation of relations. Reflective introspection and dialogical consciousness will act as a creative foundation for the community curatorial practice to operate creatively and cooperatively as a strategy for social transformation.

Translated from Korean by Rebecca Yonsoo Park.

Pascal Gielen is full professor of sociology of art and politics at the Antwerp Research Institute for the Arts (Antwerp University, Belgium) where he leads the Culture Commons Quest Office (CCQO). Gielen is editor of the international book series *Antennae—Arts in Society*. In 2016, he became laureate of the Odysseus grant for excellent international scientific research of the Fund for Scientific Research Flanders in Belgium. Gielen has published many books, which are translated in English, Polish, Portuguese, Russian, Spanish, Turkish, and Ukrainian. His research focuses on creative labor, the commons, civil actions, the institutional context of the arts, and on cultural politics.

Pascal Gielen

Between Creativity and Criminality: On the Liminal Zones of Art and Political Action*

Reimagining Utopias

Those who have been scouring biennials and arts festivals over the past decade have been treated to a veritable feast of political discussions and social debates. Sometimes art is hardly the topic anymore but, rather, globalism, neoliberalism, precarity, or ecology, to name but a few. This political discourse is mostly limited to the discursive space, which hardly moves beyond the borders of the parish of the already converted. Words and actions are still very far apart here, which means that true political activism does not materialize. However, this takes nothing away from the fact that the rofessional art world is increasingly taking a political role pon itself. The time/space that is skimped on in formal ducation seems to be shifting to biennials and theaters. dding to that the thinning of the critical debate, the ıtbacks on research journalism, and the commodification of ıe writing and speaking space in mainstream media, it seems metimes that art institutions are among the few remaining

ersion of this essay first appeared in *vocarte—Revista de Ciências da Arte*, no. eptember 2017).

places of refuge for public debate and critical political analyses.

And there is more than just room for debate. After proclaiming "the end of history,"[1] advocating the end of ideological differences and the de facto end of democracy, the idea of utopia as a possible political project was also buried. The intellectual and especially academic/scientific taboo on utopian thinking erodes the humus soil of both the political and the civil space, especially that of the *social imagination*. The current dominance of "realism" and pragmatism in politics[2] as well as in philosophy deprives politics of the chance for developing a long-term vision. Nowadays, any visionary project with an eye on an ideal society invariably runs aground on the realpolitik of budget policies. Politics has become policy, and governing seems to become more and more a matter of bookkeeping. This corners the imagination or, rather, sends it into exile to the exclusive domain of fiction. Only within the walls of a cinema, a theater, a museum, or in the pages of a novel is there still room to dream of a possibly different world. There, one can still freely speculate about a possible future society.

Perhaps the boom in fantasy and science-fiction movies in popular culture need therefore not surprise us. The first genre is a rosy escape from reality, while in the second genre utopia becomes dystopia.[3] Both genres have in common that they create an image of a truly post-political society at the end of history. Whereas in fantasy movies, all power relations have been depoliticized—as they are dissolved in supernatural and magical, but also highly moral, decisions about good and evil—the world of science fiction tends to present us with societies that are at the mercy of terror, totalitarian regimes, dehumanized camp-like situations controlled by machines, or natural disasters of apocalyptic proportions. Convincing stories about possibly different, utopian worlds are however few and far between. Our future is either transcendental or catastrophic. This popular field of the imaginary doesn't seem to offer many other flavors.

1 Francis Fukuyama, *The E[nd of] History and The Last Ma[n]* [(New] York: Free Press, 1992).

2 Mark Fisher, *Capitalist [Realism:] Is There No Alternative?* (Winchester, UK: Zer[o Books,] 2009).

3 Franco "Bifo" Berar[di, Heroes:] *Mass Murder and Su[icide]* (London and New Y[ork: Verso,] 2015).

The contrast with the boom in political and social commitment in that other segment of the imaginary domain of fiction could hardly be sharper. From the heterotopic project of Michelangelo Pistoletto to the activist architecture of Recetas Urbanas, from the political art of Jonas Staal and Oliver Ressler to the economic, postcolonial interventions by Renzo Martens, or the utopian but also highly concrete gestures of Thomas Hirschhorn—they are all concerned with imagining a possibly different world. Admittedly, many of them are reluctant to use the word "utopia," almost always stressing the direct relation their work has to the real world. Pistoletto, for example, does not just imagine *The Third Paradise* (2010) but also laid the foundation for a real functioning organization, Cittadellarte. Likewise, Recetas Urbanas is building real homes and schools that meet an acute social demand, and Martens is really rolling up his sleeves in Congo to build a museum and to transform the art exchange chain between the north and the south. In short, we see here a real praxis where actions are suited to words. Perhaps this is why these artists are reluctant to call their practices "utopian." Nevertheless, it can hardly be denied that in their quest they are hoping for a possibly different, indeed, *better* world. And although, alas, this effort is often only observed by the few in the professional art world, their actions nevertheless demonstrate the will to break out of this confinement. Driven by their imagination, they frequently jump into the gap between legality and illegality, creativity and criminality. It is precisely this imaginary potency that gives them the possibility to go further than debates about politics and civil activism. Not only are artists capable of presenting an imagined world, their skills allow them to make us also actually experience that world. Perhaps this is where their extra political potency lies.

As will be explained later, the civil space is an undecided gray zone, fallow land on which civil actions and political activism mostly settle only temporarily. However, this undecided space also provides the necessary opening that sets civil movement into motion and keeps it going. Especially here, something has to happen because no one has seen it yet or no one cares about it. And this brings us to the importance of art or, more broadly, the imaginary. In order to see what no one else has seen yet, artists can deploy their powers of imagination—powers that are being smothered in today's realpolitik. But, to understand better which strategies artists can follow, it is useful to make a more analytical distinction among the different realms in which political activism takes shape.

Between Creativity and Criminality

It is in the gaping gulf between legality and illegality, between creativity and criminality, that civil space sees the light of day. In the gray area between what is allowed and not (or not yet) allowed, civilians engage in political actions to initiate that which a government or state has not yet thought of (or does not want to think of) and for which there are no interested markets. For the record, civil action does not coincide with criminal behavior. Civil actions simply concern nonregulated domains, areas not yet covered by law. However, within a democracy, it is the legislative and judicial powers that decide whether to categorize the issue at hand as legal or illegal. At the moment of the actual action itself, this is still undecided: Will this practice be tolerated, embraced, even passed into law—or not? Civilians who invoke their civil rights are, in other words, still uncertain about where they will end up, how they will be judged. This is why a political action is mostly a risky undertaking in which one sticks one's neck out and risks one's own social position.

Civil and Civic Spaces

Because of this undecided nature of the space in which the civil action takes place, it seems wise to distinguish between the terms "civil" and "civic." Although both concepts are often used interchangeably in everyday usage, "civic" mainly refers to the government, which has "civic tasks" or sets these well-defined civic tasks to persons or delegates them to places and institutions. In other words, political actions in the civic place are already regulated (by law or otherwise), whereas those in the civil space still lay open. Or, to paraphrase Michel de Certeau's analytical distinction between place and space: The civic place is a place that is established or has taken root in policies, education programs, regulations, or laws. By contrast, the civil space, in the Certeausian sense, is a space that remains fluid, a realm where positions still have to be taken up or created.[4]

4 Michel de Certeau, *The Practice of Everyday Life*, trans. Steven F. Rendall (Berkeley: Univ. of California Press, 1980/1984).

Governments or authorities who wish to regulate civil space by, for example, guaranteeing a public square in a city, or public cultural infrastructures such as (national) museums and theaters, are transforming the civil space into a civic place. Likewise, the civil movement that demands a better legal framework for a certain issue is, paradoxically, promoting the elimination of its own reason for existence. It is no coincidence that civil movements, including independent subcultures and squatters, often evaporate once a government supports them. The movement comes to a standstill as it becomes rooted in a civic law or a civic infrastructure.

Why both the true civil action and the civil space find themselves in between illegality and legality is perhaps better understood by looking at the problem of modern or (post)revolutionary politics. As Hannah Arendt states in *On Revolution*, "those who get together to constitute a new government are themselves unconstitutional, that is, they have no authority to do what they have set out to achieve. The vicious circle in legislating is present not in ordinary law making, but in laying down the fundamental law, the law of the land or the constitution which, from then on, is supposed to incarnate the 'higher law' from which all laws ultimately derive their authority."[5]

5 Hannah Arendt, *On Revolution* (London: Faber and Faber, 1963; reprint, London and New York: Penguin, 1990), 183–4.

So, the constitutive power and the constitutive body are always outside of the constitution, since they precede it. They are therefore neither legal nor illegal, which immediately presents the problem of authority within modern democracies: Of whom is it accepted that they place themselves outside or, rather, above the law, precisely in order to establish that law? Civil space relates to civic place in a similar ambivalent manner. The former precedes the latter, running the risk of never, ever being recognized or legalized and thus remaining permanently in the sphere of illegality.

Civil and Public Spaces

Like the advocated difference between "civic" and "civil," the terms "public" and "civil" are also best kept apart rather than have them coincide. Here, too, a distinction may be productive. The civil space often requires collective initiatives and organizations. People have to make an effort, organize something, or simply "do" something in order to shape a civil space. By contrast, public space is the space we can enter freely, that is or should be accessible to anyone. It is the space of public opinion, where people can make their more-or-less idiosyncratic voice be heard, freely, and preferably with good arguments, like in the media, in public debate, or in the time-honored salon conversations.[6]

We can articulate the relationship between these concepts as follows: Whereas the public space is a space for the free exchange of thoughts, opinions, ideas, and people, the civil domain provides the framework for organizing these thoughts, opinions, ideas, and people. Within the latter space, an opinion or idea is expressed in a public action or in the form of an organization. The earlier mentioned political debates at biennials and art festivals belong, in that sense, to the public space, but they need civil initiatives to organize that space for debate. In other words, civil space needs the public domain. After all, the second constitutes the utterly vital source of inspiration for the first. Public space provides, as it were, both new ideas and new people (new citizens), but they can only claim and obtain their place in society through self-

6
Jürgen Habermas, *Th[…] Transformation of the […] Sphere: An Inquiry in[…] a Category of Bourgeo[…]*, trans. Thomas Burge[…] (Darmstadt and Ne[…] Hermann Luchterh[…] 1962; reprint, Camb[…] Polity Press, 1989).

organization in the civil domain. Vice versa, this also implies that public space is reliant on civil space, as the latter makes the public domain possible by organizing it or claiming a place for it; for example, by enforcing the freedom of speech by legal means, but also by founding organizations and institutions such as newspapers or other platforms, for that purpose. Simply put, public space is all about the free word, while in the civil domain the action takes center stage, such as in the mentioned activities of Martens or Recetas Urbanas. The interaction between both constitutes a *praxis*, where the action is suited to the word but also where actions can and may be put into words.

Commons

Before going deeper into the role of art in political activism, there is a last distinction that should be made clear: the realm of the commons. The concept of the commons has won much attention in cultural and political debates over the last decade, and it gained prominence both in recent philosophy[7] and in law research.[8] According to Michael Hardt and Antonio Negri, guaranteeing a commons is necessary to safeguard future cultural production. These philosophers have described the commons as a category that transcends the classic contrast between public property (guaranteed by the state) and private property. In the area of culture, Negri and Hardt mention knowledge, language, codes, information, and affects as belonging to the commons. This shared and freely accessible communality is necessary to keep the economy running in the long term, to regain the balance in the ecological system, and to keep our sociopolitical fabric dynamic.[9] Also, economic studies stressed already in the early 1990s the importance of the regulation of (free) access to the commons.[10] For this reason, the commons is defined here as the space where, in fact, the access to public and private goods and services is discussed and regulated. And, as is well known, much political debate and activism revolves around this issue: Who, how

7 Michael Hardt and Antonio Negri, *Commonwealth* (Cambridge, MA: Belknap Press/Harvard Univ. Press, 2009).

8 Lawrence Lessig, *Free Culture: How Big Media Uses Technology and the Law to Lock Down Culture and to Control Creativity* (New York: Penguin, 2004).

9 Hardt and Negri, *Commonwealth*, viii.

10 Elinor Ostrom, *Governing the Commons: The Evolution of Institutions for Collective Action* (Cambridge: Cambridge Univ. Press, 1990).

many, and under which conditions people may get access to debates in public space, and to civil and civic services (e.g., public libraries, museums, education, social security), is often first claimed by civil actions and, later on, organized by grassroots cultural initiatives in civil space or taken over by governments in the defined civic space.

In summary, the relationship between the differentiated spaces may be described as follows: In public space, ideas and proposals—e.g., alternative forms of (sub)cultural expressions—may be articulated and discussed, which can be worked out and organized in civil space, or they can be taken over by a government in civic space or by the market in the private sphere (e.g., the construction of and support for cultural infrastructure). But the discussion and regulation about the access to those services is a matter of the commons (e.g., who and how many people may participate, or discussions about what needs to be guaranteed by a government and what can be done by the private sector). Political activism takes place in all of those spheres, and art can play different roles in it. To understand better what kinds of forms artistic initiatives may take in those different spheres, one can relate them to shifting phases in a "civil chain of political activism," a concept developed in earlier research.[11]

The Civil Chain

Civil action is born from emotion, argues the Spanish sociologist Manuel Castells.[12] Although such actions always imply the hopeful expectation that something in society can be improved, this initial emotion is often of a negative nature, fed by fear, discomfort, or irritation. The reasons for this can be manifold. An individual may feel threatened by beggars or by drug dealers hanging around in the neighborhood. But they can also feel ill at ease because there are too many policemen, soldiers, or security cameras in the streets. Employees may feel intimidated by their boss or colleagues and may also

11 Pascal Gielen and Th[illegible] *New Civil Roles and Organizational Mod[illegible] Cultural Organizatio[illegible] Reviewing the Poten[illegible] Contemporary Cultu[illegible] and Alternative Wor[illegible] Structures* (Amsterd[illegible] European Cultural [illegible] 2016).

12 Manuel Castells, *N[illegible] Outrage and Hope: [illegible] Movements in the I[illegible]* 2nd ed. (Cambridg[illegible] Press, 2015).

experience stress because of a too-heavy workload. In short, feelings of annoyance, frustration, or injustice can have many causes. And, as may be evident from this range of examples, certainly not every negative emotional experience leads to civil action and political activism.

Discomfort can be channeled in many ways. Those who choose therapy or decide to hire a lawyer opt for a private and individual solution to their problem. Indeed, communication with a therapist or lawyer has little to do with public action or political claims. In order to "enter" civil society, we need to specifically address a collective and generate public support. The initial emotion must be recognized as a shared emotion or irritation. Civil action is only possible if we take our personal discomfort out of the private sphere, when we "de-privatize" the subject matter. However, such a step towards civil space requires an important skill: the ability of (self-)rationalization. This is required to articulate an initial intuition or basic emotion. It is the cognitive competence of analyzing one's own feelings and perhaps point out possible causes. Rationalization, and especially self-rationalization, therefore precedes communication, although the causes of certain emotions might be further clarified in dialogue with others.

And, further, after the processes of rationalization, communication, and de-privatization, the skill of organization is required in order to set the civil action in motion and, if necessary, keep it going in the long run. For instance, one must organize oneself in order to write an opinion piece, but also encourage others to do the same. Protesting in the streets or rolling up our sleeves to clean the neighborhood requires at least a modicum of (self-)organization.

Balancing between Emotion and Rationalization

What's important here is that those processes of self-rationalization and self-organization can temper the initial emotion that triggered them in the first place. For instance, having to find one's way through a maze of legal rules, being obliged to study political procedures, or having to follow the long and winding road through bureaucratic institutions in order to arrive at the right form of (self-)organization can make one lose the energy to go on. Both processes, therefore, require that we literally rationalize that initial emotion, distance ourselves from it and, in a sense, "bureaucratize" it (all forms of organization presuppose setting up a minimum number of rules and procedures and sticking to them).

In themselves, such processes are not dramatic and even necessary to initiate civil action. However, this points to the fact that the basic emotion as mentioned determines the "drive" or the energy of the civil undertaking. Or, in an analogy by Castells, it is an initial fear converted into anger that defines the engine of civil action. It is the steam that powers civil initiatives with a civil mission. This also means that political action derives its basic energy from very direct, mundane, and mostly local human experience. The chances of success and continuance of every civil initiative, therefore, depend on finding the right balance between rationalizing and organizing, on the one hand, and keeping up the energy that is obtained from a basic emotion on the other. This balance is all the more urgent as organizations "scale up" their activities, for instance, from local to regional or from the national to the transnational level. Each step up the ladder demands more rationalization and organization, and thereby one risks evaporating the initial drive and emotion as well as losing track of the local problems that started it all.

Commoning

When political activists want to reach structural change, they need to act on a more abstract systemic level (e.g., to change the "neoliberal" organization of society, work, and life; or to safeguard the welfare state; or to reduce our ecological footprint). Political activism needs to deal often with this tension between, on the one hand, "local" emotions and reasons to act and, on the other, global issues and political mechanisms. The latter are often articulated in the described public space where both visionary ideas and utopias, as well as new ideologies, can be discussed in a quite abstract way. However, ideas alone cannot produce real social change. This takes actions or acts. Citizens take initiatives to build, for example, alternative social formations and forms of self-organization in the defined civil space.

Self-organization, however, is again usually initiated locally and may therefore become stranded in localism or what Nick Srnicek and Alex Williams call "folk politics."[13] In this case, social or ecological problems are addressed for a relatively small and primarily closed community but do not build systemic change. In order to make political activism effective, it needs to organize structural change. For this reason, alternative social, ecological, political, economic, or other models must be distributed and shared—and, at that moment, the described common space comes in. Alternative economies and forms of self-organization must demonstrate their effectiveness to others if political activism wishes to generate structural effects. This necessitates the preferably free or very cheap sharing of information and knowledge, of materials and logistics, but also of business models and new solidarity structures. Political activism dealing with fundamental and deep embedded problems should also influence institutional bodies in order to have any effect. It is exactly this process of sharing, or *commoning*, that forces governments into an alternative legislative organization, as, for example, the Creative Commons license or the Bologna Regulation for the Care and Regeneration of Urban Commons demonstrate.[14] It is only when actions take place on this political and legislative level that sustainable reform may actually take place and the current social, ecological, or economic problems can be addressed in a sustainable way.

From the above, we may conclude that artists who get involved in political activism can be situated in a chain of

13
Nick Srnicek and Alex Williams, *Inventing the Future: Postcapitalism and a World Without Work* (London and New York: Verso, 2015).

14
Bologna Regulation for the Care and Regeneration of Urban Commons; regulation at http://www.comune.bologna.it/media/files/bolognaregulation.pdf/; context via http://wiki.p2pfoundation.net/Bologna_Regulation_for_the_Care_and_Regeneration_of_Urban_Commons/.

successive, distinctive operations—and that such activities will continuously have to take into account all of the previous stages in the chain in order not to alienate the activism from its own source of energy. Analytically, this succession of processes—which is called the "civil chain"—looks like this: (1) emotion, (2) (self-)rationalization, (3) communication, (4) de-privatization (or going public), (5) (self-)organization, and, finally, (6) "commoning."

Converting Emotions

By using the civil chain as a tool to analyze artistic involvement in political activism, it is possible to detect at least three transitions in which art can play a crucial role. The first one takes place at the emotional level. An initially negative feeling must be converted into a sense of positive energy, of simple enthusiasm to "get cracking," or at least of not resigning oneself to the situation. Castells gives, as already mentioned, the example of fear that must be "positively" converted into outrage and hope.[15] By "positively," we mean that outrage and hope lead to action. However negative the results of bursts of outrage may be, they always indicate an accumulation of energy. Through outrage, the paralyzing effect of fear changes from passive to active. Feelings of discomfort, irritation, insecurity, injustice, and the like, often result in defeatism or resignation. Especially when people feel they are alone in their efforts, they tend to resign themselves to the situation. Only when a sometimes-hard-to-pinpoint "spark" turns negative energy into positive energy does political action become an option.

15 Castells, *Networks of and Hope*, 247–8.

Artists or collectives such as Martens or Les Têtes de l'Art often mention observing this defeatism when they arrive at a spot in Congo, a suburb, or a local community. Sometimes citizens have already undertaken several steps in civil actions but failed to succeed. In other situations, they undertake nothing because they can see the bigger political and economic picture in which their local problems seem unresolvable, or they just don't know where to start. Artists have tools in their hands to shift those feelings of defeatism. The most effective one here seems to be simple "doing." Martens activated with his Institute for Human Activities local citizens on a Unilever plantation to make their own chocolate artworks and even to build a white cube on the spot. By engaging people in creative processes, stimulating and coaching them into realizing concrete things, citizens get a kind of positive energy and drive because they are involved in an interactive process with a positive outcome, such as a creative work, a theater performance, or an exhibition.

By taking, for example, a closer look at the activities of Les Têtes de l'Art in Marseille, we can see the same mechanisms at work. It is precisely a simple act of making art together with others or "doing things" that plays an important part. Drive is not so much communicated in words, and energy rarely comes from a well-articulated view in a debate, newspaper, or scientific report. Rather, they emerge from the activities that are organized, the artistic interventions that are staged, and the actions that are undertaken. Just like the transference of emotions can take place subconsciously and nonverbally through mirror neurons, the drive and energy are primarily communicated through the actions themselves. Artistic activities generate a "mimetic effect," which spurs others into action. Artistic interventions and performances n public space can point out the social issues within a group, neighborhood, or square. Cultural civil actions not only bring o light what is not visible but also make manifest how the urroundings, a space, or a neighborhood may be experienced differently.

In this respect, artistic activities differ from other civil ctions such as protests, opinion pieces, or petitions. Whereas uch civil actions are generally limited to social criticism, he artistic civil action has an extra element—an alternative xperience. For a little while, the artists provide an often modest ut possibly different, sometimes utopic world, which in most ases generates positive energy. Les Têtes de l'Art illustrates this quite literally with their initiatives named Place à l'Art (2007), a sort of "fair" where people in the neighborhood can together engage in all sorts of artistic activities, producing a very positive social dynamic in places where, before, drug dealers and other petty criminals created an unsafe social environment. The outrage over an unsafe environment is immediately "compensated" for with a positive alternative. At the emotional level, especially, artistic interventions provide opportunities for converting negative feelings into a positive energy.

Conversely, for some it might be precisely this alternative experience that makes them understand that their living conditions or precarious social environment are far from ideal. Crucial in this is that it is "through" the artistic process or the work of art itself that participants are given an experience of alternative possibilities. A project of Les Têtes de l'Art in Bel Horizon, a degraded building in the center of Marseille, illustrates this energizing shift very well. After a request from an inhabitant of this high-rise flat, Les Têtes de l'Art organized a collective work of several months. A group of adults and children from the tower block worked together on a script and collectively produced a fictional video about a problematic situation that affected all inhabitants. The fiction involved children and adults of the tower block as actors. The artistic vector allowed for alternative representations to the negative image attached to the place and encouraged the meeting of inhabitants in the tower. After this fiction, a second project consisted in realizing five short films about the wishes of inhabitants toward the rehabilitation of the tower. At that moment, a rather classic community art project resulted in political claims and activism.

The Bel Horizon (2010) case is just one of many actions that demonstrate how an artistic experience works within civil action. What we can observe here is how (negative) criticism of a certain situation goes hand in hand with theatrical action that generates a rather positive experience of an alternative situation. This positive experience, in turn, evokes new criticism and civil action. Or, as mentioned before, the artistic activity itself is what is keeping the energy alive. If such a positive experience no longer (or not yet) exists in the social reality, this circumstance provides artists with an interesting tool to create this experience all the same, especially in a fictional setting. A play or film creates a distance from the world we actually live in, and precisely thereby generates the context for an alternative world. It is this experience that can make participants reflect on their real social reality. For them, art generates—in the words of Niklas Luhmann[16]—a "second order observation": From the artistic, imaginary, or fictional "second order" experience, they can better observe how they live and experience their own everyday "first order" reality. In the cases of Place à l'Art and Bel Horizon, we see how this experience then encourages people to intervene in real life or, at least, to long for and demand a different reality.

16 Niklas Luhmann, *Die Kunst der Gesellschaft* (Frankfurt am Main: Suhrkamp Verlag, 1997).

Expression

A second necessary transition in the civil chain is to be found on the level of communication, as only through communication can a transformation take place from the individual to the collective level. We can, for example, test whether we really feel what we feel by consulting a therapist, in the sense that we can check whether such a professional recognizes our feelings as also occurring in others or is familiar with them from the cientific literature. It is only in that confirmation that an ndividual problem can become a collective one, in the sense hat others share our supposedly individual feeling. In the ame sense, city dwellers can have a chat with their neighbors bout street litter. This is also communication in which a basic xperience is shared and tested. Only if a neighbor confirms hat "Yes, you're right, there is a lot of litter here these days," an the feeling of discomfort become collectivized and the ossibility of action emerge.

So, without collectivization there is no civil or political tion at all. And, as underlined above with the work of Les

Têtes de l'Art, artistic skills such as play and imagination are sufficient tools to express and communicate personal fears or suppressed feelings. The modes of expression that are available in the arts make it also possible to use alternatives for words or analytical concepts to reflect on and communicate about sometimes very complex situations. One of the reasons for this is that artists can use aesthetic tools as aesthesis, in which many more senses can be activated beyond the discursive realm of words and concepts. Singing, dancing, performing, or making visuals and films are just a few ways of communicating that can be used to express and "de-individualize" unclear feelings or complex social and political issues.

We can point to the use of subversive performances by Pussy Riot in Russia, the guerrilla architecture of Recetas Urbanas in Spain, or the use of giants by the *Hart boven Hard* movement in Belgium to realize the important role of aesthetic tools to express and to communicate in different ways. A striking example of how to express controversial political issues by artistic means is the project *Ausländer Raus* ("Foreigners Out") by the Austrian artist Christoph Schlingensief (2002). He arranged for twelve asylum seekers to stay in a shipping container in the center of Vienna and engaged the public in deciding who was to be extradited through *Big Brother*-like rounds of voting. Naturally, this performance led to much controversy, but it also made people sensitive to the problems facing immigrants and refugees in a completely different way than in classic opinion pieces or political debates. This shows again that artistic tools and fiction can play an important part in making invisible feelings and private opinions visible, and in creating a communal space in which political discussion and activism may arise.

Performance

The artistic examples of collectivization by expression also illustrate that de-individualization in itself is not enough to incite civil action or get to political activism. To do so requires yet another transition, from the private to the public sphere. As indicated earlier, feelings and issues may be shared and therefore collectivized in both the private and the public sphere. For example, as long as the employee suffering from stress only discusses the problem with a therapist or only collectivizes it in a self-help group, we cannot speak of a civil action. Only when this worker articulates the initial feeling or syndrome in social terms does it acquire civil value. This means that, say, stress is no longer only explained as a mental condition but is recognized as a structural problem too. Stress is then not only about the irritated nerves of individual employees or about the annoying personal character of their boss but also about, for instance, high work pressure, about increasingly precarious working conditions such as flexible project labor, or about the decrease in long-term employment contracts and job security. In other words, in the transition from the private to the public sphere, a personal issue (being a stress-sensitive person) is not only translated into a collective problem (a stressful environment, stressful working conditions) but the cause of the problem of discomfort is then also located in broader social phenomena. This is why the transformation from the private to the public sphere implies the politicization of the initial feeling. If "the political" stands for openly shaping our living together,[17] this translation is an appeal to the political to articulate and address the issue.

So, in order to transform from the private to the public sphere, one needs to be "performative," and, again, it is artists who are very well trained to perform. The concept of performativity is understood here in the spirit of Judith Butler.[18] Far more than being simply a reference to or representation of reality, the artistic expression can be an act in itself that gives form to the social reality. One needs to organize oneself in an alternative way, and one can convince others to share this way of organizing just by performing it. For the sake of the latter, the importance of the mentioned process of commoning comes back into the picture. How

17
Jacques Rancière, *Dissensus: On Politics and Aesthetics*, trans. Steven Corcoran (London and New York: Continuum, 2010).

18
Judith Butler, *Bodies That Matter: On the Discursive Limits of "Sex"* (London and New York: Routledge, 1993).

this works concretely can be illustrated by the operations of the Spanish architect collective Recetas Urbanas. They build houses, schools, and community centers wherever associations and communities deem them necessary, with legal permission or not.

Insect House. Photo: Rec Urbanas.

La Carpa. Photo: Rece Urbanas.

So, Recetas Urbanas does not cater to the free market, or to governments, but rather to citizens who feel a civil need. In response to their requests, Recetas Urbanas offers strategies to occupy public spaces to create places of agony in which the opportunity for action, appropriation, occupation, and use of a city is given back to the citizens through architectural interventions and actual buildings. Their building projects transit often between legality and illegality, playing with the established order to rearticulate laws and urban regulations to compose new social and economic exchanges around their very pragmatic construction activities. In those performative acts, they disarticulate at the same time existing discourses and praxis by offering visionary urban projects in which citizens become the initiators of actions, appropriations, and occupations as responses to their collective needs and common necessities.

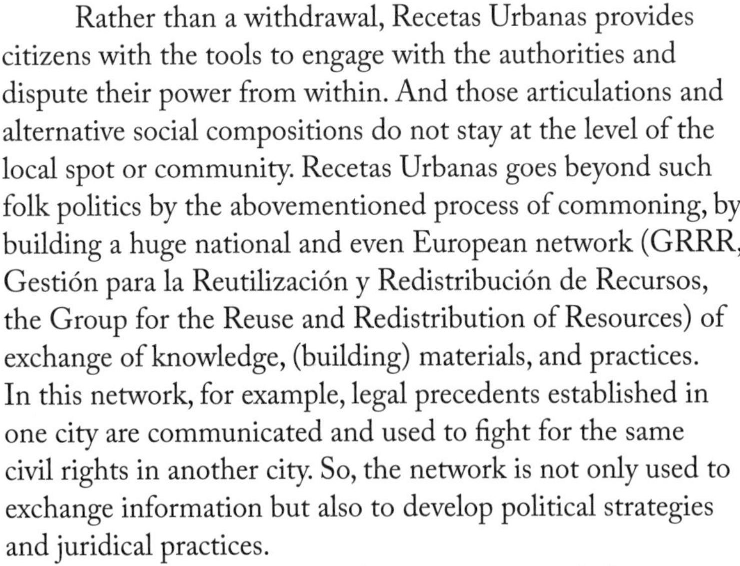

Rather than a withdrawal, Recetas Urbanas provides citizens with the tools to engage with the authorities and dispute their power from within. And those articulations and alternative social compositions do not stay at the level of the local spot or community. Recetas Urbanas goes beyond such folk politics by the abovementioned process of commoning, by building a huge national and even European network (GRRR, Gestión para la Reutilización y Redistribución de Recursos, the Group for the Reuse and Redistribution of Resources) of exchange of knowledge, (building) materials, and practices. In this network, for example, legal precedents established in one city are communicated and used to fight for the same civil rights in another city. So, the network is not only used to exchange information but also to develop political strategies and juridical practices.

Recetas Urbanas not only experiments with forms

of resistance and political activism but also performs effective strategies and practices in civil space. Those are used furthermore as testing grounds that enunciate political discourses in order to activate possible ways of civil governance. By exploring legal systems and alternative economic exchange practices, and by finding broader public support, they experiment with processes of commoning that are necessary to make political activism effective on a higher abstract and structural level.

Crossing Borders

To conclude, it can be stated that although the institutional space for the imagination of theaters, museums, and biennials may serve as a productive kitchen for political debate, artists can only really constitute civil space if they bet on the liminal zones between art and political action. Only when they venture outside of the assigned civic place by crossing the border of the museum, and go beyond the public domain of words and ideas, will they have the chance to arrive in the hazardous civil space of effective political activism. This space is hazardous because here artists step outside their acknowledged civic role, thus risking their very status as an artist. Just like those spraying graffiti on walls or trains, they run the risk of being criminalized or, at least, not being recognized any longer by their peers in the professional art world. It is only just before the checkpoint of legality and civic regulated spaces that artists sketch the contours of real political activism, in peril of never being acknowledged as artists again. This means also that artists will not build civil space by solely making political art inside the foreseen civic or market structures of museums, theaters, biennials, or art fairs. They can only realize this by *making their art political*, that means by repositioning their art and by reorganizing themselves and the original art institutions in society.

Now that the results of the presidential elections in

the USA and Turkey have familiar liberal representative democracy shaking in its foundations, the need for political activism has become clearer than ever. It only adds to the pressure on artists to cross the borders of familiar artistic biotopes. If we wake up tomorrow in a dystopia without a civil domain, we will find ourselves in a space without freedom and without autonomous art. It therefore looks as if artists have no choice but to hazard the jump into the unknown, outside the white walls of the museum into political activism, if only to safeguard their own space of imagination in the museum.

This book is published on the occasion of the symposium "What Do Museums Research?" (April 7–8, 2018) organized by the National Museum of Modern and Contemporary Art, Korea.

Series Editor
Song Sujong

Guest Editor
Kim Seong Eun

Editors
Choi Jina
Helen Jungyeon Ku

Translation
Nicholas Grindell
Lee Sunghee
Rebecca Yonsoo Park

Copyediting
John Ewing
Dutton Hauhart
Joseph Fungsang

Proofreading
John Ewing

Design
Shin Shin

Printing & Binding
Intime

1st Edition 1st Printing
December 19, 2018
1st Edition 2nd Printing
June 24, 2020

Published by
National Museum of Modern and Contemporary Art, Korea

Supervised by
Kang Seungwan

National Museum of Modern and Contemporary Art, Korea
30, Samcheong-ro, Jongno-gu, Seoul, 03062, Republic of Korea
mmca.go.kr

ISBN 978-89-6303-197-2